There are Angels in the Detail

Also by Peter Haines and Clive Birch

So You Think We're Alone?

We're Still Not Alone

Maturity and Chi Gong, a Perfect Partnership

This book is dedicated to my great friend and spiritual sister Audrey, Dave Barker and Papa Singh who passed through the great initiation during the last year. Audrey was a truly great mystic with the biggest heart that I have ever known. Dave and Papa Singh were great humans both. Also it is dedicated to all those seekers after truth and workers striving for the light. Their time is coming.

There are Angels in the Detail

The adventures and insights of a 'crazy man' continue unabated

CLIVE BIRCH

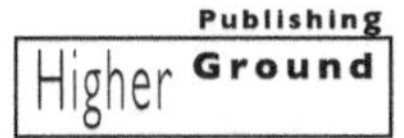

First published in the United Kingdom in 2021
by Higher Ground Publishing

ISBN 978-0-9571304-4-9

Produced by
The Choir Press, Gloucester

Contents

Introduction

'Imagination is better than knowledge.'
ALBERT EINSTEIN

Lying on friend Louise's couch, as you do, receiving Metamorphic healing, I was given inspiration for the title of this book. We were talking about what was going on in my body energetically. During the conversation Louise came out with the nugget, *'the devil is in the detail'*. After a short pause while we both digested the implications of the phrase, and which we were both not entirely happy with, Louise amended the saying. She said *'There are angels in the detail.'* My immediate response to that was *there's a title of a book in there.*

So thus was born the title for this book. The crucial point for me is that the angels thus described represent the forces of light. Within the 'detail' of this book I have done my utmost to represent the forces of light.

One day, sitting and wondering about my future writing, I battled with a negative demon of thought. This demon was telling me, 'Oh, your first book hasn't sold well. You are receiving very little feedback from those that have read it. What do you think you are doing? Do you honestly believe that you are a writer?'

Within a minute a flash of inspiration, an image, came to my awareness. I was standing at an old-fashioned French window, looking out. The wooden supports for the small panes of glass were painted in the most exquisite dark blue. The limited vision of the room that I was standing in was also painted in the same beautiful colour. I immediately realised that this message was from my Pleiadian guides. They were among those that had helped me begin my psychic journey. They were telling me that they were there for me, that this particular part of my journey was not being wasted. I was to continue. So continue I have, and I offer the following, dedicating the book to the many beings inspiring me from their realities.

In previous books the style of writing was one of looking at my adventures and views on reality through the eyes of my good friend Peter Haines. This one will be different. It is now time to present issues that are of interest to me, alone. Perhaps the reason is partly because I have the confidence to do so, and also partly to change the rhythm of writing, thus giving me a greater challenge. I trust that you will enjoy this offering.

From the subjects and incidents that I write about in this and other books it will be clear that I am fascinated with the multitude of energy patterns available to mankind collectively and individually. From meditation to visualisation to physical energies harnessed through chi gong and tai chi, through yoga (I touch the surface with this) to physical exercise systems. These have all been explored by me for development, sometimes apparently successfully, sometimes not. Mental energies, memory systems attracted my attention in earlier times. I lost interest in this latter field as my psychic and spiritual awakening unfolded and with the gradual realisation that a great intellect I was not. Over time a dawning realisation developed in me to explore the inner world in order to learn about and harness as many of these energies as possible.

I have a great interest in bringing together disparate and related views and phenomena. One lifetime is insufficient for this task so I have attempted to draw on other lives being led concurrently by my higher self.

Psychic and interesting happenings in Egypt and the US start the journey of this book. This is followed by fascinating adventures in India.

Amazing tales of 'derring-do' from other people connected to inner planes give a wider interest. I continue this journey by commenting on inner reasons and background for events that transpire in our third-dimension awareness. Sometimes stories are included because they are fascinating rather than they have an obvious inner meaning. The chapter on eccentrics demonstrates this point. There are a significant number of quotations and extracts from other writers. They are included to complement understanding of the chapter subject or to give me the opportunity to provide a different slant to the work of others. Thus an attempt has been made to create some meaning and understanding within this crazy, wonderful, difficult conscious state we call 'living'.

I trust that you will enjoy that which follows. It is a compendium of issues that complement the previous books *So You Think We're Alone?* and *We're Still Not Alone.* I certainly enjoyed preparing and writing it.

ACKNOWLEDGEMENTS

Miranda Lundy; *The Secret Qualities of Quantities:* Candace B. Pert, *Molecules of Emotion*: Drunvalo Melchizedek and his book *The Ancient Secret of The Flower of Life vol 1:* David Hamilton; *How Your Mind Can Heal Your Body:* Radio 4: Lee J. Siegel: Tina Swelzell, Pueblo Indian scholar: The Pleiadians: Jacques Rangasamy: Red Elk: Geoffrey Simcox: Sandra Ingerman *medicine for the Earth*: John Perkins *The World as you dream it:* Amorah Quan Yin: Carl Sandbergh: Robert Dale Owen: Ekhart Tolle: Mary Fitzgerald: Mary Earle: Karl Pribram: Ram Dass: Chris Thomas: Howard Broady: Suzanne Taylor: Barbara Marciniak: Marlik Hakim Johar: Joshua Lambert:Paul Valery: Chuang Tse: PapaSingh (Papa-Ji): Mama-Ji: Mark Moxon: 'Eduardo': Hazel: Louise: Ian: Joan: Pat: Kate: Jaqueline: Audrey: Cynthia: Carol: Pete: Sheena: John: Thoth: Punam: Sean: Susan: Faye: Janet: Bill: Sylvester: Katherine: Julia: Demelza: Penny: Laurie: Jansen: Ken: Henry: 'Stan': Brigid: Bryan: Melody: Pedro: Richard: Radwan: Proffessor John Lober: Wikipedia: Medicine for the Earth: Astrologer magazine: Legal Executive Journal April 2010: Gettysburg information leaflet: History channel: Lonely Planet Guide India: Savannah tourist guide: www.About.com: www.emergingearthangels.com: www.environment.news.msn.uk: www.kundalini-support.com: www.moxon.net: www.mythicalcreaturesguide.com: www.orderofthewhitelion.com/@The4elements.html: Paranormal Phenomena: www.thewashingtonnote.com: www,King-tut.org.uk/curse-of-king-tut/website: www.enlightened beings.com/kundalini.html: www.ancient-egyptonline.co.uk: www.encyclopaedia2.thefreedom dictionary.com: www.avaaz.avaaz.org: www.mumbai.org.uk/excursions/aurengbad-caves.html: www.Greeka.com: www.msn.com: www.easenews.net:www.constellation ofwords.com: www.nps/gov/hov/learn: www.discovernavajo.com:

WIKIPEDIA ACKNOWLEDGEMENTS

Boyd, T.J.M.; Sanderson, J.J. (2003). The Physics of Plasmas. Cambridge University Press. p. 1. ISBN 9780521459129. LCCN 2002024654.

Ball, P. (2004). The Elements: A Very Short Introduction. Very Short Introductions. OUP Oxford. p. 33. ISBN 9780191578250.

Science and Islam, Jim Al-Khalili. BBC, 2009: Van der Brock 1972 p146. Richard 111 of England : Spirits of the Imagination: Vietnam Veterans Memorial:

Foundation Statement for the National Mall and Pennsylvania Avenue National Historic Sometimes punctuated Indigenous "Peoples" or incorrectly "People's" Day

"Goodbye, Columbus. Hello, Indigenous Peoples' Day". HISTORY. Retrieved October 4, 2018.

"Goodbye, Columbus, Hello LBT". Science: 1070. January 1, 1993. doi:10.1126/science.1070-a. ISSN 0036-8075.

"Native American Day – Akta Lakota Museum & Cultural Center". aktalakota.stjo.org.

Thomas J. Morgan (April 9, 2009). "Brown casts off Columbus, agreeing to forgo celebrating his day". Rhode Island Journal.

Park" (PDF), National Park Service, retrieved May 20, 2010

Wunsch, Aaron V. (1994). Historic American Buildings Survey, Washington Monument, HABS DC-428 (text) (PDF). National Park Service.

Lincoln Memorial National Memorial; Washington, DC National Park Service

Bibek Debroy (2012). The Mahabharata: Volume 3. Penguin Books. pp. 184 with footnote 686. ISBN 978-0-14-310015-7.

"Hanuman", *Random House Webster's Unabridged Dictionary.*

J. Gordon Melton; Martin Baumann (2010). Religions of the World: A Comprehensive Encyclopedia of Beliefs and Practices, 2nd Edition. ABC-CLIO. pp. 1310–1311. ISBN 978-1-59884-204-3.

The name that appears on the 1909 version official map of India
"When the spirit of Kabir took over the ancient ghats of Benares". The Sunday Guardian Live. 30 November 2019. Retrieved 29 December 2019.
Rosen, Steven (2006). Essential Hinduism. Praeger Publishers. ISBN 0-275-99006-0
Khajuraho
Gray (2016), pp. 1–3.
Barrett 2008, p. 12
Flood (2006), pp. 9–14.
Bisschop 2020, Chapter 1.
Kongtrul 2005, p. 74.

Murray, Rheana. "See what happened when 3 friends set out to find their 'twin stranger'". *TODAY.com*. Archived from the original on 2017-09-06. Retrieved 2017-12-10.
Boyd, T.J.M.; Sanderson, J.J. (2003). The Physics of Plasmas. Cambridge University Press. p. 1. ISBN 9780521459129. LCCN 2002024654.
Ball, P. (2004). The Elements: A Very Short Introduction. Very Short Introductions. OUP Oxford. p. 33. ISBN 9780191578250.
Van der Broek 1972, p. 146
Praragraph headed Ghost. There is no other quoted source.

Egypt

Revisiting past life locations and enjoying new experiences

The night before Jaqueline, Faye, Audrey and I flew to Luxor from Gatwick I had a visitation immediately before falling asleep. I perceived a close energy connection between the energy known as Sekhmet and myself. It was as though there was a subtle overshadowing, the energy of Sekhmet gently providing a cover over my own personal energy. Immediately afterwards there were several 'crack' noises in the room that I was in, at least three. One was very loud. I had always perceived the sounds as signs of changes or leakages of energy and they frequently occurred around me. In addition, they have been signs for me to pay attention to the messages or thoughts that are being transmitted.

Audrey spoke of a myth in which Sekhmet became very violent. Instead of consuming those that had turned away from Ra, the sun god, she consumed the faithful also. Ra played a trick on Sekhmet in order to reverse the situation. He mixed red ochre of the earth with beer in order to make the drink appear as blood. This did the trick. Sekhmet was attracted to the liquid, drank it and became very calm and benign. Sekhmet then turned into Hathor, taking on a much more feminine aspect. Audrey saw this as the joining of the Sun (Ra) with the Earth.

Wikipedia says this of Sekhmet:

Sekhmet was considered the daughter of the sun god, Ra, and was among the more important of the goddesses who acted as the vengeful manifestation of Ra's power, the Eye of Ra. Sekhmet was said to breathe fire, and the hot winds of the desert were likened to her breath. She was also believed to cause plagues, which were called her servants or messengers, although she was also called upon to ward off disease.

In a myth about the end of Ra's rule on the earth, Ra sends the goddess Hathor, in the form of Sekhmet, to destroy mortals who conspired against him. In the myth, Sekhmet's blood-lust was not quelled at the end of battle and led to her destroying almost all of humanity. To stop her Ra poured out beer dyed with red ochre or hematite so that it resembled blood. Mistaking the beer for blood, she became so drunk that she gave up the slaughter and returned peacefully to Ra. The same myth was also described in the prognosis texts of the Calendar of Lucky and Unlucky Days of papyrus Cairo 86637.

In other versions of this story, Sekhmet grew angered at the deception and left Egypt, diminishing the power of the sun. This threatened the power and security of the world—thus, she was persuaded by the god Thoth to return and restore the sun to its full glory.

Sekhmet was considered the wife of the god Ptah and mother of his son Nefertum. She was also said to be the mother of a lion god, Maahes.

The four travellers reach the boat, the *Viking Premiere*, their floating hotel for the next week. Assorted British 'wrinklies' (I don't include wife Jaqueline in that description) unload from the coach that had brought them from the aircraft. Faye disputes this title as she is remarkably wrinkle-free despite her sixty-five years. As the stiff-legged travellers walk towards the boat along the pavement past Egyptian street-vendors and other men watching their progress, one shouts to me, 'You walk like an Egyptian.' At the time I has no idea, in my innocence, what this means.

A few days later on the street I am approached by the same man with the same comment. Clearly the Egyptian has forgotten the previous occasion. It dawns on me that this was an opening gambit to extract 'backsheesh' from the unwary traveller. I waved the attempted flatterer away.

It is time for the 'wrinklies' to visit Edfu temple, dedicated to Horus. All the travellers have been divided into three groups for the purpose of transport by coach and instruction by guides. We four are in Horus group. The temple is magnificent in its construction and size. However, something is missing for me. The energy and past life connection that I am seeking is not to be found here. For me there is a 'deadness' that takes some time for me to explain.

Horus group guide Radwan explains that this is a late period temple built by the Ptolemies, those pharaohs that ruled immediately before Egypt became a Roman colony. I realised that the profound and stunning magic that had been part of earlier Pharaonic rule had been lost in this late period. The earlier pharaohs had been priests / kings, bearers of the sacred knowledge. The late period rulers were merely kings. Egypt was in decline by this time. The five-thousand-year-old jewel of civilisation was approaching its end. The Temple of Edfu was a magnificent example of temporal power and a control mechanism of the masses who laboured for the pharoah. The one feeling that came to me here was a familiarity with the architecture. I felt comfortable in these massive columns and statues, the motifs of gods and pharaohs inlaid into the stone, the faces of Hathor peering out from the top of columns. This feeling was a mirror of the one when I had stepped off the plane: an emotion of comfort with the landscape, the shape and sandy colour of the hills. The nearest sense that I could make of this was that it was as though I was coming home. Edfu was the last great temple erected by the ancient Egyptians. The father of Cleopatra VII, she of Anthony and Julius Caesar fame, finished it.

Next stop was Kom Ombo double temple, dedicated to Horus and Sobek, the crocodile-headed god. I felt connected to the crocodile energy, partly because of a vision some years previously of a crocodile-headed being that revealed itself as part of my greater self. The other reason for my connected feeling was my knowledge that Egyptians, by building temples over crocodile pools, had communed and used the psychic energies of these creatures. I felt the atmosphere

here was magical, perhaps because the visit was made after dark and the looming massive edifices were highlighted by spotlights. The contrast of light and shade created an ambience of mystery, probably for the benefit of the milling tourists.

Parties of French tourists moved around among parties of English. Sometimes a word or phrase would be said by the English to the French and sometimes the other way round. I sensed an element of competition or edginess between the two races. Quite why this was I had no idea. It may be that old enmities could be raised in the comfort of a large support group and away from home climes.

This is what Drunvalo Melchizedek in *The Ancient Secret of The Flower of Life Volume 2* has to say about Kom Ombo.

Years ago I read of the ability of the early Egyptian priesthood to perform ceremonies that would keep the borders secure from invasion. As the civilisation declined these abilities were lost and the society moved towards collapse.

Jaqueline was very nervous about coming to Egypt. She could not explain logically why this was so. Her feelings about Turkey are more positive however. When I suggested a visit to the latter she was most positive about the idea. As the four began this journey Jaqueline asked Audrey to give her a reading concerning her worries, on the face of it unfounded, about this country of Egypt. Now for those who haven't read any of our books before, one of Audrey's talents is an ability to link to other peoples' past lives relevant to them currently. She does this by reading the Akashic record.

Audrey entered a light meditative state. She saw Jaqueline as a slave here in ancient times. She had been captured from Hittite lands. The Hittites lived in Anatolia, which is now part of modern Turkey. Thus, Jaqueline's positive and negative emotional feelings concerning both countries can now be explained. Jaqueline lived in a village in Anatolia. News reached the village that Egyptians had invaded their country. It was some time before the invasion impacted on their quiet rural life.

One day the surrounding peace was invaded by an alien roaring sound. Within minutes Egyptian chariots charged into the village. The villagers were told to march to the sea to be transported to Egypt as slaves. Jaqueline lost contact with her family. Once in Egypt she never saw them again. She was put to work as a nanny of small children, lonely and grieving for a life that was gone forever. She wasn't badly treated but simply abandoned. Thus this is the background for Jaqueline's emotional reaction to the two modern countries of Egypt and Turkey.

On the first night on the boat I walked to the front of the top passenger deck of the boat. I glanced down to the prow of the boat (the sharp end!) and saw some of the crew making their evening prayers towards Mecca. From my perspective this was approximately ten o'clock on a clock-face. To my left could be heard the faint tones of Egyptian music. Welcome to Egypt, Birchy! It was most atmospheric and relaxing.

Philae temple was next on the visit agenda. This place was particularly favoured by Faye before the trip as she believed that she had a life here in times past. As with Edfu this place was built by the Ptolemies in the Greek period. The Ptolemies were descendants of the Greek generals that Alexander left here on his journey of conquering the known world. Similar to Edfu the energies were not that great for me, neither, surprisingly, were they for Faye. *'They have all gone,'* she said with some degree of disappointment.

The temple visits were separated by other activities. One of the major interests for the three ladies that travelled with me was shopping. Retail therapy was a most important activity for them. This had to be done Egyptian style, which Jaqueline and Faye tackled with great gusto. They are both adroit negotiators. Their skills have been honed in the bazaars and markets of Delhi, Afghanistan and Mexico. No Egyptian vendor was safe from their assertive bargaining.

Audrey allowed the above two to do her negotiating. I was completely resistant to any form of shopping, as many men are. I was content to trail around, ensuring a male presence for them to eliminate the possibility of unwanted pestering. Egyptian vendors and passing men were intrigued by the presence of one man with three women. A number of them questioned why I had three wives! As a small tease I chose not to disabuse them. On a number of occasions men would approach me, offering to buy one of the wives for a number of camels. This clearly was an element of entertainment for locals and visitors, as the former are more interested in obtaining British pounds than parting with non-existent camels. However, it kept people interested and largely relaxed.

The atmosphere thus remained light-hearted. On one occasion the shopkeeper was so impressed with Faye's ability to bargain that he offered me, who happened to be listening to the process, two hundred camels to sell Faye. I demanded two hundred and fifty. The negotiation finished at two hundred and thirty. We, the two men, closed the deal by solemnly shaking hands and laughing uproariously. The English quartet went their way; Anglo-Egyptian relations had been positively reinforced.

A 3.30 am one morning an alarm call pulled Jaqueline and me out of deep sleep. Not much lazing around on this vacation. Various 'wrinklies' piled out of the boat to enter coaches with their engines running by 4.30 am. The boat was now at Aswan as far south on the Nile as it could successfully moor. The coaches headed into the desert in convoy, more than twenty of them. This convoy was not a protection against attack, or so we were told, but as security in the event of vehicle breakdown. For between Aswan and the intended destination on the Sudanese border there was nothing but desert and the snaking road. For four hours the convoy wound its way through the unchanging scene. The pristine desert sand and rocks the only unrelieved scenery.

Past a military checkpoint, necessary perhaps because of the proximity of a foreign country that was experiencing internal problems, the convoy swept into a car park. The latter was no different from the surrounding desert except the sand had been compacted. The party was at Abu Simbal temple complex dedicated to Pharoah Ramses II. A fantastic engineering feat had moved the whole complex from its original location to higher ground. As the rising water of Lake Nasser created by the Aswan dam crept higher, Russian and German engineers battled against the clock to move the temples and enormous figures in time. The cyclopean statues and temples dedicated to Ramses II and his favourite wife Nefertara, plus others, are awesome. They must be seen to be properly experienced. Photographs and film do not convey the wonder of them. For the first time on the trip I resonated with the temple complex.

The temple was built during the middle kingdom when the psychic powers of the priesthood were at their peak. This was unlike the Ptolemaic period, much later, when the old ways were in decline. I felt that I had worked here in another lifetime. The place was so familiar to me. I felt relaxed despite the enormous numbers of tourists. The visit terminated with joining a queue to enter Nefertara's temple. A Spanish man made the mistake of attempting to 'jump' the queue in front of Jaqueline. He received 'both barrels' of her verbal ferocity for his pains, in Spanish of course, and he retreated.

Since the trip had originally been mooted, Jaqueline had been keen to ride a camel as part of the adventure. I was less than keen with this idea. However, I went along with it for marital solidarity. The day dawned with my being less than excited about the project. The plan was for those in the party that wished to do this to start in the desert and then complete the ride at a Nubian village in order to experience a little of the culture of this arid region.

The adventurous souls disembarked from a motor launch, climbed the desert sands and reached a small plateau on which many camels were sitting. Tourists eyed the camels, camels eyed the tourists. It was pretty clear that the local beasts looked the most confident. Fortunately, each camel was to be led by a Nubian. The ability to stay in the saddle as the camel rose up and down is the first challenge for the untutored 'wrinklies'. Back legs came up first followed by front legs a few seconds later – camel legs that is! I lurched forward and back during this manoeuvre. I was supposed to be enjoying this. I did, however, manage to stay on board.

The party set off one at a time. My camel was about twentieth in the line. One of the issues when riding these beasts is the position of the riders' legs, for camels are much wider than horses. Another challenge was the up and down motion of the animal as it plodded along; not great for those with bad backs. The experienced locals rode their camels with their legs crossed behind the camel's neck and in front of the wooden saddle pommel. I thought about changing position from my uncomfortable one with legs dangling down by the animal's side. The fear of falling off was so intense I decided against it and continued to bounce up and down uncomfortably. A security man rode up and down the line of camels as we plodded forward; an AK47 nestled in the crook of his arm. I wondered how safe we were here.

I quickly christened my camel 'Speedy Gonzales' as it set off at a rate of knots. So much so that within five minutes of the journey it had moved up to seventh in the line. I concentrated on staying on and moving my body such that my spine would still be in alignment by the end of the jarring experience. My camel continued its race forward until it caught up with 'Mr Grumpy'. I felt sorry for the tourist on the back of this animal. 'Mr Grumpy' regularly turned its head towards the discomforted rider, bearing its teeth and making growling noises in its throat. Its stained, uneven teeth completed the unpleasant picture. At least it didn't spit at its rider, which I believe camels do if upset.

'Speedy Gonzales' immediately slowed as it caught up with 'Mr Grumpy' and didn't attempt to overtake the angry one. 'Speedy' clearly decided that discretion was the better part of valour and steered clear. Clearly 'Mr Grumpy' had clout in the camel world.

Jaqueline rode 'Mr Grumpy 2'. It started to 'play up' to the Mexican with noises of its own. Jaqueline's response was to speak pleasantly to it. *Nice Mr Camel, treat me well,* she whispered. The animal duly obliged, perhaps demonstrating that there are gentlemanly beasts in the camel world. As the party neared the Nubian village I became more confident. Instead of merely gripping the wooden pommel of the saddle for dear life I began to push it forward and back to persuade the animal to speed up. The effect was the reverse. 'Speedy' slowed, turned its head and gave me what he could only describe as the 'evil eye'. The message was clear. *Don't get excited, amigo* (or the Egyptian equivalent). *Let us be clear who is in charge.* I responded to the message and returned to clinging to the pommel. The pecking order had returned to normal. The party of camels and uncomfortable riders entered the central square of the Nubian village. I slid stiffly and gratefully from my ride. I gave my mount a last look back as I headed off. Speedy Gonzales stared disdainfully back. The journey had been survived in one piece.

We spent a little time in the village relaxing and drinking sodas. It was interesting how different the Nubian villagers were from the Egyptians we had met. The women were tall and graceful, slim and darker than the town dwellers. There were few men around apart from the camel guardians. We were told that the majority of men were working in the city.

Friday, the day off from travel and outside adventure, arrived. 'Time team' members Audrey, Faye and me gathered for a meditation in Audrey and Faye's cabin. I started the meditation by invoking the names of four beings, Sekhmet, Horus, Isis and Hathor, the latter three also being deities or powerful energetic signatures. Each of the beings was asked to place themselves in one corner of a psychically created square. The 'time team' placed themselves at the centre of the square. Next the sides of the square were drawn up, creating a pyramid. The energies of the four beings were invoked to merge with and accelerate the energy bodies of each member of the time team.

During the meditation Faye was visited by an enormously large Sekhmet who asked, *Who calls me?* Faye asked for inspirational thoughts and was told that all three humans should stand between her (Sekhmet's) paws, the man in the middle. The three were bowing in obeisance in her presence. Sekhmet gave the three the gift of power. A warning was added that much remained to be done, albeit great difficulties would be experienced in this work. The final advice was that with great power comes great responsibility. Three Hathor beings came to Faye with their legs crossed and twitching ears. Faye also saw the three members of the 'time team' working at different levels of their being. A more benign aspect of Sekhmet came to me, giving the 'time team' the gift of becoming part of her energy.

Horus, the offspring of Isis and Osiris, is the energy of the midday sun, active and energetic as well as the protector of the three members of the 'time team'. It is the aspect of that which is to be revealed. Amun (or Amun-Ra, Amun-Re) is the hidden and unknown aspect of the sun, different from the Horus aspect, representing the hidden element of that which is to be revealed or made manifest.

It is now time for the last temple visits. The 'time team' stand on a stone causeway stretching away from Luxor temple. They sense that they have stood on this royal road, flanked by sphinxes, in times past. I am engulfed by a vision of the three of us in a procession following the pharaoh with lines of priests flanking the procession. Faye, in the vision, saw herbal fronds cast on the floor releasing their perfume as the passing procession stepped on them. Palm fronds waved to cool the procession as the sun beat down from a cloudless sky. The vision was so real I could feel the heat of the sun bouncing off my white robes. I sensed that the three were part of the spiritual entourage of this pharaoh. The atmosphere was full of loud noises from cymbal, drum and horn. There was an expectant air of excitement around the event. It was as though a great ceremony was about to be performed in Luxor Temple. That was it. The vision faded and we were back in the twenty first century.

Outside the vision I thought the Pharoah was Ramses II. This temple is largely dedicated to him with a small part built by Hatshepsut. I sensed a peaceful benign energy here. We three walked towards the temple. As we moved I sensed the barrier between this density, the third-dimensional one, and a parallel one becoming thinner such that they, the dimensions, began to merge. Perhaps one of the reasons for our visit was to experience this thinning of the veil between densities or dimensions. We, mystics here-present, may have played a small part in this phenomenon.

The final temple visit was, for me, to the jewel in the crown, Karnak Temple. This was one of the three spiritual centres that I had co-operated in bringing together energetically months before in a healing meditation. The other two had been Carnac in Brittany and Callanish in Scotland. The full story of this triad of centres which were healed and re-energised is told in our previous book, *We're Still Not Alone.* It was to here I needed to come on this trip. Jaqueline and Audrey were sick. Only Faye and I were fit enough to make this journey. We stand in front of the sacred lake. Faye remembers being here in another life although not the same as her Filae life. In the Karnak life Faye was trying to escape life in the temple. As she made her escape she was pursued by a man attempting to dissuade her. The escape route was by boat through a tunnel not visible at the present water level.

As we entered the temple I felt connected and comfortable immediately. I was at home. The party entered the Hypostyle hall, the eighth wonder of the world, according to guide Radwan. This magnificent place contains 130 columns decorated with writing and cartouche from bottom to top. Each column is around fifty feet high. As I sat at the foot of one of the columns I sensed that the mass of detail around me in this powerful place was to throw the mind of the observer out of the mundane and drive the consciousness inward. The plethora of information was too much for the objective consciousness to absorb.

As we left this last temple I was already running possible places to visit and connect with energetically through my mind. I had already received an insight that I should visit the city of Alexandria, second city of Egypt, a centre of the greatest learning and deepest mystical practices for thousands of years. Other places that came to mind were Tel-El-Amarna, the spiritual centre of the Ra cult developed by

Akhenaton; this represented the power of god behind the sun. The pyramids at Giza, a return trip to Karnak and a visit to St Catherine's Monastery in Sinai would all be places that were worth a visit for this 'crazy mystic'. The final location of interest to me would be Lake Moeris, which has great spiritual power according to friend Sylvester, who visited it some years previously. We will see what the future brings.

It was time to leave Egypt and return to 'Dear Old Blighty', aka Britain. As the party prepared to leave I recalled a conversation I had with Radwan, our caring and able guide, concerning the famous or infamous Danish cartoons about the prophet Mohammed. Radwan is a well-educated man, he has a PhD, as well as being exposed to western culture and values. He had spoken passionately concerning his anger over the cartoons lampooning the prophet in a Danish newspaper. For the first time I saw the argument from the other side. Freedom of speech is a right in our society that must be protected. However, there is also the issue of respecting the views and feelings of other cultures. Muslims, even well-educated ones, such as Radwan, are greatly hurt by the lack of respect shown to their religion. I was also struck by the clash of culture between the Western libertarian and the Eastern Muslim. No wonder there are problems over the interpretation of what represents human rights, democracy and old-fashioned respect.

We also quizzed Radwan on the nature of the original spiritual and religious practices that were conducted here. He reluctantly agreed that the Isis cult was active, but was not happy to give any further information. I felt his Moslem religion precluded any involvement with the original practices. It was clear that although he was immensely proud of these fantastic buildings and complexes in his country he did not wish to investigate the meaning behind them. Perhaps later generations of Egyptians will honour this most important part of their heritage.

Postcript

There was one item that came after the trip. Jaqueline and I were enjoying a pleasant social evening with Joan and Mary. Suddenly the lights in Joan's house blinked on and off at the same time the cat flap in the back door swung forward and back violently, as though someone or something had entered the house. There was no wind outside. It was as though this someone or something was making a psychic entrance, and so it proved. That evening a spiritual being made its presence felt to Joan. It was very tall, serious natured and dressed from head to toe in black. Joan had no idea initially what the being was doing entering her consciousness. Later, friends told Joan that they thought it was a Nubian being and that it had travelled back from Egypt with Jaqueline and me.

The following week Mary, Joan and I met for their normal weekly meditation. During the meditation Mary and I sensed that this being was present to assist Joan in her spiritual work, that it was to act as a bridge between the spiritual realms and the physical in order to transmit messages back and forth when requested. I also sensed that this work was a development process for the tall being.

A couple of days before the social meeting above a very benign being came into my consciousness early one morning. This being smiled broadly and warmly at me as though he was pleased with me. I sensed that this man was Celtic in origin. At the same meditation above Mary felt that this being was there to help me with inspiration in the work that would present itself in the future.

Later that year, Audrey and I started to work with a particular energy form. Within days of starting that work I began to receive the vision of walking towards Luxor temple behind the pharaoh in ancient times. The difference this time was that the vision became stronger and stronger. It re-occurred in my consciousness time after time. There was something here attempting to break through into objective awareness. It was time to meditate deeply on this matter. I felt drawn to consult Audrey on this matter for two reasons. First of all, the reason for the enhanced vision related to my current work with Audrey, and second because we shared at least one life together in ancient Egypt in the court of the pharaoh. To date I am still awaiting any further revelations that may present themselves.

Preparation for USA Visit

Internal preparations and explorations

Inspiration came to me one night concerning my proposed visit to Georgia USA, (which subsequently turned out to be located in South Carolina 50 miles north of the Georgia border). I had been puzzled that very little inspiration had come my way concerning researching my past life there in the Confederate Army during the Civil War. Indeed, when researching the internet looking at names of Georgian combatants in order to attempt to link with one of them I discovered nothing.

I had been inspired to focus on Georgia as a venue for me to visit on my path to wholeness. This inspiration manifested in pain and discomfort to my right knee and hip. Over many months I had tried to heal it through my own and others' healing interventions with limited success. As a last resort I asked friend Audrey to 'look in' to the Akashic record to attempt to establish a meaning to this manifestation. Audrey established that the pain was in the exact location where I was shot in the Civil War conflict. The message later came to me that the above pain was a device in order to gain my attention and focus it on this part of the South. In this way the major reason for my visit there could then be revealed.

The inspiration mentioned in the first sentence in the paragraph above concerned the city of Savannah. It was broken down into Sa-Va-Nah. Perhaps this is the ancient version of the name, I thought. I was told by my inspiration that the area was host to an inter-dimensional portal, a time portal where a number of dimensions meet: a nexus point. For a few seconds I was transported into a scene of distant low mountains. The light was different from this third dimension in which our consciousness resides most of the time. Ancient Native Americans are guardians of this portal. I, in a flash of intuition, later saw again a group of Native Americans standing around a campfire in another dimension. These, I believe, are the guardians. They made their presence known to me some years previously.

I was puzzled by their sudden appearance again. Now I understand the connection is beyond time. This portal is not stable in the third dimension. It moves around the area growing larger, as big as the whole area sometimes, and smaller at others. It moves much as a torch-beam does in the dark. It is my view that my presence at this location will assist in the stabilisation process. Anomalous phenomena may surround the portal because of its great size and power. The ghost story told later may be one example of this phenomenon.

At a subsequent time I sensed that friend Bryan's energy would be a bonus during this visit. Bryan feels imbued with light energy increasingly, so much so that as he walks sometimes his legs lift effortlessly as he takes each step.

A further insight that came to me related to a phenomenon proposed by Jacques Rangasamy. This stated that throughout our many lifetimes, including this one, we 'slough off' fragments of ourselves, our personalities, our soul personalities caused by the traumas and heartaches that we experience. That is, these parts of our being separate from us. These fragments, although not integral to our spiritual psyche, nevertheless remain connected to us by psychic threads. Further, Jacques proposes that, through our spiritual work, we can reclaim these semi-detached elements. To do that we offer back to source (God, our higher selves) those parts of our being that become separated from us and stopped us being whole. We were thus separated from our authentic selves.

As we reclaim ourselves the Holy Spirit enters our bodies, thus preparing us for the next stage. In order to live we please our egos so that we can cope with life's vicissitudes. The insight that I received was to the effect that the Sa-Va-Nah portal was a perfect environment for facilitating these psychic reconnections. Indeed, for me, the two propositions that attracted me to Georgia (and South Carolina), namely healing my life in the Confederate Army and the stabilisation of the portal, were now part of the same work.

OK, let us open up this debate a little more. I am of the opinion that our future and past lives are constantly interacting and learning at a subliminal level from each other for the development of the soul personality. A major trick here is to, first of all, realise that this is happening and then find ways of working with this for our advantage. This brings an interesting point relating to the calling back of those elements of ourselves that we have lost because of pain, anger, guilt, grief and other negative emotions. Does this proposition mean that we are only calling in those elements from 'past' lives? If the so-called 'past' and 'future' lives are running concurrently from a cosmic perspective then surely we are in a position to heal 'past' and 'future' at the same three-dimensional reality. Indeed it could be that our 'future' and 'past' lives are also involved in this healing work. Our 'present' life is the one in which we are focussed right now.

There the story rested for some time until I, suffering from writer's block, contacted the 'lion person', from another reality, that had suggested some years ago that I would write a book. This communication was in the form of as meditative request that the said 'lion person' inspire my efforts. That very night I was woken with information relating to the Merkabah. The latter is the interlacing tetrahedron shape that is said, in mystical teachings, to surround our physical bodies and, which it is believed, is the sacred geometric key to our initiation into a higher realm of existence. My perspective on this phenomenon began some years ago when I read an account by Amorah Quan Yin, the Pleiadian channel. She wrote of the presence of our original eight cells from our conception residing in our perineum. Later I was given the insight that these eight cells were aligned in the form of the Merkabah within each person's perineum.

The insight that I received at the beginning of the above paragraph was that our development could be quickened if we, using visualisation, perceived our whole body imbued with these Merkabah structures uniting eight cells in each case. Secondly, that I should work on the Merkabah surrounding my body and that this stronger sacred geometry of my being would assist in grounding and stabilising the energy portal in Sa-Va-Nah. In a further flash of inspiration I found himself in the presence of the Native Americans living in another dimension again. I knew this because there was something different about this mountainous desert environment. The vibrations were somehow stronger and more alive. I had been in their company once before but, at that time, had no idea what I was doing there. This time I knew that these were guardians of Sa-Va-Nah.

Later that same day I tuned in, during a meditation, to the Native Americans. I joined them around their campfire as I had done previously. One of them was standing, a tall man with a single feather in his braided hair. The other two were sitting by the crackling fire either staring into it or meditating. I could not see which as their eyes were hooded. I felt that they both were aged. I joined them and sat cross-legged at the fire. I felt that they perceived me as a ghost. They were not startled by my presence. They had been expecting an event. I then asked them for help in stabilising the energy portal. The two seated men continued in the same vein as far as I could tell. The third standing man immediately went into a dance, shaking a rattle and chanting as he circled outside the fire. The three of us joined him.

A little later we three sat again around the fire. The leader of the dance went and stood by a nearby sacred rock, making various passes with his hands that I could not perceive. All I knew at this point was that the rock was sacred. I also realised that the three Native Americans did not have any answers and that their current activities were designed to evoke inspiration from yet higher realms. My contact finished as the four of us sat in a square, a symbol of stability, around the fire. I sensed that this was a move designed to start the stabilisation process. Through the four seated figures the portal passed straight through the fire and on down to the third dimension. There it would open out to be much larger in size.

As the meditation deepened the energy of the portal flowed down in white, tendril-like spirals. The four beings deepened their meditation connection, stabilising further the course of the energy as it moved down into the third dimension; looked at from above the square rotated slightly to give the impression of a diamond shape, with one being seated at each corner. Straight lines of force reached from corner to corner, further stabilising the energy in the fourth dimension. I, as a last vision during this meditation, moved my consciousness back into the third dimension, looking up at the portal entry point stabilised by the straight lines of force. I then returned to sit with my companions for some time until I came out of this meditative state.

It was time for me to return to my body, reluctantly. I would have preferred to stay but there was work to do on my ego and psyche that would keep me in this lower reality. In a subsequent meditation friend Mary intuited that I needed to perform a medicine wheel ceremony before leaving for the US in order to strengthen the work of the stabilisation.

The Native American beings demonstrated that they have a wider spiritual support remit for me than the portal stabilisation work in Sa-Va-Na. In order to assist a Mexican woman cruelly and wrongly imprisoned for a murder she did not commit, I decided to conduct a medicine wheel ceremony at home. She was about to be sentenced, so urgent support for her plight was required. During the ceremony, completely unexpectedly, the beings came into my awareness. I was considerably heartened that they should appear. I believed that their visual intervention was a sign that they were contributing their energy to the task. I later realised that the medicine wheel, a Native American spiritual tool, was probably the link that enabled their participation.

'It's Bryan, Clive.' The familiar voice rang through the telephone earpiece.

'Sadly I will not be able to join you on your forthcoming trip to Georgia and beyond. However, I feel that your journey should include some time in Vicksburg Civil War ceremony. Visiting Gettysburg would also be great for you to do. It is a place of strong energy, particularly with your connection to that conflict. I would suggest that you fly into Chicago O'Hare airport and drive down to Savannah from there.'

So, I was not to be joined by Bryan and his energies. At least I could now start planning the trip. I placed great credence on Bryan's advice. His contact with psychic forces was powerful. As the day wore on I felt less and less comfortable with Chicago as the flight destination. Neither did Atlanta seem to have the required energies. Almost idly I opened the map of the US that I had originally obtained before my 1999 trip. My glance ran across the map from middle to right-hand side until my eyes locked on to Washington. My eyes seemed to be trapped looking at this spot and the energy began to flow through my body. *Well,* I thought. *This is right next to the Virginias, where a lot of Civil War action took place. I could wheel to the right into North Virginia and then south through to the Carolinas into Georgia.* Thinking in those terms brought home to me that my journey was almost a military operation in its own right.

It was as though the basis of the first part of the trip was unveiling in my mind with little mental intervention. As I contemplated the journey the words 'Bull Run' and 'Appomattox' came into consciousness, both battles in the war. As the words sank into objective consciousness there was a click in one corner of the room similar to a rifle being cocked. Many times in my spiritual and psychic work unexpected and unexplained sounds will confirm the flow of advice sourced from my intuition.

I could complete my work with the Civil War energy and then move onto the portal work in Savannah.

As I continued to contemplate, the words 'journey of healing' entered my consciousness. My eyes then swept back up the map through Atlanta then to Memphis, Little Rock, Oklahoma City (both places with recent traumatic history), then to Amarillo and Albuquerque, New Mexico.

It is meditation day with friend Joan. I feel a little insecure about landing in Washington. After our meditation Joan intuits that all will be fine. I will be looked after by the spiritual forces. However, it would be beneficial to rest in Washington before the travelling. In addition, she senses that travelling alone will be better; that my energy will be all that is needed for the tasks ahead. I feel better after this information and plan to stay in Washington for two days, resting and working there.

Later as I thought about my journey starting in Washington, the face of a Native American came into my awareness. Very strong and full of personality he was. The face filled my vision. Perhaps this is a sign of the proximity of his presence. The name of the local football team is the Washington Redskins. However, Jacques Rangasamy has said *'The North American Indians call themselves the red man not because the skin was red but because the hearts were red with the flame of the soul lit in the heart.'* In fact, their skin is brown in colour.

In a meditation conducted with friends I received some interesting feedback from them as well as an insight of my own. The latter insight presented the name of the recently arrived Native American guide, who announced himself through my intuition as Red Elk. One of my friends perceived a well-known Native American being in the background orchestrating the journey; his name is White Eagle. Before the meditation I let slip that I was nervous about this trip and not my usual confident self. My friends said that it was important to be confident in my spiritual self and that everything would be taken care of. Red Elk and a protective Native American would ensure a safe and productive trip. In addition, it was not necessary to become dependent on the magical practices of the past such as medicine wheels.

It was sufficient to ask that the situation, problem, issue be healed. The cosmic would take care of the rest. Fellow meditator Ian said that he felt impelled to give me two objects to take on this journey; one was a seashell and the other a crystal. This latter was to be used in the visionary work of creating rainbows of light between the centres that were to be worked on and in. The above and the following insights and work was leading me to a similar situation before my six-month trip to the Americas in 1999. Then, as now, psychic changes and insights manifested in my being.

> *What do you know about the eight shafts of light emanating from the Pineal Gland? Can you ask the new guide that will be arriving shortly. Sorry to be so obtuse but that is all I am getting at the moment, apart from seeing these inside my head!*

The above message arrived from Ian via email, apparently unconnected with other work that I was doing. Still, what do I know! I replied:

> *I received a vision with shafts of light, 7 of them, going in and out of the pineal. The 8th one, I sensed but did not see, went straight up into the cosmic realms. The shafts can be associated with the Buddhist eightfold path. Probably this is only on one level of reality. There must be other meanings. The shaft going straight up is a way out of this third dimension, a path to higher dimensions. In order to access it we must dispose of all our baggage otherwise this path will not be open to us. Drunvalo Melchizedek says that the eye of the pineal looks straight up. This path would be our final initiation in this reality. The new guide will present him/herself when the time is right, either to you or to the group.* (I was wrong. The new guide for me was Red Elk, mentioned above. In addition, at our meditation meeting Ian picked up that all members of the group now had one new guide each with a Native American orientation.) *There could be others.*

Subsequently further reading caused to me to email Ian again:

> *This is in the Drunvalo Melchizedek book you loaned me. We actually have six of these sensing rays – not just one, but six. They all come from the centre of our heads, the pineal gland. One ray comes out of the front of our head at the third eye and another goes out the back; one goes out of the left and another out of the right side of our brain; and another goes straight up through the crown chakra and the sixth straight down through the neck–the six directions ... This might be why the American Indians and native people all around the world find the six directions so important.*

Reviewing my vision I latterly saw four rays entering the front of the pineal and four entering the back with the ninth going up through the crown. I missed the one going down through the throat. This last vision seems kosher to me. A subsequent meditation with Joan brought up the information from within that this pineal work was to clear me more so that experiences in the upcoming US trip would be strengthened. I would be more absorbent of experiences and information there. Finally, more experiences absorbed would enable more to be shared with 'crazies' back home. Another insight gave me the information that I should meditate on the trip during the outward-bound flight.

As this psychic and physical preparation proceeded one other strand came in to join the party. On the same day that I booked my flight to Washington I received an email from Sheena, my 'buddy' on the Brittany/ Malta/ Gozo trip of the previous year. (This trip is documented in our previous book *We're Still Not Alone.*) This email advertised a trip to India, a place that I had not felt drawn to work in despite my past connection to Paramahansa Yogananda and other Indian mystics. Immediately this struck a chord with me.

As the day progressed I realised that I was being impelled to start a period of working in the east. Further, it came to me that, given that it was successful, this current trip would be my last for a while in the

West. There was a sense that this trip to the US, besides the work to be completed, was also a doorway to another energy form and work pattern in the East. The trip to Egypt written above was also a forerunner of this work. When I told co-writer and friend Pete about this US trip he was enthusiastic about including it in our previous book. I was less enthusiastic, as I knew that the energy pattern was different from previous. Later I realised that the work in Egypt, in the US and in India were all connected and would therefore form the basis or spine of this book.

Advice concerning this trip continued to filter into my consciousness by psychic and human means. Audrey called me to say that she sensed it would be to my benefit to trace the place of my shooting in the Civil War life for a healing to take place. I could help myself by psychically exploring a map, she continued. My intuition around the same time suggested that I relax during the trip and not rush around, as is my wont.

This is from the tourist guide to Savannah.

Savannah was established on February 12, 1733 when General James Oglethorpe founded Georgia. The city was named for the Savannah River, a local waterway. Oglethorpe carefully planned the city's streets by using a grid pattern with 24 park-like squares. Savannah has the distinction of being the first city in the state of Georgia.

There are numerous attractions in Savannah to increase cultural awareness and make Savannah the 'Hostess City of the South'. Savannah is home to a National Historic Landmark District of 2.5 square miles, and more than 1,100 architecturally significan tbuildings.

Friend Suzanne Taylor, who lives in Beaufort and who I plan to stay with, says Savannah is an old, old historic city, she believes that they imported slaves from another country (possibly European) to build it and there are many restless spirits there.

St. Helena Island was territory occupied by people from Africa with deep voodoo roots. I think in the 1800s a great hurricane came here and wiped out most of the inhabitants on the island.

Suzanne recently had a session with a shaman apprentice and much was revealed. There is a feminine vortex in Beaufort, South Carolina that runs to Savannah, and it is wobbling, Suzanne was told. This could be the vortex that I seek to work with. The shaman called Suzanne a sister and said she was needed. The shaman also said Suzanne needed to open her lower three chakras, and that she was a galactic traveller. Suzanne could have exited this life many times but she hasn't. Suzanne is a determined person. The shaman revealed a couple of nasty endings to past lives, but she saw the goddess rising up out of the sea with dolphins all around Suzanne.

She said the pain she was carrying was not her own. It needs to go. She also sensed that there are vibrations in her house that aren't resonating with her level of awareness.

I have a friend, Laurie, who also has a connection with some of the work I will be doing on this trip. He has a perception of fighting in the US Civil War in another lifetime. The difference between him and me in that conflict is that he fought on the side of the north, the Yankees. He has said in that lifetime we may have been in conflict rather than the harmonious spiritual work that we do together today. There is also two other connections between us. First, we have the same birthday, although our births were ten years apart. Second, on photographs a number of people have mistaken one for the other, although in the flesh we don't look that much alike. What these last two points mean I have no idea, except that they highlight the connections between us. He asked me before the trip began to bring back three condor feathers from Native American sources, if possible. He uses feathers as a cleansing device for the aura.

As I meditated during my last night at home I recalled visiting Austin, Texas, in 1999, seeing the governor's residence and state legislature. This was occupied by George Bush, who was soon to be president of the US but was then governor of the state of Texas. On the 10th of October I planned to visit the national legislature and

White House, occupied by President Bush, who would soon be ex-President Bush. There is symmetry between the two events. I have been here at the beginning and at the end of this presidency. Perhaps I, and others, ushered him in and out of his presidency. I mean this in an energetic sense. He is much criticised as a president. Perhaps he was elected to teach the American public some things on their path to maturity. In every situation there is opportunity for learning. It is an ill wind that blows no-one any good. The incoming president will be very different if for no other reason than the American public will demand it.

In 2003 again I had been in the US, this time at the Spring Equinox, March 21st. Sitting in a motel room in front of the TV, I watched the 'shock and awe' attack on Baghdad. I wonder if this visit will mark another symmetrical event with that one. If so, let us hope that it is not a violent one. In a recent meditation, friend Mary saw me, during the course of my US visit, protected by an enormous brown bear standing behind me. The Native Americans identified previously were also there. Mary and Joan will be in Greece for one week from October 16th. Joan sees the three of us continuously connected on our two journeys. Later I felt that the symmetry I mentioned above was, in fact, an end marker for my work in the West, mentioned above at least for the time being. Also it was a marker for the beginning of work that I was to do in the East.

In the crystal Ian had given me as a gift for the Native American shaman, Faye saw a lone wolf. This wolf is my power animal. It is certainly significant and symbolic of my lone journeying. The wolf is also a pack animal so it can happily co-exist and co-operate with others or work and live independently. I am much the same. Audrey saw a knight in shining armour. Maybe Audrey's knight is a symbol of potential or actual protection. If this is so then it will be much welcomed.

USA Part 1

From Washington to South Carolina

As our aircraft banked over to one side in preparation to land at Ronald Reagan Airport, Washington DC, I looked down on a scene of bug-like vehicles snaking along the highways. The pollution cloud, although hanging at a higher level, was not evident at ground level and was not as ubiquitous as in LA. I put this down to the pollution-freeing effect of many thousands of trees that are in and around the city. An evening walk around the block from the hotel enabled me to stretch cramped limbs and to open constricted lungs to fresh air. The temperature is a balmy one so a relaxed perambulation is possible. The cicadas are in full chirp. There is one chirp that is different. It has a metallic, hollow, resonating quality and is lower in tone. I realise that some of these insects are positioned under the cars parked along the sidewalk. Their calls are bouncing off the metal undersides of the cars. The taxi driver who takes me from airport to hotel says that the temperature has been 78 degrees Fahrenheit today. This is the second week in October. In England this day's temperature would be around 58 degrees. The taxi journey had driven past the Pentagon. I did not get a great feeling from it. I asked the taxi driver why I could not see the damage caused by the attack on it. He replied that it had been on the other side of the building.

Friend Hazel had given me a beautiful tiger's eye crystal to place on my third eye in quiet periods during my trip. This was the case for the first thirteen days of my journey until it disappeared without warning. It had completed its work with me and moved elsewhere by that time. This is a common occurrence with me on such journey quests that an item will disappear when it has finished its work. I recalled the intuitive advice that I received to watch where I was treading carefully. I was given a stronger message on the aircraft from Heathrow to Boston. Somehow my trainer shoe sole became stuck in a metal strip that runs the length of the aisle along the outside of the seats. The sole was half ripped away from the shoe as I attempted to disentangle. A most bizarre and unusual accident resulted in me flap-flap-flapping my way into the US customs hall. This pair of trainers was now useless for the remainder of my trip. Perhaps this was a small price to pay for a significant warning concerning my safety.

In cosmopolitan cultures such as England and Washington DC different races are now ubiquitous. The white race, genetically, is now on the decline, arguably, as cultures mix creating hybrids of the old separations of white, brown, yellow and black. This can only be advantageous to humanity. This mixing will aid in the ridiculous mindless racisms in individual and group psyches. Homogeneity will, at last, bring together the combined gene pool of our species. This mixing will also significantly change the old Judaeo-Christian culture exemplified in Western Europe and the United States. There are those that will resist this move toward a homogenous society. There is still rampant racism is some areas of the south of this country. Recently I watched a shocked British TV presenter as he was confronted with the 'n' word in a TV interview. It was the first time that he had heard it spoken. The resisters and racists are fighting a losing battle.

Through the efficient subway system in Washington I travel to the heart and towering symbols of political power in this country. The Washington Monument pierces the sky. Its impressive presence dwarfs the observer. The effect is increased as the monument is set on a mound. Its purpose, for those that would rule us, is an energy antenna it appears to me. Some call the people that would rule us *the Illuminati.* I call them, *those that are hanging on to the past.* In my mind I pay it little attention for the moment. My mind is set on visiting the Lincoln monument. Abe looms large in my attention and interest. I can almost feel his energy and smell his Victorian style clothes, replete with mothball tang. He has a quiet strength. What happened to that trait among current politicians?

The base of the monument is circled by US national flags on flagpoles; the latter look like matchsticks in comparison to the mass of the monument. Could one aspect of the symbology here be the piercing male member penetrating and subjugating the more passive female? Amazingly, on a platform near the monument, two women are dancing in a sensitive and flowing manner. They twist and twirl to what sounds like Hebrew music. There are bright Hebrew letters on flags placed around the dancers. One flag has a large wolf's head on it. All the while loud helicopters buzz around the monument and the twirling dancers. The music of the latter is fighting and straining to be heard over the harsh, brash helicopter engines noise. I sense that the helicopters are deliberately here to negate the female influence of the dancers. The scene, the noises and the very vibrations seem to me to be a clash between the peace vibrations of the dancers and the aggressive energies of the helicopters. The latter seem to me to be supporting the status quo masculine influence of the monument. This is truly a battlefield energetically between the energies of the past and those potential energies of the future. Here I am to witness and record it.

Many people walk by unaware of the energetic nature of what is going on. Their consciousness is in a different reality. I catch the word Binyamin written next to the wolf's head. Audrey later tells me that it means Benjamin. The energy in this place is just phenomenal. I talk to the women dancers later. One of them tells me that they are celebrating with the creator. It is my view that those that would rule us would work towards inserting themselves between us and the creator. The power over humanity is their objective. For thousands of years they have been in charge on this planet. They sense their power slipping away. Their time is over.

This whole area is laid out in swathes and circles with the phallic monument in the centre dominating. I wonder if other people here understand the symbology.

OK let's go see Abe. Well, the energy here becomes weirder and weirder. Before I reach Abe's monument there is a war memorial. I reach into my bag for my camera; no camera. I am nearly paranoid concerning keeping my camera close to me. I retrace my steps. There the camera sits on the wall facing the dancing women. I have no recollection of leaving it there. (When describing this part of the incident to friend Carol later, she felt that the camera had been removed from my bag by spiritual forces and placed on the wall in order to bring me back from the war memorial and to pay attention to the need for ritual work.) I glance over towards the monument and feel called to approach closer to it. I hop over the low boundary wall onto the grass beyond. As I do so I spy a brown bird feather in front of me on the floor. I pick it up and approach the monument.

As I make my approach the monument I am inspired to tile (walk round it in a ritualistic manner) it anti-clockwise carrying the feather. As I perform this apparently, to outside observers, simple ritual, I feel impelled to chant internally the ancient Rosicrucian chant, Aum-Ra-Ma-Oom. On this occasion the male-female Ra-Ma becomes transposed in my awareness and the chant becomes Aum-Ma-Ra-Oom. In this way the female now takes precedence over the male. I move around the monument in a slow even pace without outward show of performing a ritual activity. At the completion of the first circuit around the monument I am inspired to move inward toward the monument so the second and third circuit change the complete movement into a spiral. At the end of the third circuit I sense completion. By this time I am physically close to the monument and to finish the ritual touch the marble stone of the monument in order to ground the energy. The ritual is complete. This return to psychic work was cosmically inspired. As I wrote these notes after the ritual sitting on the low boundary wall, the bird feather blows away and quickly disappears before I can retrieve it. We have, the feather and I, completed our work together.

This is from the internet:

> *The Washington Monument is an obelisk within the National Mall in Washington, D.C., built to commemorate George Washington, once commander-in-chief of the Continental Army (1775–1784) in the American Revolutionary War and the first President of the United States (1789–1797). Located almost due east of the Reflecting Pool and the Lincoln Memorial, the monument, made of marble, granite, and bluestone gneiss, is both the world's tallest predominantly stone structure and the world's tallest obelisk, standing 554 feet 7+11⁄32 inches (169.046 m) tall according to the U.S. National Geodetic Survey (measured 2013–14) or 555 feet 5+1⁄8 inches (169.294 m) tall according to the National Park Service (measured 1884)*

I photograph Capitol Hill from the monument. There is a straight line between the two flanked by boulevards with lines of trees. I believe that the boulevards and the lines of trees are assisting in the focussing of energy along the straight between the various locations. This appears particularly so from the monument to Capitol Hill. This energy is palpable for those that will stop and tune into it. From the other side of the monument I can see the war memorial and Abe's monument. Now that I have completed this work I will return to the war memorial and then visit Abe.

The war memorial is truly beautiful. An oval of water nozzles spout water in varying intensities. This outer oval seems to represent individual states of the Union. These spouts are smaller in size than the two large inner spouts. The latter represent the Pacific and Atlantic theatres of war in World War II for the US. Between the war memorial and Abe's memorial is a rectangular, smooth, unruffled lake. The lake will be familiar to those who remember TV pictures of demonstrations against the Vietnam War. The war memorial is situated halfway between the Lincoln Memorial and the Washington Monument.

I am drawn to the Vietnam War memorial wall of names, which is set to one side of the other monuments. I walk slowly down it looking at the names with respect. I ask my inner self that any discarnate souls that are still troubled by that conflict be released and find peace. The energy and emotion of the place is almost too much to bear in its seriousness. My eye catches the name of George P. Custer. This name is reminiscent of a previous, internal to the US, war. For some reason I think of my mother Joyce Birch and her loss of my father in World War II. I take a photo of a monument of suffering soldiers being attended by nurses. The statue is dedicated to the nurses in the Vietnam War. One man, in his compassion, places his hand on the head of one of the figures as he passes.

This is from the Wikipedia:

> *The* ***Vietnam Veterans Memorial*** *is a U.S. national memorial in Washington, D.C., honoring service members of the U.S. armed forces who fought in the Vietnam War. The 2-acre (8,100* m^2*) site is dominated by a black granite wall engraved with the names of those service members who died as a result of their service in Vietnam and South East Asia during the war. The wall, completed in 1982, has since been supplemented with the statue The Three Soldiers and the Vietnam Women's Memorial.*
>
> *The memorial is in Constitution Gardens, adjacent to the National Mall and just northeast of the Lincoln Memorial. The memorial is maintained by the National Park Service, and receives around 3 million visitors each year. The Memorial Wall was designed by American architect Maya Lin. In 2007, it was ranked tenth on the "List of America's Favorite Architecture" by the American Institute of Architects. As a National Memorial, it is listed on the National Register of Historic Places.*

I walk to Abe's monument. The statue of the great man is sitting looking out towards the Washington Monument. The statue is huge, maybe sixty feet tall. I wonder what he thinks of current political activity. I take his photo. An empathetic person takes my photo next to Abe's statue.

'Hi Abe, how are you doing?'
'Fine, Clive, how are you?'

I muse on this imagined conversation.

This is from Wikipedia

The Lincoln Memorial is a US national memorial built to honor the 16th president of the United States, Abraham Lincoln. It is on the western end of the National Mall in Washington, D.C., across from the Washington Monument, and is in the form of a neoclassical temple. The memorial's architect was Henry Bacon. The designer of the memorial interior's large central statue, Abraham Lincoln (1920), was Daniel Chester French; the Lincoln statue was carved by the Piccirilli Brothers.

I walk to the White House. By now I am wilting. It is 2pm by the time I reach it. Visitors are, it seems to me, not welcome here. There is a sidewalk (pavement) from which photos can be taken through narrow metal bars. That is all. There are no private cars in the blocked off, well-policed street. There is no point in remaining here for very long. Do I have the energy to walk to Capitol Hill? I need to be back in the subway by 3.30pm in order to miss the rush hour. I feel myself running out of inspiration as I run out of energy.

There was one final drama associated with the Washington Monument. From the White House I attempted to cross the grass area around the Washington Monument. This was in order make a short cut towards the Capitol Hill. As I crossed the grassy knoll and reached the other side I became completely disoriented and ended up facing the wrong street. Worse still, initially I couldn't work out where I was. This puzzled me greatly in the moment because, normally, my sense of direction is very good. I looked over to my left and saw a bandstand that was similar to the one where I had watched, entranced, the dancers earlier in the day. In that moment I assumed it to be another one, although similar music was issuing from it. In fact it was the same one but my straight line walk across this highly energised place had totally confused me. Eventually I managed to re-orientate myself. As I looked back across the grassy mound, on which stood the monument, I realised that the paths for walking around the monument were organised in a circular fashion so that people coming to visit the monument would walk in spirals toward it. By walking in a straight line I had been working against the energetic flow that had been set up. It was a strange and unnerving experience. I was bucking the trend of the manufactured circulation of energy. Interestingly my spiral walk around the monument, cosmically inspired, was anti-clockwise. I believe that my spiral walk was negating the energy of the clockwise movement of many people here.

Two years later in a meditative state I received another insight into the strange events above. I was told by my intuition that my walk across the Washington Monument mound was not an accident. By walking across the line of energy I created a line of dissonance. This line of dissonance could then be worked on by spiritual cosmic forces in order to break up the energy creative mechanism. This energy creation had been used for nefarious purposes by alien entities and their servants. It had been decided by the highest forces that this energy dynamo was to be broken down completely. I trust that it has been. The anti-clockwise walk that I did which is mentioned above was the first phase of this breaking-down process.

I liked the elderly manager of the Days Inn Hotel here in Washington where I was staying. He was gentle, quietly spoken and respectful. His name, which I cannot remember, looked as though it was Iranian, Afghan. Certainly it was Middle Eastern. He has a strong accent, not American. I wish him and his hotel well.

I woke up on October 11th ready for my driving assignment to Manassas (Bull Run), site of two Civil War battles. Immediately I focussed mentally on this place a piano keyboard came into my consciousness. I think that this indicates a change of octave of energy from Washington DC. Or perhaps there is some other explanation? In addition the woman who had been my wife in the Civil War life came into consciousness. I felt an impulse to send her, in her present incarnation, healing. Perhaps this is part of the necessary work for me on this journey.

This is from Wikipedia:

> *The First Battle of Bull Run (the name used by Union forces), also known as the Battle of First Manassas (the name used by Confederate forces), was the first major battle of the American Civil War. The battle was fought on July 21, 1861, in Prince William County, Virginia, just north of the city of Manassas and about 30 miles west-southwest of Washington, D.C. The Union's forces were slow in positioning themselves, allowing Confederate reinforcements time to arrive by rail. Each side had about 18,000 poorly trained and poorly led troops in their first battle. It was a Confederate victory, followed by a disorganized retreat of the Union forces.*

As I was driven to the car rental pick-up at Ronald Regan Airport the taxi driver, who lived near Manassas, spoke of the ghostly voices and noises of battle that can still be heard at night. He claimed that the energies from these souls were so powerful that they had been recorded on audio equipment. The armies of the southern Confederacy called the site of the battles Manassas because they were defending the town thus named behind them. The Union forces called the actions the battles of Bull Run because the river thus named was as far as they reached in their charges on the Confederate troops. The Manassas Park where much of the action of both battles took place is a haven of peace, on the face of it, during the day.

A filmed re-enactment of both battles focussed my mind on that particular part of my life in those times. A subsequent talk by one of the Rangers made me realise why the trauma of my part in the Civil War has been with me to this day. He spoke of the effect of the low velocity lead shot fired from the muskets of that time. The low velocity caused an entry wound but not an exit one on any flesh that it penetrated; with lead being a poison, the limbs thus affected would be cut off if the shot could not be dug out. All this would be done without the aid of pain killers. So whether a wounded soldier died immediately or from the effects of lead poison, from the surgical intervention or even from subsequent infection was a moot point. Of course this war was long before the use of antibiotics or blood transfusions. The bayonet used in that war was triangular which, because of its shape, created a wound that would not heal. These bayonets are now banned by the Geneva Convention. Even if one survived the trauma of a penetration injury the lifetime trauma must have been terrible. Sometimes it may have been kinder to be killed by a bullet or bayonet. Thankfully the latter did not kill many. If a soldier had been unable to load his muzzle-loading musket in time and saw a charging opponent running towards him then most would adopt a 'discretion rather than valour' technique and take to his heels.

The following is taken from an advertising leaflet at the site.

On a warm July day in 1861, two armies of a divided nation clashed for the first time on the fields overlooking Bull Run. Their ranks were filled with enthusiastic young volunteers in colourful new uniforms, gathered together from every part of the country. Confident that their foes would run at the first shot, the raw recruits were thankful that they would not miss the only battle of what would surely be a short war. But any thoughts of colourful pageantry were suddenly lost in the smoke, din, dirt and death of battle. Soldiers on both sides were stunned by the violence and destruction they encountered. At day's end nearly 900 young men lay lifeless on the fields of Matthew Hill, Henry Hill, and Chinn Ridge. Ten hours of heavy fighting swept away any notion that war's outcome would be decided quickly.

In August 1862, Union and Confederate armies converged for a second time on the plains of Manassas. The naïve enthusiasm that preceded the earlier encounter was gone. War was not the holiday outing or grand adventure envisioned by the young recruits of 1861. The contending forces, now made up of seasoned veterans, knew well the realities of war. The Battle of Second Manassas, covering three days, produced far greater carnage – 3,000 killed – and brought the Confederacy to the height of its power. Still the battle did not weaken Northern resolve. The war's final outcome was yet unknown, and it would be left to other battles to decide whether the sacrifice at Manassas was part of the high price of Southern independence, or the cost of one country again unified under the national standard.

I didn't receive any strong healing or psychic feelings in this place; perhaps it is sufficient to send healing thoughts and suggest that any discarnate souls still trapped here that wish to escape should turn to the light and ask for release. I completed a tiling on the area around the administration buildings and left. There is one possible explanation of the strange noises at night other than that of ghostly visits. Perhaps the strong emotional energy at the time of the battle has impregnated the surrounding countryside with the sights and sounds of the time. This would be a little like the sounds and pictures imprinted on a CD or DVD. It is believed by many that rocks and landscape can trap, hold and release impressions of events that happen in those environs. I had such an experience one time that I camped high up on a shoulder of a mountain in Snowdonia. As soon as I crawled into the tent and lay down I was assailed by a plethora of images. There was no rest during that night. Faces, clouds events piled one on top of each other into my consciousness. The rocks in the area are granite, which, I believe, are particularly adept at storing information. As I was about to leave Manassas I saw and sensed a rising of light upward. Perhaps this was my imagination or perhaps there was a genuine release going on of the energies trapped there.

It is time to move on and drive to Gettysburg.

I am visiting the sites in chronological order. Not that this was planned by me but it has turned out to be the most economical from a travel point of view. I arrive in the small town of Thurmston just over twenty miles from Gettysburg. Small niggles have arisen. The SUV that I was persuaded to rent by the car rental salesman will not work on the electronic key so I am using the physical key. I can't open the boot. There are small scratches on the driver's door that weren't noticeable when I left the gloomy cavernous car rental warehouse. This town is heaving with people. There is a regular market going on. I was forced to take the last hotel room available in the town. It is a smoking room; uuggh, disgusting. I keep the widow open day and night to attempt to drive the smelly fug away. My voice is weak here. Is this the effect of smoke inhalation on my asthmatic chest or an emotional reaction to Manassas? There is a painful insect bite on my hand. Everything else is fine. Perhaps I should not have halted my journey in this town. I called on the cosmic forces to keep my chest well this night.

Eventually I get it. This is a lesson in creating positivity out of apparent reversals and a succession of niggling issues. This is not about thinking positively alone. It is about bringing positive events into one's life and turning situations around from the apparently challenging and negative. This is the attitude I should be adopting from here on in. It is part of the higher awareness. I should be in this place. Wherever one is located is the right place to be. Morning arrives without worsening chest or asthma issues. Thurmston, however, continues to create small blocks. I called Jaqueline from the hotel but couldn't get through. So, I went to buy a telephone calling card with my debit card. The request to use it was declined by the computer system. OK, time to get out of here and drive to Gettysburg.

Gettysburg marks the furthest north that the Confederate forces reached. I stand on a little hill overlooking the plain. This apparently innocuous place, key to the Union armies' left flank, was occupied five minutes before the arrival of the Confederates. All day the Union forces were attacked but held out to greatly contribute to the final victory. On these small margins great events are decided. This hill was immortalised in the film *'Gettysburg'* which I had seen in England. It was a great thrill for me to stand in the spot where the battle and the war were decided. No other person in the tour, all US citizens as far as I could judge, had seen this film. Bizarrely only the foreigner knew of it.

The Union victory was achieved despite the fact that Union General Sickles ignored his orders to place his troops on the hill and next to it. Sickles moved his forces too far forward, placing the victory in jeopardy. Sickles was quietly removed from his post by General Grant after the battle in a diplomatic manner. The reason for this diplomatic sacking was partly because he lost a leg in the battle and partly because he had friends in high places. Sickles had been a politician before the war began. He knew Abraham Lincoln personally and the then current secretary for war. This seems to be a case of *'who you know'* rather than *'what you know'*. With less political influence Sickles would probably have been publicly disgraced. In any event the battle was won and the tide had turned. Lincoln, viewed as the father/hero figure of the nation, regularly changed commanding generals in the early part of the war while it was going badly for Union forces.

After four days Confederate commander General Robert E. Lee marched away, never again to set foot in Union territory. The battle was lost for the Confederacy and, ultimately, the war. The tour, very well conducted, was too intense for me to write notes there and then. I was busy 'drinking in' all the information given by the tour guide and absorbing being in this terrible but powerful place. Being here was enough. I did not feel drawn to conduct a healing. Perhaps my energy was enough to make a small difference to the energies stored in the land. It was time to move on again; to drive south on interstate Highway 81 towards Appomattox.

The following is from Gettysburg site information leaflet:

On June 3rd 1863, a month after his dramatic victory at Chancellorsville, Confederate Gen. Robert E. Lee began marching his Army of Northern Virginia westward from its camps around Fredericksburg, Va. Once through the gaps of the Blue Ridge, the Southerners trudged northward into Maryland and Pennsylvania. They were followed by the Union Army of the Potomac under Gen. Joseph Hooker, but Lee, whose cavalry under Maj. Gen. J.E.B. Stuart was absent on a raid around the Federal forces, had no way of knowing his adversary's whereabouts.

The two armies touched by chance at Gettysburg on June 30. The main battle opened on July 1 with Confederates attacking Union troops on McPherson Ridge west of town. Though outnumbered the Federal forces held their position until afternoon, when they were finally overpowered and driven back to Cemetery Hill south of town. During the night the main body of the Union army, now commanded by Maj. Gen. George G. Meade, arrived and took up positions.

On July 2 the battle lines were drawn up in two sweeping arcs. The main portions of both armies were nearly one mile apart on parallel ridges. Union forces on Cemetery Ridge, Confederate forces on Seminary Ridge to the west. Lee ordered an attack on both Union flanks. Gen. James Longstreet's thrust on the Federal left turned the base of Little Round Top into a shambles, left the Wheatfield strewn with dead and wounded, and overran the Peach Orchard. Farther north, Lt. Gen. Richard S. Ewel's evening attack on the federal right at east Cemetery Hill and Culp's Hill, though momentarily successful, could not be exploited to Confederate advantage.

On July 3 Lee's artillery opened a two hour bombardment of the Federal lines On Cemetery Ridge and Cemetery Hill. This for a time engaged the massed guns of both sides in a thundering duel for supremacy, but did little to soften up the Union defensive position. Then some 12,000 C onfederates advanced across open fields towards the Federal centre in an attack known as' Pickett's charge'. The attack failed and cost Lee over 5,000 soldiers in one hour. The Battle of Gettysburg was over.

I have noticed that the battle sites that I visit have Civil War re-enactments. There are similar events in England. I believe that this re-generates the consciousness, the energy of the conflict. It may be one of the factors in re-energising the psychic phenomena of the ghostly visions and noises throughout the decades and centuries. It is my view that healing ceremonies regularly performed would be a much more positive approach. This would also cause those visiting the battle sites to leave with a much calmer, less martial perspective. The tour guide makes the observation that it would be wonderful to stay in some of the Gettysburg wooden buildings that date from the conflict.

'As long as you can stand the paranormal activity,' he continued.

So the energies of the past are still active, partly for reason that we have discussed. I wonder if he is joking or attempting to fuel tourist interest. There are a number of businesses in the town that thrive on the local ghost 'industry'.

An amazing event brought me to my next overnight stop. I was intending to stop much further south but was held up by an accident on Highway 81. Fortunately, it appeared that no-one was hurt as I passed the faulty vehicle. By 5.30pm I was tired so I pulled off the highway when I saw a Hotel 8 sign. Mount Jackson was really a 'pit stop' with gas station, trucker stop as well as the motel. I felt good immediately as I pulled up. This was partly because the sun was shining on the well-tended front of the motel rooms. My room was fresh and clean. When I spoke to the desk clerk I was staggered to learn that the location had a special place in the Civil War. It was neutral in the conflict and became a hospital centre for the wounded of both sides. So, it could be argued that this is where the healing of the conflict began. In addition here I am more than 140 years later attempting healing in a different way. If it hadn't been for the delay of the accident causing the traffic jam, I would have driven past Mount Jackson unknowingly. This stop was a metaphor for the Civil War part of my trip. The visit was cosmically inspired.

This journey down Highway 81 took me past, right and left, the Blue Ridge Mountains and the Appalachians. Apart from a 'pit stop' for fuel and Burger King the next day I needed my concentration for the road. So sightseeing could not be on the agenda this time round. As I contentedly munched my Burger King burger I thought of friend Pete, who loves this particular food and would have much enjoyed being here. As I ate I surveyed the local women who were sitting in the diner. I wondered how many of them would vote for Obama. I surmised that it would not be many apart from the Afro-American girl taking the orders. This looks, pretty much, to be 'redneck' country.

I am in another diner, on my way to Appomattox. I sit next to three 'good ole boys', local men of a certain age. The subject of the upcoming election is the topic of their conversation.

Ah'm gonna vote fer George Wallace, the man closest to me declares. This was the Republican governor in the 1960s who tried to prevent the integration of black children into white only, at that time, schools. Perhaps the 'good ole boy' was frustrated by the quality of the available candidates in his eyes. I nearly asked,

Are you going to dig him up first? The good governor had been dead for decades. However, I thought better of it. I mean no disrespect to the governor's family.

It takes me four hours to drive from Mount Jackson to Appomattox. When I reach the area I am amazed at the low-key nature of this historical place. First it was difficult for me to find. There seems to be no great triumphalism. Very few people came to visit while I was there, compared to Manassas and Gettysburg. Consequently I have the space to become aware of the sombre atmosphere here. I am able to relax, watching a film about the place in the tourist centre. This is a welcome relief from the concentrated driving. The atmosphere, although friendly and lively from the staff, is somehow respectful and careful. Gone is the gung-ho spirit of Manassas and Gettysburg.

One interesting way of informing those that come here about that time period is acted out literally. I drive to what I take to be the main commemorative site of the battle. An actor, dressed in period costume talks to groups concerning the events that led up to Lee's surrender here. I found this most evocative, from a civilian's rather than a military person's perspective, and most interesting. The actor spoke of individual human acts that covered other aspects of the war compared to the mass events that had been spoken of at the other two sites. In one story he spoke of a Confederate soldier hiding behind a tree and, from his hiding place, shot dead a Union cavalry colonel. Reviewing his shot he kissed his musket, saying that it had done its duty, put the musket against the tree and walked away from the battle and, of course, the war. I read of the sadness of the victorious General Grant when taking the surrender from his opponent Robert E Lee. I visit the building where the surrender was negotiated and carried out in Appomottax Court House village before leaving. The wooden walls exude solemnity and sadness too. At last the killing was mostly over. The courage and intense companionship engendered by the conflict was also over. I drive away from the site with the imagined words of Robert E Lee in my head saying '*thank you*' for my work. I am not sure what I have done apart from heart-centred healing as I left the site.

It is of interest to me to speculate on other possible timelines when I am connected, by imagination, to places and events of interest. This is true of the American Civil War. Historically, South Carolina forces fired on Fort Sumter without a 'by your leave' to the remainder of the Confederacy. This pressured the US congress to, in its turn, pressure a newly elected Abraham Lincoln to call for 50,000 volunteers to defeat the rebels. These forces were arranged to muster in front of Washington DC. This last act stimulated the state of Virginia to create an army to defend itself against what it saw as northern aggression. Before this pattern of events unfolded Virginia had decided to leave the Union but *not* to join the Confederacy. Virginia had seen itself as the buffer between the north and the south. The Fort Sumter attack blew that plan out of the water.

If there had been more control of the Confederate forces early on and the attack had not started there and then at Fort Sumter, there would have been manoeuvring room for a political solution. President Lincoln had not, at this point, asked for the abolition of slavery, but that slavery should not be allowed in the newly opening up western territories. If the south had gone along with Abe on this then slavery and the old southern way of life could have, perhaps, survived for decades in the southern states where it had been established. It may have survived into the 1960s. In this scenario the freedom marches would not have been about racial equality but about the abolition of slavery. This may not be as unbelievable as it sounds. There are still some countries that quietly and secretly have slavery as internal policy. I sense Abe giving a wry smile at my imagined scenario which, incidentally, now has a reality created by my consciousness.

Antipathy to the north and its latter rape of the south by General Sherman and the carpetbaggers is still rife in the southern states. US citizens from the north are still referred to as Yankees by many white inhabitants in the south. Resentment is still strong. On a previous visit in 2003 I saw a bumper sticker that said *'The south will rise again'*.

The journey moves on. As I wake one morning in Durham, North Carolina, I sense that, somewhere, the land has been punctured as with a knife thrust. This was a negative energy penetration. At first as I woke further I thought that this was the energy portal work in Savannah. As I focussed it felt as though this particular energy portal was the land in which the hotel was situated. I sleepily asked, '*How many people were involved with this?*' Immediately came back the response to my consciousness, '*Approximately nine hundred students.*' From this reply I realised two things, first that the source of this information was from the Native Americans with whom I had been working. The second was that the word *student* referred to the workers building the foundations and structures of the hotel. The numbers of students referred to was so large I assume that the hotel was part of a complex that was built at the same time. This land must have been sacred previously. These 'students' were less spiritually evolved humans, hence the polite way of referring to them. I contacted the Native American who had arrived in my consciousness once I had decided to fly to Washington. Almost immediately I saw all the Native Americans together. This time four were grouped in a square at the points and a fifth at the apex of a pyramid rising up from the square. This geometric figure and the presence of the beings in it will generate tremendous energies and help with this work that I am doing. As I lay in bed I worked on healing the knife wound penetrating the land and also later as I moved around the hotel I continued the healing. I plan to start my journey later today as I need to rest. This journey requires much focus of physical, mental and psychic energies.

I perform the following meditation in order to help the land here as I sit on the floor to make my connection as strong as possible. I visualise the pyramid with the five beings in the geometric shape described above. In addition I see myself underneath the pyramid creating a diamond shape. The diamond fills with light and begins to rotate into a vortex. I feel my coccyx vibrating strongly as the energy moves through my body into the earth beneath me. Eventually the work was complete.

The previous evening I had driven past this hotel building missing the entrance. I then drove round looking for an alternative place to stay. Eventually I returned to the entrance of this hotel passing no other on the way. I know now that I was guided to be here. When I arrived in the lobby to book a room the receptionist said, *'I'm sorry sir, we have no rooms available.'* My heart sank.

'Oh no, I have been driving for hours and have been unable to find another place.'

She took pity on me and offered a room for the disabled. This was all she had. I snapped it up. The room was spacious and fine for my needs. As I walked to it I thought to myself humorously, *'If I didn't have a room here tonight I would have felt disabled.'*

This is not an insult to disabled persons but a reflection of my near exhausted state.

The next morning a journey of several hours found me, in the early evening, in Beaufort South Carolina. A pleasant social evening was spent catching up with friend Suzanne Taylor, who I had met on a tour last year in Brittany and Malta. The following morning I went to practice kung fu in her yard. I asked permission of a tree there to use it as a focus for my movements. Back came the reply, *'No, use that one over there!'* This took me aback as well as making me smile. This was the first time that a tree had spoken to me, although I do know of others that communicate with trees. I went over to the other tree asking it for permission. There was no reply so I took that as a *'yes'*. Perhaps the first tree was the boss of this particular grove and thus dished out roles and responsibilities to the others. My feeling was that the consciousness of this second tree was elsewhere and was unconcerned with my presence. I completed my exercises, thanked the tree and left. Friend Mary told me a story, one time, of a group of people who regularly communicated with trees in a particular wood. Recently they returned to continue their annual contact. They were told quite strongly at this latest visit to *'Go away we are not communicating with you anymore.'* Trees are a great link between earth and sky. Their roots are ever deep in the ground and their branches reach up to the energies of the sky. I believe that they pull in energies from both sources, creating a harmonious mix of the two.

Suzanne tended not to be an early riser, which is the opposite of my pattern. While I stayed in her house I would take an early morning walk down the street where she lived. The wild life was wonderful in this heavily wooded area. Buzzards 'hung out' on the roofs of houses. Suzanne told me that they ate road-kill. They are large birds that resemble vultures. Perhaps they are of the same family. Later Suzanne and I drove around looking for the vortex, which I knew was very large and could, quite easily, extend from Savannah fifty miles to the south. We found no energetic trace of the vortex, which puzzled and concerned me as this was a central reason for my journey to this part of the country. I decide to work on this issue overnight and concern myself with it on the following day.

The following morning Suzanne took me to see her old family home. This was an old wooden building situated next to the river estuary. The whole scene was very southern. The house was surrounded with Spanish-moss-festooned trees. The hot steamy atmosphere completed the southern feel for me. As we sit by the estuary a most amazing sound is heard. It could almost be an electric motor whining away. Suzanne tells me that it is the local large cicadas making their music in the trees. This does feel the place to do vortex work by building a medicine wheel here. I sense that the other one should be completed in Suzanne's yard. Suzanne feels the same. I had come to this latter decision at 5am lying in bed. When I woke I was puzzled at my inability to locate a place to perform a ceremony to stabilise the portal. As soon as I tuned into the Native Americans in the other reality at this time I received the prompt response to build two medicine wheels here in Beaufort.

Later we both went behind Suzanne's house and built the medicine wheel in her yard and performed a ceremony invoking the presence and power of the four elements, earth, water, air and fire and the power of the four directions, north, south, east and west. We took a break before creating the other wheel by driving into town to perform some errands. As we drove, I felt relaxed, as though a burden had been lifted. The job was half done. We arrived at a doctor's surgery for Suzanne to have a painful shoulder checked out. As we waited we watched the ubiquitous, in the US, TV. The channel was showing positive coverage of one of the presidential candidates and ignoring the other one.

'They have sold out,' said Suzanne, referring to the channel directors. This biased reporting would never be allowed in the UK I am sure. I am not the greatest fan of some institutions in my home country but in this regard we have got it right.

I had the intuitive impulse that the medicine wheels should be left untouched for three days. During this time the energy of the cosmic forces would work on them, grounding and stabilising energies. Medicine wheels function a little like tent pegs do for a tent. They create a stable structure. Suzanne asked if the medicine wheel also created a link upward for Earth energies and human contact to cosmic realms. I believe that they do. I also believe that the medicine wheel in Suzanne's yard will assist in the creation of a positive environment in the surrounding area, for Suzanne and her home.

One of my friends had suggested that three-dimensional structures are unnecessary and that all that is required is intention. That can be true. However, in this case, it was important for Suzanne and me to use the medicine wheel as a focus in the invocation of energies. It is also the case that the medicine wheel is a traditional mystical tool of the Native Americans who inhabited this land before the arrival of the white man. The destruction of the Native American culture through white man's diseases, plus physical and social pressure, stole the land from its ancient heritage. My contact for this work has been the Native Americans in another realm. I am sure that they would be content with the use of these devices. Indeed, I believe that it was their inspiration that guided me to use the medicine wheels.

We built the second medicine wheel in Suzanne's family home yard. No-one lives there right now. We performed a ceremony to the four directions and the four elements. As we did so it was as though the local animal kingdom woke up and rejoiced to the energies. Squirrels raced up and down trees and birds started to sing. The active scene was watched by two toads which poked their heads from their holes. When the ceremony had been completed Suzanne and I strolled along the jetty that poked out from the family property into the estuary. As a final act we were treated to the most beautiful birdsong. We drove away with the feeling that the work was now complete.

Suzanne has a great empathy and healing power with animals. One time she took care of a racoon that was hurt. She ignored warning comments from a friend that a bite from this animal could generate a dangerous disease. The conversation from the friend went something like this:

'Gaahd, Suzanne,' the friend spluttered in her South Carolina accent. *'Wut if yew get bit bah thet theng?'* (Please forgive my feeble attempt to capture the local accent).

The animal never did bite her. Indeed it would allow her to cuddle it, giving it loving affection. In the past, before moving on to a shaman's path she, by her own admission, carried a lot of anger. This was backed up by a strong and determined personality. One time she was railing on the telephone to a friend concerning a third person.

'I'm gonna round up a posse to get that person,' she said.

The friend replied, *'Suzanne, If anyone can round up a posse, you can!'*

It is self-evident that a posse would have been easier to round up 150 years ago in the era of the cowboy out in the Wild West.

Suzanne tells the story of a man who worked with purifying stretches of water through positive affirmation and thought. One day, when this man was working in this way on a particular stretch of water the body of a dead woman rose to the surface. The body had been under the water for some considerable time. The water thus surrendered its secret and was disposing of that which was polluting it. For thousands of years mystics have believed that water possesses its own intelligence. Books have been written of the conscious magic of water.

In the old family house Suzanne tells the story of the lower level, the ground floor, being rented out to a young family after the death of her father, who lived there previously. There had been a dispute within the family that the father was not happy about. The young family were startled many evenings when a door would open of its own accord with no physical human interference. The same thing happened to Suzanne's mother after the young family left the house. Suzanne believes the door opening by itself was her father demonstrating his displeasure concerning the family dispute. This door was one that he would frequently use in life. Suzanne and her boyfriend Mark told the story of a couple having problems with their car while on a drive in the local area. The husband gets out of the car to attempt to solve the problem. The wife falls asleep and doesn't wake up until the next morning. To her horror she finds her husband hanging, by his neck, from a tree. (Other versions of the story say she finds her husband's torso minus the head.) The upshot of the story, carried forward to modern times, is that, on that same stretch of road as the legend, a ghostly figure engulfs cars during the hours of dark. Some say that it is the spirit of the husband looking for his head. This is certainly a good story for the tourists.

In holiday information mode, Beaufort has one of the last surviving outside cinemas in the south. I ask Suzanne why these once popular places of entertainment had declined. Suzanne was at a loss to explain it. I suppose tastes change. Maybe people have turned their backs on being in nature, she concluded. After a final meal with Suzanne and Mark before leaving Beaufort we drove back to Suzanne's house in Mark's car. Suddenly a loud beeping noise erupted in the vehicle. Mark said that it was an alarm that detected police radar in the area. He said that it was legal to have such a device here. I wondered if such a device would be legal in England. Somehow I doubted it.

Before I left I gave Ian's crystal to Suzanne. She truly is a shaman.

The fact that she is not Native American is not relevant. She is doing the work for the Earth and the animals in and on it. After the gift was made Suzanne disappeared for a few minutes and reappeared with a crystal that looked as though it had come from the same family as Ian's. *'I have had this crystal since I was sixteen. Please take it with you.'*

When I returned to England I gave the crystal to Audrey, asking her to 'look into' a life that was relevant for Suzanne. This is what Audrey came up with after attuning with the Akashic.

Suzanne had a life as a puritan in England with brothers and sisters. Her father was a landowner who was very strict. It was not a happy family environment. There was no singing or dancing. The civil war started and the father went to fight. Difficult times arrived. The father was killed and the mother died from an illness. A Royalist came to Suzanne's home and took the place over. Suzanne became housekeeper to the Royalist. The rest of the family scattered. Suzanne had an affair with the Royalist. This was her first taste of freedom. He rode out one day and was killed by Cromwellian supporters. The Cromwell people turned on Suzanne because of her affair. Other Royalists killed the murderers of their colleague. Suzanne was left homeless. She walked across the country and got a job as a barmaid by the time Charles the Second came to the throne. Suzanne caught a chest infection and died despite the landlord's wife being kind to her.

Then Audrey came up with a reading of another life.

Suzanne lived in the Far East, probably Japan, centuries ago. Her father worked in the temple playing drums. Suzanne's mother arranged flowers in the same temple. At this point her life was calm and peaceful. Things changed. There was civil strife. Soldiers arrived and destroyed everything. Suzanne's father was killed and her mother dishonoured by the soldiers. The mother then hung herself. Suzanne somehow escaped the abuse and left the area and was taken in by some people. Over time Suzanne developed spiritual powers. People would come to Suzanne for healing and advice. So this life ended in happier circumstances than the last one uncovered by Audrey.

I think that is enough for this chapter. It is time to move on.

USA Part 2

From South Carolina to New Mexico

Before continuing with the story of my journey I would like to take the time to give an explanation of what a shaman is, because we will come across another one later on in addition to Suzanne Taylor in the previous chapter. This is from *Medicine for the Earth* by Sandra Ingerman.

Shamanism was the first spiritual practice of humankind. Evidence suggests that it dates back at least forty thousand years. Some Anthropologists would argue that it is more than one hundred thousand years old. Shamans are found in many cultures worldwide, but the word Shaman comes from the Tungus tribe of Siberia. A shaman is a man or woman who heals the spiritual practice of illness: diagnosing and treating illnesses, divining information for the community, communicating and interacting with the spirit world helping souls to cross over to the other worlds ... He (Michael Horner) found that the practice of shamanism is distinguished by what is called the shamanic journey. Mircea Eliade, author of 'Shamanism Archaic Techniques of Ecstacy', describes a shaman as a person who journeys in an altered state of consciousness, outside time and space. Through these journeys the shaman retrieves healing help and information for patients, family and community.

One of the beauties of shamanic journeying is that it allows for direct spiritual revelations. Recently fires burned out of control in the rain forests of South America. Out of desperation the government called in shamans to make rain. Two days after their arrival rain came. What resource did the shaman use?

While in the Dutch resistance during World War 2, Jack Schwarz was captured by the Gestapo and tortured. But before his torturer's eyes his wounds healed. Later on public TV, he had needles put in him, then healed right in front of the camera. What resource did he use?

... Schwarz says he heals himself through heightened consciousness and attuning to the universe.

... In shamanism, we do not use our own energy in doing healing work; we work in partnership with the spirits. The shaman is the hands and heart that the spirits work through. Thus when I am doing shamanic healing work such as restoring lost power, returning lost soul parts, or removing intruding spiritual energy, I merge with my helping spirits. The helping spirits and the compassionate spirits are the conduits of the power of the universe. In merging with the helping spirits, an expansion of consciousness is necessary, since the ego must stand aside for this union to take place.

A second subject I would like to discuss is that of Columbus Day. I was in the US on this day but was unable to review it from my perspective, or research it, as I was in Gettysburg. Thus I had other things to work on at the time.

The first report is from Wikipedia:

Indigenous Peoples' Day is a holiday that celebrates and honors Native American peoples and commemorates their histories and cultures. It is celebrated across the United States on the second Monday in October, and is an official city and state holiday in various localities. It began as a counter-celebration held on the same day as the U.S. federal holiday of Columbus Day, which honors Italian explorer Christopher Columbus. Many reject celebrating him, saying that he represents "the violent history of the colonization in the Western Hemisphere", and that Columbus Day is a sanitization or covering-up of Christopher Columbus' actions such as enslaving Native Americans. It was instituted in Berkeley, California, in 1992, to coincide with the 500th anniversary of the arrival of Columbus in the Americas on October 12,

1492. Two years later, Santa Cruz, California, instituted the holiday. Starting in 2014, many other cities and states adopted the holiday.

The following information is a précis of a Radio 4 programme about the beginnings of the US.

It is alleged that President Roosevelt started Columbus Day in order to please Italian-American supporters of his Democratic party. Roosevelt linked western going settlements with Columbus. Native Americans grew maize, squash and beans together harmoniously; wheras early Spanish settlers grew crops that exhausted the land. From the new world came staples for Europe potatoes, turkeys, maize. On the debit side tobacco and venereal disease. Disease more than steel and bullets caused the Native American collapse. Plymouth was the first European settlement founded on a village ravaged by smallpox and measles. Decimation of the Native American population opened the way for European settlement theologically, legally and practically. The Native American population fell from five million in 1492 to half a million by 1650 due to Western illnesses.

I realise that the above is a negative perspective. However, this is the reality of this celebration for me and for many others. I explore a much more positive subject later when I visit an Obama campaign headquarters. For me exploring the positive and the negative is exploring reality. Please stay with me.

It is time to explore through travelling again. I drive from Beaufort to Savannah, Georgia, the focus of the energy portal that Susannah and I worked on in the medicine wheel work. I stop only to pick up advertising information on the region for a student back home in the UK. Savannah was spared from destruction by General Sherman because Abe gave it to him as a Christmas present. Perhaps the president had enough of the pyromania and wanted at least some building to remain standing in the south. Then I drive up Highway 16 to Macon and on to Atlanta which the good general burned. On the road there were hurricane warning signs. I am pretty sure that we are past that time of the year when these cataclysmic works of nature occur in this region.

I stop for a meal in a waffle house. The probably poorly paid black workers are happy and friendly. They clearly enjoy working together. Their harmonious chatter helps to create a bright atmosphere in the place.

'You all have a nice day now,' is heard as customers leave.

Atlanta becomes my stopover for the night. My tiring attention and the wall-to-wall concrete of the city highways and buildings don't mix very well. Atlanta appears to me as an outsider to be a megatropolis of zooming traffic, the aforesaid concrete jungle and confusing directions. It is time to take an overnight break. If anyone in the South has an inferiority complex about being southerners in this country I would advise that they come to Atlanta. The success, in material terms, is for all to see. The hotel receptionist where I decide to stop is abrupt and unwelcoming. If I had the energy I would move on to another place. I am just too darned tired. I treat her with respect with plenty of *please* and *thank you.* I pass a restful night and am ready to move on the next morning. The receptionist has warmed to me in the interim. She is pleasant and wishes me a safe journey. Perhaps other customers have not treated her with the respect in the past, hence her early negative attitude to me.

There is not time to stop for anything other than overnight stays en route as I have work to do in New Mexico and my plane for home leaves Albuquerque on October 30th. I have the good fortune to have the offer to stay with my good friend Cynthia Walker in Placitas, New Mexico. Onward I drive up the Interstate 75 to Chattanooga, which looks to be a really interesting city as I drive by. A short but sharp pang of regret shoots through my body as I continue on my way. The straight highway is relieved by a curving road and a lake on one side as I pass by. I sing the line of the song that I know about this city, *Pardon me boy, is that the Chattanooga choo-choo?* I assume the song is talking about a railway train. On such small entertainments my starved intellect seizes on during monotonous driving chores. For that is what they are to me. Driving long distances is a means to an end for me and not the greatest pleasure.

The road winds past the lake and up into wooded hills. There are signs off the highway to interesting places such as *Indian mounds* and *Civil War battlefield sites.* My desire to lapse into tourism grows stronger. I fight it off. The spiritual work is why I am here in this country. At least I have, now, 'clocked where they are'. If I have the opportunity in the future I would fly into Savannah, explore that city then drive up this stretch of highways to explore. We shall see. The last leg of this day's driving sees me in Jackson, Tennessee. Driving for seven hours, including breaks, is enough for me. There is a warm sun so I am looking forward to relaxing in the motel that I have booked. Friend Pete emailed me a couple of days previously to tell me that England had its first frost. Perhaps there is some compensation for being on the road in the southern states of the US. I hate the cold and damp weather of my homeland.

There are a lot of Christian religion billboards along the highway in Georgia and Tennessee. I realise that I am in the 'Bible belt'. They are of the '*Time is short but not in eternity*' variety, allegedly signed by God; there is no pressure here, folks. Get in line or feel the guilt! This reminded me of something that Suzanne had spoken of. She said that the Christians had now appropriated December 21, 2012, as a date for the arrival of their saviour. Have they no shame stealing the date of cosmic alignments and possible Earth changes that mystics have spoken of for millennia? Mystics have been persecuted by said Christians for their pains and such beliefs.

I eat another meal in a waffle house as I relax after my drive to Jackson. The black women and girls serving and cooking seem full of life and fun. I spoke with them on the difficulties of understanding each other. One of the women said that she had the same problem when she moved to Jackson from Iowa. She coped with the situation by changing her accent to the local drawl but changed back to her original accent when returning to Iowa. I explain that my conversation is affected in the same way. I orient the way I talk to include

North American pronunciation. I became tired of saying the same things several times in my normal English accent in order to make myself understood. When these 'waffle house' women are speaking together I cannot understand what they say. This experience for me was similar to the one in the Georgia waffle house. Generally many young black women in hotels and restaurants are very self-confident with an *I'm black and proud of it* attitude.

My journey continued the next day into Arkansas. A 'pit stop' in this state did not go so well. The energies of the place that I stopped at felt depressed. The restaurant building looked uncared for. The woman serving was quiet and unsmiling. I suppose if I worked in such an environment then I would not be happy. A happier experience was encountered in the Arkansas tourist centre. The helpful desk clerk said that this was the harvest season for rice and wheat in the state. Arkansas exports rice to China. I wondered if they did the same to Mexico, homeland of my wife. I know that Mexico is an importer of this food as it has a skyrocketing population. Since the 1950s the population has risen from 29 million to 146 million in that Latin country.

I drive on to Fort Smith on the Arkansas/Oklahoma border. More by good fortune than planning I end up in a downtown hotel rather than one next to the interstate highway. After booking in I walk down the main street. It feels so relaxing to be back, for the first time on this trip, in Little America rather than interstate highway restaurants, shopping malls and wall-to-wall concrete. There are brick buildings of all ages higgledy-piggledy giving me a relaxed and comfortable feeling. Thank God, whatever you perceive her to be, for lack of planning. Increasingly our lives are planned from cradle to grave. Even the first National Bank occupies an ancient, by American standards, five-storey building: the white stone complementing the different hues of brown brick. I walk up and down Garrison, the name of the main street. I wondered, at this point, if it was named after a be-whiskered father of the community in times past. I thoroughly enjoyed the human-sized structures and environment. I was saddened by a number of abandoned shop fronts. Perhaps I am watching the demise of small-town America. Later I was told by a woman in a coffee shop that keeping the lid on the amount of activity in the town was a deliberate policy of the city council. Perhaps the city fathers obtain more tax revenues from the out-of-town shopping malls and complexes.

This woman had set up her neck and shoulder massage chair in the coffee shop. She offered me a five-minute session for five dollars. I was pleased to accept in order to feel the strain and pressure of all the travelling so far be eased away. The massage was 'just what the doctor ordered'. I felt refreshed and invigorated afterwards. I went to visit one of the historic buildings set just off main Garrison, which was used by the early and mid-nineteenth century state political bosses. This building had been used by the military as a troop garrison headquarters. Perhaps that is why the main street is so named. It was also used as a prison and court house. Another less than positive use, in my view, was as a centre to quash the resistance of the Native Americans against white rule. I plan to return a little later and conduct a healing here. The prison was in the cellar part of the building with no natural ventilation and little light. Prison guards used to sprinkle sawdust between this basement and the ground floor. This was in order to eliminate the stink of urine and unwashed bodies from the courthouse above. This must have been horrific to live in and barbaric in the extreme.

I gotta move on. I do enjoy using the vernacular. The next morning I was on the road before first light as I was planning to drive the most number of miles in any one day. This drive is from Fort Smith (goodbye Little America) to Amarillo in the Texas panhandle. Once over the bridge out of Fort Smith I am in Oklahoma, where '*The corn is as high as an Elephant's eye.*' This is another cue for a song to relieve the driving boredom. There was no corn in sight as I drove through the state on Highway 40. Oklahoma is flat as far as the eye could see, with Oklahoma City sitting in the middle of the state like a cherry on top of a cake. What a strange comparison. I don't have a clue where that came from. There must be more to Oklahoma away from the interstate highway for those that have the time to explore. I don't stop until I reach the Texas border; except to enjoy an egg, sausage and bacon breakfast on the way; lovely stuff. It is a calm day with hardly a movement from the blades in the wind farms` as I pass. The I-40 (interstate highway) passes various internal border signs signifying the beginnings and endings of tribal lands before Texas is reached. I am not drawn to stop. There will be time to work in tribal lands later.

If Oklahoma is flat then the Texas panhandle, viewing from the interstate, is flatter. I imagine playing pool on its surface. The panhandle is so named because looking at a map of Texas the main body of the state is round, a little like a pan. In the north is a squarer, narrower area, thus the pan and its handle. I look forward to finishing this quite boring part of the drive. Relief floods my being as I reach my hotel in Amarillo and a much-enjoyed hot pool that the receptionist calls a sauna. An early night's sleep was delayed by a screaming child in the next room.

Why do I attract this to myself? flashes through my mind.

I speak to my higher self, asking that it speaks with the higher self of the child in order to persuade it to calm down. Incredibly this works and the child quietens immediately. I settle down to a peaceful night's rest. Perhaps the lesson here was to trust this route of communication more often. As I peep out of my motel room the next morning I see that the weather has changed overnight from warm balmy conditions to cold and windy. My drive to Albuquerque should be taken with care.

One unexpected development came up in Amarillo. The crystal, which Hazel had given me to place on my third eye during the trip, disappeared. I am scrupulous in checking motel rooms before I leave them. I had left nothing. However, when I reached Cynthia's house the next evening the crystal was gone. This is not an unusual phenomenon for crystals to move into other realms of existence. It is also a common occurrence for those on spiritual journeys to have objects removed from their persons or baggage. When I tuned in later, my guidance informed me that the crystal was now in the Earth, in another dimension, using the energy that had been generated on the journey up to that point for the benefit of reality. The crystal disappeared on day thirteen of the trip; this is a most auspicious number in mystical beliefs.

It isn't until I reach the first New Mexican city of Tucumcari that the energy of this state hits me in the heart. It is a great lift. A few miles before that feeling strikes me I pass mesas, breaking up the previously unrelieved flatness of the countryside. They appear to be the energy outposts of this, my favourite US state. It seems as though they could be contributing to this energy change. It is as though they are saying *you are now entering a place of high energy.* Until this point the flat material Texas energy has dominated. I didn't notice the Texas energy until changed by that of New Mexico.

As a major part of my work in New Mexico I plan to work in Hovenweep, which is actually in Colorado, a wonderful place of the heart. I spoke to Cynthia on the phone the previous evening and told her of my plans to arrive the next day. She has a room in her house for me to use. Part of my work in this region will also be to go up to the Four Corners, a place of spiritual significance as well as being the place where the states of New Mexico, Colorado, Utah and Arizona meet.

OK, back to the present. I reach the town of Santa Rosa the second city on Highway 40 between the Texas border and Albuquerque. I stop for fuel and breakfast and eat the latter in a Mexican–American restaurant. The owners are speaking Spanish as well as English. They seem to have little interest in interacting with me, their lone customer. At the end of my meal I ask the woman owner if she is Mexican. This is an innocuous type of social contact that I have made along the way. She speaks with a hard voice back to me, no eye contact and no smiles.

'No, we are New Mexican and speak Spanish too.' The words are normal enough but the delivery is short and sharp. I think to myself

that the subtext of this is, '*You've had your food. Get your sorry ass out of my restaurant.*'

I find out later that there is a community of old Spanish families from before this area was taken over by the US. I also realise that, in some peoples' eyes, Mexicans, who have come here to work, are sometimes looked down on. Perhaps those two points explain the owner's attitude to me. A little later, as I continue my drive along Highway 40 towards Albuquerque, the food that I had eaten and which had been excellent was not resting easily in my stomach. I realise that the less than pleasant contact with the owner had affected my feelings about the food. So, I blessed the food and asked my inner self that it should be honoured and used to positively fuel my body. Soon afterwards I felt better. Perhaps with a kinder attitude to customers the owner would have a better business. Alternatively, perhaps she was just having a less than positive day.

I arrive in Cynthia's house in Placitas, New Mexico, a few miles north of Albuquerque. Cynthia is a good friend from the, for me, momentous journey that I took with Don Alejandro and the Maya in Guatemala during 1999. I had stayed with Cynthia in 2003 in a small adobe house that is on her property. Cynthia works as a teacher and healer with the energies of Maya, Native American and Celtic traditions. On the first evening here I relax by watching a fictional film about Avalon with my friend. There is an interesting exploration, in the film, of the tension between the ancient goddess religion and the form of Christianity promulgated since the Council of Nicea in 325 AD. This is reflected, in a similar way, during the present historical times, except that today the goddess's spiritual form is on the rise, whereas the present form of Christianity is declining, in my view. The times they are a'changing.

Cynthia spoke to me of the Mayan Baktun. This is the Maya time period of 5200 years ending on December 21st 2012. She said that this period was initiated by invasion and destruction caused by invaders from the north. This is often the direction from which successful invasions are carried out. I feel that we are already in that age, and many things are changing. Cynthia also talked of the story of St Patrick clearing the snakes from Ireland. According to her this is a cover for the eradication of the Druids in that country. The asp (snake) was a symbol of Druidic energies and healing.

Some of the Native American reservations have casinos in them because they are subject to different laws compared to those of the state around them. I am not an enthusiast for gambling. However, there is a delicious irony, for me, in the knowledge that previously abused Native Americans are relieving the white man of his money. Thus the abuser and the abused have changed places. It's an ill wind that blows no-one any good.

My perambulations around Bernallilo, the town a few miles away from Placitas, brought me in front of an election office for Barak Obama. I was intrigued, given my experience on the trip already mentioned, to find out more. I went into the office and asked, as a writer, if I could talk to some of the volunteers working there. My request went to the supervisor, who duly agreed. The first person I talked to was a student, Christina, a young woman from Brooklyn, New York. She had come from her home city to offer her services, without pay, to the campaign. I asked her why she was here giving of her time in this way. She said that the other major candidate, Senator McCain, represented the way of the past, the status quo, a continuation figure. She continued that Obama represented change, a chance that the country wouldn't normally have. Many people were involved for the first time. The single event that persuaded her to commit was the convention of the Democratic Party when Obama was elected as presidential candidate. She was impressed by the man. She continued that this should be where we are going rather than where we have come from. As the campaign moved on the two options set forth by the two major candidates became polarised. This young lady was also greatly concerned at the choice of Senator McCain's vice-presidential running mate. (I came across two incidents related to this topic.)

One evening in a motel I watched a program hosted by a black comedian. He spoke of attending a rally of the Republican vice-candidate. The comedian was dumfounded by the level of hate towards Obama being created at this rally. Much later I read a piece that spoke of the church of this candidate being burned to the ground. Was the burning a karmic backlash from the before-mentioned hatred generated? Obama was bringing more people to the election process and he was looking to improve healthcare in the country. This is a great country that ordinary people can assist to change. Christina was aware that foreigners, Europeans, Mexicans, would be happier with Obama. *'There has never been an election like this,'* was a common theme of her talk to me. There were a lot of first-time voters that were interested in what was going on. People are joining because they feel that they can make a difference in New Mexico, a swing state. That is a state that could vote either way.

The second person I spoke to was a woman who had taken a break from work, Sidney was her name, to volunteer for the campaign. I would say that she was from the middle classes. This is a synopsis of what she said.

> *This is a community project providing opportunity with purpose. Normally there is a very low turnout in this state and this county. This time we are registering new voters all the time. One of the new voters was eighty-three years old! This office is open twelve hours per day. We are providing a non-threatening, non-intimidating environment for people that are prepared to come and work here. One of the reasons we are here is to help people get through the voting process.* (At this point she showed me the voting paper. Everyone from president to local dog catcher seemed to be on this long document.) *We don't want people to feel humiliated when at the voting station. Obama has thirty to forty offices in this state alone. People in poor areas are concerned about health care. This thinking is in line with Obama policy. The real story about this election is that it is about people coming together. Bernallilo sits at the edge of Albuquerque. There are people from many backgrounds here: sophisticated and intelligent,*

> *Native American, traditional Spanish, Mexican, poor peoples. It is a delight to co-ordinate the energies of different peoples and to find a way where people are empowered. We are all working with the Obama precedent that people can engage in civic life so that they will be less afraid of each other. Obama will give a new perspective for citizens of this country also will develop a new perspective of the US for foreigners. This movement is not just about the election. Door-to-door canvassing, which is a new thing in the US, has been incorporated into the election process. Ordinary people have welcomed this phenomenon. I met Obama. He was warm and friendly without any celebrity pretensions. I believe McCain realises that he has made a mistake with his vice-presidential running mate. We have even offered to babysit so that one voter can get to the polls.* I have a personal endorsement of the regret of McCain concerning the appointment of his running mate. At the meeting where he conceded defeat and thanked his workers the body language relating to his running mate was telling. I never saw him look at her or refer to her. She was not allowed to speak at this event.

The third and last person to be interviewed was Deborah, a Native American woman from the Laguna pueblo nearby. This is what she said.

> *My Pueblo is just off Interstate 40. We are used to people always travelling through our land and interacting with them. Our Pueblo has the same agenda as many Americans looking for change and new policies with respect to health care. Importantly we need to keep our pueblo traditions and culture alive. We support Obama. Ninety percent of our people are Democrat supporters. We want to make sure that people vote whatever their background and party support. There have been a lot of subtle threats to our sovereignty through Supreme Court legal decisions. Judges are appointed politically here. There are only a handful of lawmakers who understand tribal sovereignty. We need a person at the top who understands the issues and guides the*

lawmakers. Obama has promised to have a Native American representative in the White House. There are twenty-two tribes in New Mexico alone. Congress needs to understand Native American issues. I believe Americans will vote in large numbers. (She was certainly correct in this assumption.)

I left the office pleased and heartened at the welcome and openness of these three women, all from different strata in US society. Their enthusiasm was reflected later in the turnout and success, as far as they were concerned, of the US election. So did the Obama presidency satisfy the yearnings of the American people? The following quote is from Bertice Berry, at www.azquotes.com.

When you walk with purpose, you collide with destiny.

While I was in the Obama office I was told that the Democratic presidential candidate (as he was then) would be speaking at a rally in Albuquerque the next day. That evening I discussed this with Cynthia. She was most enthusiastic that I should attend this event, as she was interested in my 'reading' of him and the rally. I agreed to put my visit to the Four Corners and Hovenweep off for one day to go to the rally. In the meantime I had added the Aztec ruins, which are in the same area, to this trip. My agreement to go to the Obama rally was really to please Cynthia, although it would have been interesting to be there. That night I awoke from sleep with the most unpleasant feeling in the pit of my stomach. Two possible causes entered my awareness. The first one was that I had eaten something that disagreed with me. The second possible cause was that I was being affected by a negative energy source that Cynthia and I had been discussing on the previous evening. This negative energy source had been discussed between us so that I was warned of possible potential barriers on the trip to the Four Corners. In order to attempt to clear this negative energy I mentally opened the acupuncture points on the bottom of my feet in order to bring in positive energy. I then attempted to raise it to the lower abdomen and clear that uncomfortable feeling there. This exercise helped as long as I was concentrating on it. As soon as I stopped concentrating the uncomfortable feeling returned. So, this was not curing the problem. It came into my awareness that this discomfort was not due to a physical cause but resulted from an energy imbalance in my sacral or second chakra. Temporarily I abandoned the problem and fell asleep.

The next morning I woke with a start. A feeling of unease beset my being. I arose and began some stretching exercises, as I often do. As I stood on one leg performing a balancing routine, it came to me not to attend the Obama rally. It was more important to continue my journey of the sacred to the Four Corners and the other places in the region. Immediately my being relaxed and I felt comfortable that the best decision had been made. Attending the Obama rally would have been fun and interesting, but was not related to the spiritual reasons that I had made the trip. I was back in focus. All the feelings of unease had disappeared.

(Years later I reviewed that which I had written concerning Obama. For me the comments still held true in the context of that time. There was much speculation among the spiritually awake that Obama was then, or perhaps always has been, of the dark persuasion. His election was a massive con trick some say. Certainly he was subject to tremendous pressure to conform, as other presidents have done, to those that would rule us. The events that will overtake us in the next few years may render his presidency redundant. Much will change.)

Clive's personal note: The above concerning Obama is now a historical document, but in the context of my journey worth including in this book.

Before I left, Cynthia spoke to me in a serious manner concerning the journey I was about to make. She asked me to open the map and we peered down at the road I was due to take. Cynthia pointed to a stretch of the road and told me of a danger that was present there. This is what she said to me:

On the right-hand side of the main road is an underground base for aliens of a negative persuasion. There have been rumours and evidence of abductions here. These beings are extremely unpleasant. On no account should you stop on this stretch of your journey. I know a shaman who lived in this area. Other Native Americans living in the reservation that contains the area of the base have seen some amazing things. One series of sightings was of cars being lifted by no apparent physical means but by the power of a blue pillar of light. Allegedly genetic experiments with human body parts are part of the alien work being done here. I have never told anyone, in so much detail about this phenomenon. So do take care.

Her words were so sobering that indeed I did take care not to stop in this stretch. Fortunately, I did not see anything amiss when driving there.

So, I drove to Farmington to rest for one night before going up to the Four Corners. I made a wrong turn after booking a room at the Motel 6 in Farmington and ended up going towards Aztec ruins first. This place had been planned to be the third and last place to visit on this mini trip. As I drove into the parking lot I realised that I had been here before in 2003. This time the energy of the place was much stronger. I could not tell if it was me, the ruins, a combination of the both that had increased in vibration. Perhaps it was the combination. Inside the large reconstructed underground circular kiva I was fortunate to be there alone. I took the opportunity to tile inside the kiva and finished by touching the central altar stone to ground the tiling.

This area is a great and sacred land. A prayer offered by its ancient inhabitants, the Anasazi, recites '*our daily life is like a prayer, a constant quest for balance and harmony.*' The civilisation flourished from 850 AD until the late 1200s. The people left their homes and land suddenly, mysteriously and disappeared. No-one knows exactly why. Many indigenous people of today are claimed to be their descendants and maintain strong cultural and spiritual ties to the site. The latter point is a most important one. The spiritual ceremonies performed with great emotional and spiritual feeling over the centuries vibrate still in the ruins and the landscape. This is what I sense, honour, and, perhaps without knowing it, am helping to reactivate as Mother Earth gathers herself for her vibrational and consciousness uplift.

Later, when I reviewed the visit in a nearby restaurant, my body was shaking with the vibrations of the visit. Quite what the reason was for me being at the Aztec ruins I cannot say. Suffice to say that it had been necessary. (Later I sensed that this place was a portal of energy from cosmic realms. It had already been opened by the indigenous peoples. My energy had been used to open it more. Also being in this place had wakened me a little more to higher consciousness. These latter insights comforted me greatly. There are times that I do spiritual work in far off places and receive no feedback. I suppose on those occasions it is necessary to trust that the work has been done.) I fought my way through the Farmington traffic. Thankfully there were large signs that directed me back to Motel 6. A restful evening and night was a good preparation for me to rise early and drive towards the Four Corners monument. I reached the monument at 7.15am. The entrance was locked as the opening time was 8am. This turned out to be a blessing. I was able to perform the Four Corners routines from my chi gong practice, to tile and to perform a short meditation before anyone showed up to open the site. The site was owned and administered by the Navajo Native American Nation. To one side the crimson sky announced the imminent arrival of Ra, the life-giving sun. My ceremony was the reason for my visit. Once the site was opened visitors arrived and I was no longer alone. I couldn't have, effectively, completed ceremonies with non-sympathetic people here. The energy changed completely to a more mundane one. The early wake-up call and drive had been cosmically inspired in order to do the work unhindered.

My original plan was to drive next to the city of Cortez, book a hotel and then find Hovenweep. After driving for a few miles from the Four Corners monument I suddenly came upon a sign for Hevenweep so immediately turned to make the forty-plus miles journey to the sacred place of the heart. This drive was through dry, arid desert relieved by a few small settlements along the way. The visitors' centre at Hovenweep was as I remembered it. I immediately started the two-mile walk around the canyon of Hovenweep, where people had lived until eight hundred years ago. The sense of peace and awesome quiet relaxed me after the concentrative drive. The only sounds that could be heard were that of an occasional bird chirruping in the underbrush and the crunch of my shoes on the gravel path. This place is special. Similar to the Aztec ruins, the energy of the heart-centred ceremonies performed time after time resonated from the rocks. Until recent times they had been locked by the vibration of the past. Now they were released to perform their great work and to thrill those sufficiently attuned to appreciate them. If any person needs healing this is the place to meditate and renew oneself. As I write this later, just thinking about Hovenweep attunes me with the place. Regretfully I pulled myself away in order to start the long drive back to Placitas. I realise that by the time I reach a restaurant it will be nearly twenty-four hours since I have eaten. My energies are waning and need replenishing with material food and liquids.

The following is from www.nps/gov/hove/learn:

> *The towers of Hovenweep were built by ancestral Puebloans, a sedentary farming culture that occupied the Four Corners area from about A.D. 500 to A.D. 1300. Similarities in architecture, masonry and pottery styles indicate that the inhabitants of Hovenweep were closely associated with groups living at Mesa Verde and other nearby sites.*

As I drove across the dusty, northern New Mexico plain there, in the distance loomed the mighty and massive Shiprock. The morning haze gave its castellated top a mysterious blue colour. This is a most sacred mountain of the Navajo nation rendered more powerful by its surroundings of flat plain. On a previous visit I attempted to approach it but could find no roads that would take me towards it.

All I could do was circle around it miles from its rocky crags. I am sure that the Navajo have their routes that are not available to outsiders. I can understand their desire to keep out those that are not part of the great work performed there. The following is an extract from the internet.

The following is from www.discovernavajo.com:

> *Located 15 miles southwest of the town of Shiprock, New Mexico is a unique towering, bird-like volcanic rock formation that can be seen for miles in all directions. Shiprock, as this mighty sand-colored column was named by Anglo settlers, is known to the Navajo as "Tsé Bit' a'í", or rock with wings. The peak is 7,178 above sea level, and is at the center of three volcanic pressure ridges that pushed the rock skyward millennia ago.*

This was a long driving day. I struggled to keep my eyes open on the straight, minimally trafficked roads. At one point I was jolted back to safe driving awareness by the ghostly vision of my four Native American co-workers on the windscreen of the car. I am sure that they were anxious for my wellbeing. I felt better and much more awake after this vision. The adrenaline was flowing again. Further, I was able to refresh myself with pecan pie and orange juice in a restaurant seventy miles from my destination of Cynthia's house.

There is a national network of retail stores in the US called 'seven two (to) eleven'. The title is related to the hours of business that they are open for. That is, they open from early morning to late at night. Mystics claim that eleven is a mysterious number. The relationship between eleven and seven were considered so important by the ancient Egyptians that they used it as the structure for the design of the Great Pyramid.

Having written the above I wondered if those that named this very successful business venture knowingly or subconsciously tuned into the vibrational harmony of the numbers. This tuning-in would be in order to attract the positive features of sacred numbers. Alternatively, is there some other explanation? I assume that seven is the planned opening time and eleven in the evening is the closing time of each store in the chain (maybe).

The following piece is from the Astrologer magazine and is as good an epitaph for my journey as I could imagine.

> *On November 1st (2008) Neptune stations direct at 21 degrees Aquarius, calling us to further embrace the ideals of the Aquarian age, honouring freedom and equality, shifting from hierarchy to collaboration, and fulfilling the Hopi's prophecy 'We are the ones we have been waiting for'.*

This is also from the Astrologer magazine.

> *What are your dreams? What are your fears? What is your truth? Remember: When one door of happiness closes, another opens; but often we look so long at the closed door that we do not see the one which has been opened for us (Helen Keller).*

I am aware that my three-week trip here is winding down. I have visited and worked in the sites that I have been guided to. It is time to relax, do some shopping and prepare myself for return to the UK. I went to a store in Bernallilo purchasing some small gifts for friends at home. Speaking with the storekeeper she talked of her son, remembering a previous life when he was three years old. His mother asked him what he remembered of it.

'There were trees all around,' he replied.

'Did you like it?' his mother asked.

'No, it was hard,' the boy said.

Later the boy's grandfather brought a picture of ancestors to show mother and boy. This photo showed rugged, tough men.

'What did they do?' Mum asked.

'They were lumberjacks,' said granddad.

So, was the boy remembering a previous life or was it a racial memory projected into his consciousness from his DNA, or is there some other explanation? This story reminded me of my own experience of recalling a life in Atlantis. This memory was triggered as a result of seeing toppling skyscrapers in a childhood comic. My childhood home was a rigid Christian one. Even so young I learned to keep my mouth shut about issues that did not suit the home theological framework.

With three days remaining of my stay in the US I have the opportunity to rest and recover before re-entering the rhythm of family life in England. The first day was difficult for me in health terms. I felt nauseous, weak, with stomach or second chakra issues. This, I realised, was my personal adjustment to the energies with which I had been working. There was a sense that those energies with which I had been working were returning to me as a gift. The strength of these energies was such that my body and being initially struggled to cope. Cynthia, the friend with whom I had been staying, was away from the house. I spent much of the day calling on the forces of the universe to assist in integrating these energies into my being. I discovered a harmonious corner in the house and, sitting on a fleece, was able to move towards a place of harmonium. This was assisted later by a slap-up meal in the aptly named *'Flying Star'* restaurant. On the second day of the three, I planned and built a medicine wheel in Cynthia's yard. There is a flat piece of land that attracts me for the project. The wheel's purpose was for honouring my journey and helping to 'ground' the energies generated in this reality. I explained to Cynthia that I build my wheels, mostly, out of twenty-nine stones. My medicine wheels consist of a cross inside a circle.

Traditionally the structure is oriented towards the north so that the crosspieces face the four cardinal directions of north, south, east and west. Thus, there are four stones, one at each cardinal point and one at the centre. Each of the four arcs of the circle and each one of the four cross pieces are constructed from three stones each. This is my preferred structure. Others will construct their wheels according to their own inner promptings. Once constructed I then perform a ceremony as my inner consciousness dictates.

From my point of view the situation is changing as far as the last sentence above is concerned. There are other non-Native Americans who are attuned with medicine wheel work.

A valued friend stated that it was not necessary to use three-dimensional constructs, such as medicine wheels, when attempting to perform spiritual acts. For me this is not the case. The performance of rituals utilising intention and attention is focussed by medicine wheel construction and ritual for me. I am reminded of a comment that another friend made when I first started travelling abroad to sacred places as a result of intuitive and spiritual influences. He believed and stated that it was not necessary to travel to these places in order to perform attunement rituals or healing. Again, for me, my presence in these places is a requirement for Earth energies transmitted from cosmic sources through my body and being into the earth of these places.

On the last day in the US, before my journey home I spoke with the owner of a café. She described how she had moved from a discriminatory environment in southern Florida to run a business here in Placitas, New Mexico. She said that discrimination was rife in northern Florida also, of a different kind. I didn't enquire about the nature of that discrimination. It didn't seem to be of overriding importance. I felt sad that this negative treatment of someone could drive them away from their home environment. One of the presidential candidates is of mixed race. Perhaps (I wrote this immediately after the Obama election), the new president can begin the process of not only the eradication of this discrimination, but also to assist in the healing of its wounds.

The day of my departure from Cynthia's house and from the US duly arrived. The trip had been 'awesome' for me, to use the common parlance here. The animals around the house were more active as they prepared for hibernation. When I arrived I was greeted by a chipmunk, the first I had encountered, tiny and busy with its business. The larger nocturnal animals, bears, mountain lions and bob cats were around, although seldom seen. Cynthia's house is on the edge of the Cibola forest, a protected environment.

Well, there is change all around. Cynthia talked to me about Guatemala. She said that Alvaro Colon, the new president of that country, is a student of Don Alejandro, the Mayan shaman and leader of his indigenous people. The inauguration of the president was held in the main plaza of Guatemala City instead of the confines of a stiff and formal palace; as with the US, the people are expectant and yearning for change in that war-ravaged country. In the ceremony Don Alejandro carried the staff of power for the Maya people. He gave it to Alvaro Colon to hold. The latter, encouraged by Don Alejandro, promised to work for the best interests of his people. Let us hope that this really is a new beginning for this small country. Cynthia also said that the political and financial elite, those with most money, are holding themselves aloof from the change. I told Cynthia that those who place themselves in a bunker mentality are doomed to cut themselves off from the very lifeblood that has sustained them in the past.

So, this is the end of the trip, goodbye to the sixteen states, if the district of Columbia is included. From Washington DC to New Mexico I plied my trade of 'mad mystic', working with healing and grounding new energies. I enjoyed the trip immensely. I felt fulfilled, although there were many challenges along the way. The 3,000+ miles of travelling was completed successfully with help from my spiritual protection. This had been of concern to me as I don't enjoy driving at all. It is a necessary chore as far as I am concerned. I was, at the last, grateful for the comparative luxury of the SUV that I had hired in the nation's capital. I was also thankful for the help and support provided for me by friends Suzanne and Cynthia. So, it is back to England for recovery, reflection and review, as well as re-connecting with friends and family.

Postscript to USA

Reflections on a most amazing journey

On the Sunday after my return from the US I attended a meditation group meeting. Having given the group a taste of my contact with Abraham Lincoln I was asked to lead a meditation in order to make a positive contact with him. After the attunement I asked for feedback from the other members of the group. All of them spoke of a harmonious vibration and a calm relaxed contact. My attempted contact with Abe's spirit contained the request that we think well of the American electorate over the last few days in order to assist in the creation of a positive vibration. (This was immediately before the US presidential election.) This I did and I asked my fellow meditators to do the same. At the same meeting friend Joan said that she saw my face being overshadowed by a Native American during the meditation. I was impressed with her vision. Perhaps it is one of the five that I worked with during my trip. My subway stop was called Rosslyn in Washington DC. I wondered if the naming of this place had anything to do with Rosslyn Chapel in Scotland. This is a place of great interest for mystics. Throughout the US trip I perceived interesting side issues that it would have been great to pursue. However, I had a 'shopping list' of places to work which took priority. There was no time for other things in the three weeks that I had allocated for the trip. This was particularly so as the spiritual forces had directed me to other places that I had not planned to work in. Still, that is the norm on my trips.

There was a downside to this trip upon my return. During the first few days I was the recipient of the most powerful jet lag that I have experienced. As soon as I recovered from that I was struck down by a very heavy virus and cold which took some time to clear up. I should have expected some backlash. I operated in a high vibration on this trip. Inevitably a coming down to Earth should have been expected.

My two major journeys that year had been to Egypt and this trip to the US, including the Four Corners. As far as I was concerned there was no connection between the two until I read the following. This is from the *Ancient Secret of The Flower of Life* by Drunvalo Melchizedek.

> *There was an astrologer who had an amazing idea about this diagonal, which has to do with the stars and a specific area of the United States. Once the astrologer saw that there was an astrological chart in the sand around the Great Pyramid she wanted to know about the diagonal line at A(not necessary to show here) that seemed to be important to the ancient Egyptians. I can't quite explain what she did because I'm not an astrologer, but she took the astrological wheel and related it to the North Pole and aligned it somehow to Cairo. Then she looked to see where the other end of the line would point. It marked a specific point on planet Earth. In her understanding, it was the four corners area of the United States, where Utah, Colorado, New Mexico and Arizona meet. To the Hopi and other native peoples, the Four Corners area is marked by four mountains, which create a much smaller area.*

I was intrigued by the connection that Drunvalo highlighted between the two trips that I had made. So I, first of all, consulted my guidance on the matter. I was shown a series of visions by guidance which did not make coherent sense to me. The first one was the curve of the Earth as though from some miles up in the atmosphere. The next was the line between the two locations mentioned in Drunvalo's piece. This line opened up in the form of a crack in the Earth with brilliant white light shining through. I later sensed that this image was demonstrating the Earth's evolution into a higher vibration. My guidance spoke to me strongly on this vision saying, *get this.* The next image was of one segment of a ball of light with a being of light leaving it and flying off. The meaning of that was revealed in a meditation that I will discuss later. The penultimate vision was of a wise being standing on a ledge above me. The being had a head of an owl. The final vision shown to me was of hieroglyphic writing that I did not understand. Guidance told me that it was Atlantean.

There was no time to continue the contact with guidance after the above for, fortunately, I was due to meet with a meditation group that morning. It would give me the opportunity to discuss the matter and obtain feedback from this group of attuned mystics. In fact, I felt that the whole thing had been set up by the cosmic forces so that my interest would be sparked in time for the meeting. I duly laid out the above to the group and we entered meditation to attempt to piece together the disparate elements of the visions. During this meditation I was given much more information concerning the ball of light which the being floated out from. I was told that light possessed its own conscious awareness, hence the being in my vision. It was more than just vibration. Advanced beings utilise this consciousness in order to increase their awareness to a greater degree. The information went on to say that this light consciousness could be used as an enhancement for the benefit of the group and for each of us individually.

Friend Hazel received the information that the owl-headed being was one from a higher dimension. These beings were on a path of development also. Some were highly advanced and some not so advanced. These beings would contact us, creating visionary scenarios in their own consciousness for their benefit. These connections may or may not be for our development or in our best interests. Hazel highlighted this potential, let us call it danger, with a story. She spoke of her return from Egypt some time before. She had not returned alone. During a group meditation she was joined by an Egyptian being that wished the group to participate in a ceremony during which certain symbols would be placed over the head of each member of the group. Hazel became uncomfortable with the progress of this work because the being was directive and not participative. The work was thus rejected. Thus the original image was telling me, I believe, to be discerning in the work that was undertaken with discarnate beings. That is not to say that such contacts should be viewed with suspicion. I should, however, ensure through my normal intuitive faculties that the contact was for my highest good and that of the universe.

Louise, another member of the group, provided more information concerning the hieroglyphics. She said that they were indeed Atlantean. These writings were stored in the Earth and were available to advanced beings from a number of realities to access. They could be used to enhance wisdom and knowledge. They were also available to our group to use. These hieroglyphics were not just linear explanations of concepts or ideas. They were gateways to sacred elements of conscious awareness, I believe, akin to Reiki and runic symbols. Ian was told during the meditation that the line from the pyramid in Egypt to the Four Corners in the US was reciprocated on other parts of the Earth surface. One line went to Peru. Louise saw one terminating in Canada. Ian was given the Himalayas as the termination point and the snake journeyed along it on its recent relocation from Tibet to Peru. This snake is the kundalini of the Earth being. (There is a further explanation of kundalini in the postscript.) Drunvalo say that the Earth's kundalini has moved to northern Chile just south of Peru.

It was also said that my visit to Egypt was a reference point, as I did not go all the way to the pyramid. The contact point of my visit to the Four Corners and the reference point visit to Egypt was enough to complete the work along that line. Other people independently were also working in a similar way in those two places. Thus the availability of the information stored in the Atlantean symbols was improved.

The outline of one of the symbols presented itself to me again later. Much more complicated than Reiki symbols and runes, this one was with swirls, circles and projections. It hints of possibilities for the race and this third-dimensional reality. Generally, these symbols also create a resonance to improve the communication between beings in different sectors of reality. Different items of knowledge can be revealed by one Atlantean symbol depending on the vibrational resonance and level of development of the person receiving. Regular meditations on symbols that present themselves will reveal different scenarios of knowledge and potential action. These symbols are dynamic and, once perceived, will work with the observer in his particular reality. They can work in a similar way to a rune of protection, for example. The latter can be invoked at any time that a person is in need of its help. The Atlantean symbols can be more significant in that they possess the ability to work with many possibilities for the person fortunate enough to be in tune with them. Groups and individuals that work with these symbols do not necessarily need to be aware of the detail of a symbol to be worked with. If the group is sufficiently attuned and developed then meditating on the idea of the symbols can create harmonic resonance and connection, bringing in Atlantean knowledge and action scenarios for dealing with current and future issues. Revealing the mysteries of these symbols can be assisted by drawing or writing them, thus bringing them closer. The symbols can work by embedding themselves in our cells. Thus revelations of their knowledge may appear at times totally unexpected as they have their own consciousness and will work outside linear time. The symbols are particularly helpful to those individuals that feel connected to the Atlantean experience, or believe that they had lives on that continent.

In a subsequent meditation a friend of mine suggested that these images were connected to my next planned trip to India and that further revelations would follow. I feel that the symbols are those that Thai and Indian writing grew out of. Friend Mary drew a line on a map from the Four Corners to Egypt and then onwards. The line continued into the middle of India. Thus all three of my trips in that year are connected at least by the line of energy. We will see what that brings to the fore. There we will leave this for now and continue the story of the energy line at a point in the India chapter.

The inauguration of President Obama, like the election, is creating a lot of interest in the US.

Hazel's group, also before the inauguration, meditated on the January 20th difficulty. I received a number of pieces of information from guidance. As soon as I 'tuned in', I perceived a golden energy around the situation. This was replaced by a stronger, vibrant bright light energy that was so strong that my whole body vibrated with its pulsation. My guidance informed me that the protection around Obama was so strong that he would not be killed by those opposing him while in office. I was informed that the forces of light had learned well from the assassinations of Abraham Lincoln and the Kennedy brothers. Protective energies were now much stronger. The energies and cosmic forces would also assist the new president in the development of policies that would aid his country as well as the world. This protection would not inhibit the inevitable karma that was coming to the people, the nation of United States. Learning the lessons of the new energies was likely to be difficult for many in this country. Obama could not change this karmic course of events. It was almost as though he was a citizen of the universe loaned to this nation for their development. Part of his task was to cleanse the presidency, which had been besmirched by the actions and thoughts of previous holders of this office. In this way the nation and its institutions could begin the process of renewal. If the nation chose not to follow Obama or support him then the downward spiral of this once great country would continue.

As I write this the day before the presidential inauguration there seems to be an almost hysterical expectation of the new presidency. I realise that, particularly in the US, many people were heartily sick of the previous incumbent. Supporters at home and abroad will need to be patient and be aware of the realities. The expectation is almost as though Obama will recreate civilisation. Only the mass of the people can do that. There is another side to this debate. Pharoah Akhanaton was in his own way a trail-blazer, but was perceived as a failure by conventional history. However, the deep mystical truth is that this pharoah planted, in the Akashic record of the mass consciousness, a practical vision of the purity of a spiritual vision to be accessed later in human history. It may be that Obama also possesses that deep spiritual credibility to prepare the way for the future, as well as providing a vision for action now.

This is from www.emergingearthangels.com;

> *Know as well that Barack Obama is here to provide stability for these changes to occur. His role is in holding the energies as stable as possible during the final shifting and crashing so that it will be as comfortable as possible for everyone. The shifting and crashing will continue on until December of 2012. Obama's destiny was to be present at the helm during this time. His grandmother passed away the day before his win was announced. She left as she knew she had completed her purpose ... to raise him to fulfil his destiny, and his destiny was now intact. Making her transition the day before the election results were revealed, was proof therein that he had indeed won the election and things were now in order.*
>
> *Placing Obama on a pedestal or expecting one man to save the planet is not the intention of his role. His purpose involves embracing many, uniting the whole, and spreading this energy in order to form a higher level web of stability to hold things as stable as possible while we complete the final phases of the shift. This is why his background involves so much diversity and why he does what he does. He is simply creating a huge grid as his soul knows exactly what it is doing. (Please, please do not contact me about Barack Obama in any negative way, try to convince me that he is 'reptilian' or some other low level interpretation of his beingness. He is a high level being who is doing exactly what he came to do, just as George W. Bush (and his administration) did as well, and thus creating what is needed at the time for the higher purpose of this planet.)*

A meditation brought Obama to Mary's awareness. He took her to the edge of a place where those of the dark persuasion were preparing activities not in the best interests of humanity. He asked Mary that our group work on this problem by asking the highest spiritual contacts that we could muster to contain the threat. We were not to work on this issue ourselves as the dangers to our beings would be too high. The negative powers would be overpowering for our human physical and spiritual being. Obama was so intense that he asked Mary twice to initiate this task. Thus another area of work opens up for us. I am aware of the dangers of confronting the dark forces directly. It can be a very dangerous proposition, which my previous experience verifies.

No doubt there will be those that will strive might and main to restrict, side-track and embarrass Obama in whatever way is open to them. A press report, soon after Obama's election, stated that a half-brother of the president had been arrested and then released from police custody on a charge of possessing a small amount of drugs in his home country of Kenya. The charge was dropped and the half-brother claimed that he had never used drugs. So, was the latter lying or had he been 'set-up'? We may never know.

During the same meditation Mary saw a representation of the six humans that are part of this group; they are Mary, Joan and Clive, who are incarnate and Paul, Kate and Terry (my father) who are disincarnate. The next day I remembered that as Mary recounted this story I was aware of the Nubian, who had arrived after my Egyptian trip, as a guide for Joan. It was as though he was saying, *I am here too!*

Postscript to Obama: From a later perspective I know not if the information on Obama is valid or not. Perhaps it doesn't matter. As my friend Bryan says, *'Everything is in divine order.'*

Our final two stories in this chapter are based around Suzanne Taylor. Suzanne emailed me concerning the irksome warplane engine noise that afflicts her home town and her home. It seems that the engines of Marine Corps warplanes are tested on the ground, making a horrendous din that can go on for hours. When

I was in Beaufort I certainly was bothered by the noise. Suzanne asked me for help in finding a way through meditation and visualisation to eradicate the noise. I emailed her back, telling her of the Greenham Common women in England. In the 1960s the US government persuaded Britain to house nuclear missiles aimed at Russia on English soil at Greenham. Effectively this country became an aircraft carrier for US foreign policy and thus a potential target for retributive action from the Soviets. The resistance to the housing of the missiles here was spearheaded by women who camped outside the missile site for years in peaceful protest. Many people thought that they were mad. There was thus no way that the foreign policy of the greatest super power on Earth could be deflected by a few hundred scruffy hippy women, or so people thought. Guess what! Eventually the missiles were withdrawn. The power of the feminine focussed meaningfully is awesome. I told this story to Suzanne to encourage her with this success story to work on her perceived problem in Beaufort. We will see what happens. The power of the feminine is seen by many masculine cultures as a threat. Thus the pressuring of women to become second-class citizens has been rife throughout history. The slaughter of the alleged 'witches' in the middle ages and the branding of women's menses as being unclean are other examples.

One final story from the bizarre end of the spectrum concerning the US was emailed to me by Suzanne.

> *Of course, y'all know of the big bail out on the auto industry in the US. Well, a church actually had a SUV on an altar!!! Unreal, maybe they were praying for the SUV's soul . . .*

Maybe they were. It could be argued that any object has the consciousness of those elements that compose it. If we add the consciousness of the people that built it directing awareness as they worked on the vehicle then perhaps a car does have a nascent form of consciousness. This awareness would then respond to other consciousness. I talk a little more about this in the chapter on healing. Although giving such an object a soul may be taking things a little far. We may not be in the position, just yet, of seeing 'Herby' running around our streets. However, as we rise in consciousness in these enhanced energetic times, who is to say that those things around us will not also rise in awareness?

OK, I think that we have finished with the energy of the four chapters concerning my US trip. We will explore issues surrounding my India trip next.

Postscript

This is from www.enlightenedbeings.com

Kundalini is the supreme cosmic enlightening energy that resides inside us, deep at the core of our being. Kundalini is the most powerful force in the Universe, and brings enlightenment to our world. Your Kundalini awakens the manifesting being in your life! Anything you wish to manifest is possible with an awakened Kundalini.

In ancient text the Kundalini is often described as a female serpent coiled 3 and 1/2 times at the base of your spine. She is sleeping away, waiting for you to awaken her energy and rise up your spine. It's a bit bizarre that such a divine all-powerful energy would be taking a nap at the base of your spine, yet she truly contains the most awesome power you can imagine in the Universe.

'Each of us has a spark in life inside us, and our highest endeavor ought to be to set off that spark in one another.'
~Kenny Ausubel

Your Kundalini will reside at the bottom until we are completely awakened, living 24 hours a day knowing we are The Divine All-powerful God-Being we truly are. When we awaken her infinite Shakti power for the first time, we receive a spiritually enlightening experience (Satori) that can last for days, weeks or months. We then realize who we are is something much bigger than anything we presumed before. We see we are this unlimited consciousness, eternal energy, outrageous creativity and divinely inspired intelligence at all times. The Kundalini allows us to realize this, not as another ego trip, yet through annihilating the ego we can see the bigger Truth exactly as it is. This constant realization and surrender to the God-Being that is here now is called samadi.

Preparation for India

The beginning of the process into Indian immersion

Peter Owen Jones, BBC reporter on the religions of the world (possibly not in post now), in a TV program spoke of India as being the most spiritual country rather than a religious one. This was a description that I particularly enjoyed. It suggested a sense of toleration and the ability to look beyond the dead hand of dogma and theology. Thus a true sense of a relationship with God was available by all in India.

From London, Heathrow, I plan to fly to Mumbai, home to the Zoroastrian faith in India. There are estimated to be only between 1–200,000 adherents remaining in the world. In India they are called Parsees. For every newborn Parsee in India there are four deaths. The other centre of this religion is in Iran, where the numbers of adherents are increasing due to high birth rate. This is a non-proselytising religion. It doesn't seek to convert others. This is a good thing in my view. Throughout history the proselytising religions have raised armies to convert the 'unbelievers' to the 'correct path'.

Perhaps one good way of starting this chapter is to give some background to Hanuman, the monkey god of India. The following is from Wikipedia:

> *Hanuman is a Hindu god and divine vanara companion of the god Rama. Hanuman is one of the central characters of the Hindu epic Ramayana. He is an ardent devotee of Rama and one of the chiranjivis. Hanuman is also son of the wind-god Vayu, who in several stories played a direct role in Hanuman's birth. Hanuman is mentioned in several other texts, such as the epic Mahabharata and the various Puranas.*

The latter is an interesting twist on the notion of virgin birth. Perhaps I will come across the work and influence of Hanuman on my forthcoming trip.

India has a great historical background in mathematics. Our way of writing the number 2 comes from India. We call our way of writing numbers as being Arabic. A mathematician speaking on BBC Radio 3 recently said that, in fact, we should call these numbers Indian–Arabic, their true historical root. The mathematician told a story on the same programme concerning an Indian ruler who offered a wish to a mathematician. If he, the ruler, could not fulfil the promised gift then half his kingdom would be given to the man of numbers. The latter asked that a grain of rice be placed on the first square of a chess board. Thereafter each square should receive double the number of grains in the series 1, 2, 4, 8 etc. The ruler thought that this was such an easy request that there was no problem at all. However the power of numbers became apparent when the exponential power of such a series became apparent. Long before the sixty-fourth square was reached the ruler would have been required to find enough rice to cover the whole of London as far out as the M25 motorway. The ruler was thus tricked into giving half his kingdom to the crafty mathematician.

Friend Ian is of the opinion that part of my journey will involve shutting down old energy centres so that new ones can thrive. If this is the case the likelihood is that I will be unconscious of such events and I will be unlikely to receive feedback afterwards. At a group meditation I was given a couple of passing shots. Mary Earle, who had recently visited India, received the message for me to 'watch my back'. Friend Mary Fitzgerald suggested that I invoke the Egyptian deity Anubis, the patron of travellers. She spoke of a friend of hers who visualised flying on the back of the jackal-headed god on her travels. These two messages were a sobering reminder to me of the dangers as well as the exciting opportunities on pilgrimages.

A few days after this suggested connection to Anubis I was asked to perform an energetic clearing in friend Pete's house to attempt to dismiss unpleasant energies that had permeated the family's living space. Before I drove to the house I quietly went inward to seek guidance for this important work. Immediately I felt comfortable connecting with Anubis's energy, which filled my being, giving confidence for the proposed energy clearing. Thus Anubis had a supportive role, for me, in other work as well as being an aid for travellers.

www.ancientegyptonline.co.uk has this to say about Anubis:

Anubis is one of the most iconic gods of ancient Egypt. Anubis is the Greek version of his name, the ancient Egyptians knew him as Anpu (or Inpu). Anubis was an extremely ancient deity whose name appears in the oldest mastabas of the Old Kingdom and the Pyramid Texts as a guardian and protector of the dead.

He was originally a god of the underworld, but became associated specifically with the embalming process and funeral rites. His name is from the same root as the word for a royal child, "inpu". However, it is also closely related to the word "inp" which means "to decay", and one version of his name (Inp or Anp) more closely resembles that word. As a result it is possible that his name changed slightly once he was adopted as the son of the King, Osiris. He was known as "Imy-ut" ("He Who is In the Place of Embalming"), "nub-tA-djser" ("lord of the scared land").

He was initially related to the Ogdoad of Hermopolis, as the god of the underworld. In the Pyramid Texts of Unas, Anubis is associated with the Eye of Horus who acted as a guide to the dead and helped them find Osiris. In other myths Anubis and Wepwawet (Upuaut) led the deceased to the halls of Ma´at where they would be judged. Anubis watched over the whole process and ensured that the weighing of the heart was conducted correctly. He then led the innocent on to a heavenly existence and abandoned the guilty to Ammit.

The ancient Egyptians believed that the preservation of the body and the use of sweet-smelling herbs and plants would help the deceased because Anubis would sniff the mummy and only let the pure move on to paradise. According to early myths, Anubis took on and defeated the nine bows (the collective name for the traditional enemies of Egypt) gaining a further epithet "Jackal ruler of the bows".

This is from encyclopedia2.thefreedictionary.com:

Egyptian myth a deity, a son of Osiris, who conducted the dead to judgment. He is represented as having a jackal's head and was identified by the Greeks with Hermes

Arrangements for my planned trip to India were going well, organised by 'buddy' Sheena, who I met on a previous trip to Brittany and Malta. The trip had been paid for from half of my remaining savings. The visa for India had duly arrived and I was preparing to arrange my flight to Mumbai, the start point of the itinerary. The day before the booking a news announcement spoke of the horrors that had broken out in Mumbai the previous day. Terrorists had opened fire on unarmed civilians in that city. Hostages had been taken in a number of locations and more than a hundred people killed. How was I to react to this news? First I believed that one must not be intimidated. For this attack was the work of the dark forces in my view. One must show courage in the carrying out of the tasks that one has volunteered for. I realised that this trip must be connected to the light and I was being tested as to my 'stickability' to the task required.

The terrible and sad events convinced me that the work to be undertaken in India was important. If this was not the case, why would this particular city be targeted in this way? There are no accidents, no chance, neither is there good or bad luck in my view. I 'girded my loins' for a backlash from wife Jaqueline on the evening that she had heard the awful news. As she left for work that day I heard the comment '*I don't want to be a widow,*' as I stared at her disappearing back. The evening discussion on my proposed trip would probably be much stronger. I contented myself with the thought that when my father strapped himself into his aircraft in World War II to fight the Nazis he was not looking for security but to protect that which he held dear. I visualised myself strapping myself into an aircraft seat to begin this trip, being aware that I was working in an equally positive way. Anyway the trip was three months away. There was plenty of time for security in the city to be beefed up.

When meditating on the proposed trip and the Atlantean symbols identified in a previous chapter, I was told by guidance to buy a travel book on India, to study the itinerary and to work both together as a first preparation.

It was my view that security will be raised after such a terrible event. Terrorists don't usually strike in the same place twice. This crime against humanity reminds me of the attack on the skyscrapers in the US by the aircraft flying into them. Terrorists of all persuasions tend to attack icons that have deep roots in the psyche of a community. Deep down they know that this will severely affect the people and the confidence they have in their societies. I understand that Mumbai is the financial centre of India. Embittered, jealous and angry people will attempt to attack such targets. They are organised by those who have no compassion, no feeling for the people of the Earth. These are people intent on the destruction of all that has true value. We will not let that happen. *'Thank god the terrorist were from Pakistan and not India,'* said friend Sheena. *'The consequences for the Muslim community in India would be horrendous otherwise,'* she continued. Perhaps one of the important issues of our trip will be to perform healing meditations there, which will help in the recovery of the land and the people from this abuse.

This is from avaaz@avaaz.org:

We're all feeling the shock of the awful attacks in Mumbai. All our hearts go out to the victims and their families. I'm writing this because I feel we need to honor their memory.

The attacks were aimed at our people, our prosperity and our peace. But their top target was something else: our unity. If these attacks cause us to turn on each other in hatred and conflict, the terrorists will have won. They know that hatred and chaos feed on division. As radical extremists, their only hope of disrupting society as a whole is by turning the rest of us against each other.

On occasions, when in the midst of the most terrible carnage, remarkable feats of survival manifest. Simon Heleas, a British university lecturer, was shot in the arm and the leg during the terrorist attack on the Taj Mahal hotel in Mumbai. He narrowly avoided a grenade blast also. He avoided death, remarkably, when a bullet was prevented from entering his chest by his wife's glasses case, which he carried in his breast pocket. The case deflected the deadly missile. Terrible tragedies invoke their equal and opposite human traits of compassion and healing. The England cricket team, who were in India for two test matches, donated half of their match fees to the Mumbai appeal fund.

Perhaps there is room for one more disturbing note on the tragedy. This was posted on www.washingtonnote.com on November 30th 2008. It was headed 'Things aren't always what they seem':

What interests are served by these attacks?

Washington is intent on using the Mumbai attacks to:

1) *Foster divisions between Pakistan and India and stunt the process of bilateral cooperation and trade between the two countries;*
2) *Promote internal social, ethnic and sectarian divisions in both India and Pakistan;*
3) *Justify US military actions inside Pakistan including the killing of civilians in violation of the country's territorial sovereignty;*
4) *Provide a justification for extending the US led 'war on terrorism' into the Indian sub-continent and South East Asia.*

It is vital that we of good heart are eternally vigilant and counteract the negative. The being called Thoth has said that he has been fighting the negative forces for thousands of years.

The Indian government is blaming the Pakistan government for being complicit in the attack. The Pakistanis are asking for proof. The news alleged that India had been warned by the Americans of an impending attack by terrorists. In November 2008 British Airways cancelled flights to Pakistan; this did not make the main news but was indicative of security concerns in the region. This whole region remains a volatile one with the two nuclear states of India and Pakistan at odds with each other over a number of issues. Security remains a concern for the whole world as these two former segments of the British Empire seem unable to live in harmony.

Friend Sheena asked me to consult guidance on the creation of a calendar celebrating Obama's election. This is what came through from my guidance.

> *Any calendar that Sheena creates should be a CELEBRATION of Obama's election. It could be linked to successful presidents of the past, Washington, Abe Lincoln, the two Roosevelts, Kennedy (particularly him as well as Abe. Kennedy generated the same opportunity for change spirit in the US.) The calendar could celebrate the triumph of the will of the US people in other areas as well. It was suggested that there be a page for each month with Obama highlighted in November, the month he was elected, and the positive spirit of the US people in December. As for the rest of the calendar it was said that Sheena has enough creative ability to make a success and a complete WHOLENESS to the finished article.*

OK, this is a continuation of the story concerning the energy line running through the Four Corners, through Lower Egypt and into the heart of India. India is on a continuation of the energy line going through the Four Corners area in the US and continuing through Egypt. There must be some synchronicity here. I was not aware of this energetic relationship until friend Mary looked at the relationship on a world map. Before a recent meditation Mary, Joan and I checked in the map of the world to find that the straight line runs just to the north of Mumbai. Thus this confirmed the integrity of the intuitive information that I had received concerning this energy line location. Once in the meditation I asked that the cosmic forces assist in the healing of Mumbai after the recent murderous attack. It seemed to me that this attack was an outpouring from the negative forces using weak individuals to block the opening of this line. Secondly, in visualisation I saw the curve of the Earth, as if from outer space, with the energy line opening up. The line opened in the shape of a long lip with the energy pouring through from beneath the surface. The final scene was of a human face picked out in light facing the lip as though receiving something from it. I took this to be a symbol of the information and its energy being made available to mankind as a whole. I recalled a previous vision where I had been told that this energy had previously been available only to high beings from different dimensions and areas of reality. Now with the line opening up there was greater access to the wisdom and knowledge. In a subsequent meditation the subject of a new spirit of Christmas came to the fore. It was perceived by those in the group that contacted this new spirit that subtlety and compassion linked to the Christ Consciousness was at its heart. Those attempting to break from the tired materialistic version we are confronted with each year would be the potential beneficiaries of this energy. Inspiration from the higher realms was linking to the ancient spiritual energies. The knowledge and energy of the latter was flowing from the metaphorical crack in the Earth that had been identified previously. So this work was proceeding apace.

I was relieved, as I prepared for the trip, to discover that I did not need additional injections to combat the diseases of northern India. One thing that the nurse who advised me was unsure about was the need for malaria tablets. '*Ask your travel company for advice,*' were her parting words. This I did, emailing tour organiser Sheena. The reply came back that this was winter in India and such medication was not necessary. Her reply was strongly against the use of such drugs as this would interfere with the high energies that we were to experience. This advice facilitated a strong connection for me with a powerful vibration that I took to be a guide or an energy that was associated with the trip. During a healing with friend Sean he had sensed the presence of a being connected to the India trip, which was close to me now. Each time that I 'tuned in' to this energy I could feel its powerful vibrations suffusing my body. It was so powerful that I could tolerate the vibrations for seconds only.

I spent a day and a half at friend Audrey's house before the flight to Mumbai. I relaxed, was well fed and slept deeply. It seemed as though I was a stone placed in a sling before being flung out into the latest adventure. Audrey, friends Faye, Sylvester and I performed a meditation and visualisation as a preparation for my trip to India. Statues of Anubis and Bastet, representing Sekhmet, were placed in the centre of a table. Sekhmet has been an important messenger and protector for me in the last three years. This is Faye's vision from that meditation.

Faye saw herself as Derga, the huntress, riding a tiger with a bow and quiver on her back. Faye (Derga) and the tiger arrived at a banyan tree with roots going into the ground. Hanuman, the monkey god, was sitting under it wearing a little gold waistcoat and a small crown on his head. A triple headed cobra surrounded the banyan tree. Hanuman took me (Clive) by the hand and we rode into the sky along bridges of light. He and I met a monk. I spoke with the monk who placed a string of beads around my neck and handed me a peacock's feather. Hanuman and I flew back over Amritsar. As we looked down people were dancing surrounded by rainbows of light. We all went to visit Anubis, who stopped people other than me from approaching. We entered a dark doorway together and spent some time there. When we emerged Anubis held up his ankh as a blessing for me.

Audrey saw Anubis as a being who confronts us with our

negativities and dark thoughts. She saw Sekhmet as an opportunity to look into her eyes and replace the popular perception of her as an object of fear with an opportunity to possess courage. After the meditation Sylvester explained that a jackal – Anubis is the jackal-headed god – buries its prey and eats it later when it is poisonous to all other creatures. Anubis represents transmutation and turning negatives into positives, mouldy meat into sustenance. Anubis is a guide, a mediator between realities, said Faye. She added that at the end of the meditation she saw me in a grove of trees writing up my diary. The scene was very peaceful with the trees and the sunlight.

As we prepared for the meditation Audrey received a phone call from her acupuncturist, Tony. He invited me – we met on a previous occasion – to a demonstration of chi gong in Pinner, Audrey's home town. An interesting element of the invitation was that he could not have known that I would be staying overnight with Audrey. The chance of me being there when the demonstration was taking place was at least one hundred to one against. Intrigued, I attended the demonstration, which was totally different from my experience of chi gong in the past. At the session Tony introduced a Chinese woman, Dr Yang. Tony described the doctor as a master of the art and had been consulted by and examined by scientists and doctors. Her skill consisted of having the ability to see and feel people's energy fields and chi flows. From this she could diagnose illnesses and conduct cures by adjusting an individual's chi.

After an explanation, the twenty or so attendees began a meditation supervised by Dr Yang. We were asked to stand, to relax and to gently close our eyes. In other words, we were taking part in a standing meditation. We stood and we stood. I lost track of time. As we meditated we had been told that Dr Yang would walk among us performing a chi healing and balancing. I became aware of various energetic sensations impulsing my body. My lower left arm began to make circles without conscious initiation or control. Surges of energy moved through my body. Months later I realised that this healing meditation had begun the process of surfacing the miasms (ancient illnesses and pains) from the cells of my body into conscious awareness.

We had been asked to visualise ourselves standing on a cloud with a tube of energy running through our bodies from above. I came back to this vision time after time as I attempted to re-focus my meditation. I received a final perception of vortices of energy pulsing through my body. After the meditation I made my escape as the session returned to more talking and discussion.

The next day, the one of my evening flight to Mumbai, I felt weary in the morning and afternoon. Could this be the aftermath of my chi healing from Dr Yang?

And so to India.

India

From the Arabian Sea to the Himalayas

Mea Baba and Yogananda both said that India is the country closest to the astral realm. For me the energies of India were so strong. Perhaps this is one reason why many newcomers to the country experience much sickness as they struggle to cope.

My aircraft to India left two hours late, thus perpetuating my normal travelling fortune of experiencing difficulties on most of my 'pilgrimages'. The passengers wait in the departure lounge. An airline assistant eventually calls for first class, the disabled and mothers with young children. There is a mad scramble resulting in a scrum at the entrance as around 200 people are desperate to begin their journey. I assume that they are visiting relatives or are desperate to return home. A few of us vacationers and the more 'laid back' of us watch in amazement. The assistant appeals for calm, for people to step back and allow the mothers and children through the scrum.

The journey in the plane is boring for the most part. The one break from tedium is the battle for 'lebensraum', living space, with the large gentleman seated on my left. Travelling in the 'cattle truck' part of the aeroplane is beginning to get to me. I would like to push the boat out and trade up in future. The gentleman has rolls of fat that flop over to my side of the seat as we both attempt to sleep, or at least rest, in this tube of noisy discomfort. I retaliate to this fatty invasion by sending in my shock troops. This consists of my bony left elbow which I dig into the approximate position of the large gentleman's ribs. The rolls of fat slither back over the border. The battle is over but is the war won? I pass some of the time by working on my eye exercises to relieve the tired muscles and assist my eyesight. This exercise consists of rolling my eyeballs around the sockets, first to the left and then to the right. This is not a pretty sight but does help to relieve eyestrain. As I reach the end of the rotational movements I catch the eye of aforesaid large gentleman, who is staring at my gyrations open mouthed.

'Yes, I am mad,' I think at him without saying a word. I glare at him with all the fierceness that I can muster. He retreats back over the border again. At the end of the flight a peace treaty is confirmed between us as we smile at each other and say goodbye. I am sure that he is as happy as I am to be leaving this torture chamber.

A shuttle bus picks me up at Mumbai airport. We drive towards the south and the sea where my hotel for two nights is located. The first smell to assuage my nostrils as I pick my bag up is that of the drains. The smell is identical to that of Mexico City. As we drive there are no road markings, no traffic lights and no road discipline that I can see on the part of road users, nada, nothing. It begins to make Mexico City look like a haven for good drivers. I never thought I would be saying that. Pedestrians, cyclists, motor cyclists, tuk-tuk three wheelers, and motor vehicles of all types jostle for a little bit of road space. It is total chaos viewed from the point of view of this newcomer. Welcome to India, Clive. The one saving grace is that they drive more slowly than in Mexico City. The parts of the city that we drive through are extremely poor. Apartment blocks appear ready for condemning and demolition from this westerner's point of view. There are people living on the streets. However, people also live on the streets of San Diego in the country of the 'Home of the free'.

One bright spot as we drive is the elegance of the women in their brightly coloured saris. They look clean and wholesome in contrast to their surroundings. We pass one zebra crossing in the half hour drive. I wonder if anyone uses it. Most pedestrians appear to dash across the road, having an innate knowledge of the traffic chaos. To be fair to Mumbai, I did come across some road markings the next day as well as traffic lights. Later in the trip I saw roundabouts in Varanasi. The discipline of giving away to traffic coming from the right in England is not part of Varanasi driving. All traffic hurtles on to the roundabouts. The road discipline seems to be of the 'who blinks first' variety and who applies their brakes at the last possible second.

I am reminded of a Mexico City story. A combi (Volkswagen micro bus which squeezes thirteen passengers into its space) knocked over a pedestrian and severely injured the unfortunate person. He then backed over the prone figure, killing the person. His reasoning was that a dead person was less hassle than a live one. A live but injured person would have sued for damages which the driver could not afford. I can't see the better-tempered Indians doing such a thing. Am I being naïve?

It came to me in a flash. India is the mother of all countries. Perhaps a fuller meaning of that will surface later.

The next day the whole party meets up and is treated to a lunch with a 'Bollywood' star, Tanuja, a good friend of Sheena. As I was to find out Sheena is well connected in India. Tanuja was a most charming and generous host as she told us her story. She was sent to an English finishing school in Switzerland by her family in order to learn languages before an anticipated career in the diplomatic service. She was called back to India when the family finances took a turn for the worst. A career switch saw her make her first film at twelve years of age and broke into the big time aged fifteen. And the rest, as they say, is history.

The lunch, held in a five-star hotel, was a microcosm of the film star lifestyle. At the table next to us sat a couple of models who were being filmed as a marketing exercise for the hotel. On the other side of the restaurant another Bollywood star was sitting eating lunch. This was a most bizarre way of starting our India journey.

The previous evening I had been sitting on the hotel wall overlooking the beach and Arabian Sea. A young woman, perhaps one of those who lived on the beach, began begging. She carried a small child and possessed a beaming smile. Not at all like the victim consciousness that I was used to in beggars. I gave her a small coin and she said she would be back tomorrow. We would be gone by then on our travels. I was struck then and later at the apparent lack of jealousy of those that have so much by those that have apparently little. Perhaps the awareness of karma is imbued in the mass consciousness of the population here. So many people seem happy with their lot. Perhaps we in the West can learn from this attitude.

The next morning, a Sindi (originating in Sind province) wedding party arrived at the hotel. The Sind culture is said to foster a good business environment. The bridegroom, who is from that culture, was marrying a woman from the Indian equivalent of the Jewish culture, according to Sheena. The match would unite two strong business families. This was another interesting slant on Indian culture for me.

I felt 'well into tourist mode' when the group visited the *Taj Mahal* hotel, location of the November bombings. The atmospheric environment perhaps arose from our personal perceptions of the tragedy. We thus projected our own energies, our own vibrations into the matrix of energies that already existed there. Stone and apparently inanimate substances absorb the energies of humans and will project those energies back into the environment. This is my experience.

The main building will be closed until December of that year. The annexe, a magnificent multi-storey block, was not attacked at the time of the tragedy and is now fully operational. We had tea in the restaurant; very gentile it was. I drank masala tea, attracted to the taste the previous day. Susan, a member of our tour group, was gifted with a psychic experience in the hotel. She walked to the pool area on her own and felt emotions of fear and anger pervading the place. She also felt that souls of the murderers and victims were trapped there. She said a prayer asking the souls to be released and the energies cleansed. If there was any one reason why the group should be in the hotel, this was it.

The smiles and good humour of the people throughout Mumbai continue to be a prominent feature. Even the poor and the destitute appear to be content. The contrast with the aggression and threat of Mexico City puzzled me greatly. Papa Singh, Sheena's father, began to throw light on the issue. One lunch-time he described how the

Indians, certainly the majority population of Hindu, were vegetarian. In addition, alcohol seems to be consumed in relatively small quantities by most people. Meat in large quantities and alcohol are both staples in Mexican societies that I have been in contact with. I wonder if these are key features. I am not criticising Mexican society, the diet or its approach to civil life. I would like some answers to the conundrum of the disparity in good humour of the two societies if anyone out there knows.

There was one blip that contradicted the peaceful experience of the group on this trip. As we left a hotel on our travels one day our coach was forced to take a detour. The normal route had been blocked off and barricaded by youths who demanded money from vehicles going through. The day was a Bank Holiday. It seemed that the police were taking a more relaxed view of lawbreakers on this holiday.

McDonalds had great difficulty in establishing themselves in this country. Beef fillings were most definitely not acceptable and the taste of the American/European bun was obnoxious to the Indian palette. Success was assured when the company re-formulated these products. A bun to suit Indian tastes was developed together with vegetarian products. As with the world over McDonalds is now a favourite with young people here.

I stare out of the coach window as we move around the city. A lithe, slim and elegant young woman walks along the street. Her apricot-coloured sari is trimmed with silver. I stare in appreciation until she bends forward and spits on the floor! Oh well, another dream shattered. This incident is typical of the dichotomy of India. Goodbye Mumbai. It is time to move on.

I have had the strangest third day. First my watch stopped at around midday. This is not unusual as watches regularly stop when I wear them or the straps break within days or weeks of using them. Next, I nearly left my passport and boarding card in the airport. The situation was rescued by Punam, our trusty guide. I did leave a heart-stone in the airport. Perhaps this will play a healing role in the recovery of this great city. Finally, and most disconcertingly, on the flight to Aurangabad I leave my only pair of spectacles, which I need for reading. So what was going on here? My intuition told me that watch, passport, spectacles were all symbols of a situation that I needed to be aware of. I was to take less account of the material trappings and to work and trust with the inner promptings and energies of the tour.

We fly to Aurangabad and pass through the airport. A monk of a Hindu sect wearing an orange robe and sandals sits in the arrival hall. The sandals are set on two blocks of wood similar to the platform soles of the 1970s, much loved in England then. Sheena tells me that the structure of the sandals are designed to suppress sexual appetite; suppression, suppression, when will it end. I respect the right of the individual to run their life as they wish, so there is no criticism of the individual. I will say more about this later. The population of Aurangabad is one million, approximately – small compared to Mumbai. We drive through industrial areas on our way to the hotel. The roads are full of motorcycles dashing hither and thither. Hundreds of others are parked in ranks on the side of the roads. What a posh hotel we are staying at in Aurangabad. The *Taj Residency* is in the same group as the taj that was bombed in Mumbai.

Papa Singh, Sheena's father and a participant on the trip, told me the following story. At the time of the partition of India on August 15, 1947, Papa was serving as an officer in the Indian army commanding a unit of Muslim soldiers. As the violence and killings began to take hold between certain sections of the Hindu and Muslim communities, Papa commandeered an Indian army three-tonne truck and drove into what had so recently become Pakistan. Papa's ancestral home was now on the 'wrong' side of the border, as far as his Sikh culture was concerned. The ancestral home of his family still housed his parents, grandmother and other family members. It took him nine hours to drive overnight, accompanied by four of his soldiers, to within a mile of his home village. He stopped by the end of the metalled road.

Papa offered to take as many of the villagers as he could cram into the truck and deliver them into what was now the state of India. Papa's father was a village elder who was loath to leave his community. Papa's mother said that she would stay with her husband. Papa gave everyone until 10 am to make up their minds whether to stay or to leave. Eventually Papa dragged his father into the cab of the truck, thus ensuring that his mother would leave also. Thirty souls, approximately, together with a box of possessions each, piled into the truck and Pappa drove away. As he drove he could see fires burning. He surmised that the Muslims in the village were burning the Sikh homes once Papa's group had left. Pappa never saw his ancestral home again. Many others were forced to leave the village later and took up to two months on the trek to safety in India. As I write this the emotion and poignancy of this story hits me in the heart. Sheena said of her father, with tongue in cheek I suspect, that as an army engineer he built bridges (presumably on the advance) and then blew them up (presumably on the retreat!).

I 'lifted' the following from Sheena's tour guide information:

> Aurangabad is named after the Mughai emperor, Aurangzeb. From ancient times Aurangabad has been place of great importance due to its location on the famous 'silk route' that runs across the breadth of Asia to reach Europe. Textiles, embroidered finery and various kinds of beads made in nearby Paithan were exported to markets of Greece, Rome and Egypt. The first Buddhist cave monuments of Ajanta date from the second and first centuries BC. During the Gupta period (fifth and sixth centuries AD), many more richly decorated caves were added to the original group. The paintings and sculptures of Ajanta, considered masterpieces of Buddhist religious art, have had a considerable artistic influence.

www.mumbai.org.uk/excursions/aurangabad-caves.html has this to say about the Aurangabad Caves approximately thirty miles from Ajanta:

Situated just on the, fringes of Aurangabad are the caves that were carved out during the 2nd to 6th century in Maharashtra. These caves are ten in number and have been shaped out of somewhat soft rock. Tantric Hinduism has been the inspiration of their architecture and iconography. Aurangabad Caves are to be found at two different locations, at a distance of a kilometer. These two locations are referred to as Western Group Caves (Cave 1-5) and Eastern Group Caves (cave 6-10).

Regarding Western Group Caves, the architecture is absolutely fascinating. The majority of the caves are monasteries, excluding Cave 4 that is perhaps the oldest cave and represents the prayer hall of Hinayana phase amidst its ridged roof and stupa in the forefront. The monasteries essentially represent the early style of Buddhist monastery having an open court, encircled by open cells. Cave 3 is the masterpiece amongst all, with its beautifully carved pillars and sculptures depicting scenes from the Jatakas. Other caves are essentially monasteries, which usually have an open court encircled by open cells.

The Eastern Group Caves are no less than the former group in terms of design and architecture. Cave 6 is considerable for its amazing picturization of women, specially their hairstyles and ornamentation. Outside this cave, you can see amazing figure of both, Lord Ganesha and Buddha. Whereas Cave 7 is the most remarkable of all the caves in Aurangabad, principally for its sculptures that portray figures of women meagerly dressed and richly ornamented. It also indicates the augment of Tantric Buddhism during the period. A visit to Aurangabad Caves would give an insight into the rock-cut architecture of India.

Some of the group are in cave four at Ajanta. We gather in the end room where massive statues of Buddha, in different poses, loom over us. We sit and wait as other tourists leave the room. The quietness is interrupted by the slow reverberation of the sacred sound 'Om' gradually building in the voices of the group. The room responds by echoing the sacred sound back to us. We enter a different state of consciousness as we continue to chant. As the sacred sounds rise and fall I sit on the floor, feeling the vibrations of this place coiling upward through my palms and into my body. The sounds gradually die away.

The magic atmosphere is broken as Buddhist monks, clad in their saffron robes, enter. Instead of the expected sacred salutations and prayers the monks flourish digital cameras and pose to have their photos taken. The incongruity of it strikes me as the monks play at being tourists. Meantime, we, the tourists, stand and wait to continue our chanting and meditations. Welcome to India!

I leave the caves before visiting them all. I am exhausted by the heat and the amount of walking up and down. I take the Indian version of the sedan chair back to the entrance. After dismounting a haggle arises over the price of the ride. After paying the agreed price my face must have demonstrated some dissatisfaction. One of the carriers follows me and almost begs for my good humour. I smile and we part good friends. There are not many places in any part of the world that I have visited where such an exchange would take place after the fee had been paid. I feel a little guilty over my attitude, given my comparative wealth and their precarious existence.

One evening we stop at a small roadside village after visiting some of the caves so that we can experience the village life that so many live here. At first we are welcomed by the residents as we view the inside of a house. We give small gifts of food that we have collected on the way. Gradually the atmosphere changes as the children, particularly, begin to ask for money and beg aggressively. The food that we have brought is snatched from my hand. I leave somewhat disenchanted. Others stay a little longer. Sheena says later that she believes that the adults in the village had influenced the children to beg aggressively.

On March 4, the day of the goddess Saraswati, we all dressed in traditional clothes, most of them purchased by Sheena. A ceremony was conducted in a small plaza in the hotel in the cool night air. Rose petals were strewn across the floor. An altar was created on a nearby wall. A picture of the goddess was placed on the altar. This was accompanied by a book and a pen. The goddess is patron of the arts, crafts and wisdom. I was particularly delighted as Sheena had selected a copy of our book *So You Think We're Alone?* to be placed on the altar. We all lit a candle and made a wish to the goddess at the altar. Sheena 'smudged' each person with a peacock feather, so enlivening our auras with the energies of Saraswati. We were now initiates of her sacred order. That night I tuned into the goddess and asked for attunement for the next day. I actually received a throat virus, which needed an anti-biotic. Perhaps the gift was one of clearing negativities from my being. The goddess was active later, however, not in my timescale.

The goddess Saraswati was patron of arts and culture in ancient times along the banks of a river that is now dried up. Vedic priests lived in communities here and wrote their epics, including the Vedas.

One of the cultural interests for me was to see some of the young men walking around holding hands. I was told that this was not the behaviour of homosexuals but is an expression of friendship, of taking care of one's friend.

At many cross-roads and in front of some houses and shops can be found swastikas painted in order to attract good fortune. They are not the same as the ones used for perverted aims in the West by the Nazi regime. The Indian swastikas have the end lines or arms pointing to the right. This is the opposite of the past European perversion.

Outside our hotel *Taj Residency* in Aurungabad can be heard the faithful being called to prayer. At 4am the Muslims start the process. As soon as they are finished the Hindu priests make their call. The last ones to call the faithful are the Sikhs. This is a great country for religious tolerance. This secular state allows all religions to practice and to flourish. It stays out of the religious debate. The political system is said to be rife with corruption. Perhaps this is a price worth paying in order to avoid assaults on personal freedoms in other areas of Indian life. It is all very well for the rich and affluent in other countries to strive for impeccability in public life. It is altogether another thing to achieve in the struggle to support oneself and one's family in the much poorer east.

I saw a poster with the pictures of four politicians advertising themselves prior to the elections. They all had the most scary and sinister faces. Negativities blasted forth from their likenesses. It looked most bizarre. Perhaps it could be argued that at least they are projecting their true selves. In the West many politicians cover their true identities with so much 'spin' and public relations one never knows what the true person inside is.

We are in Aurangabad airport in the exit lounge awaiting a flight to Varanasi. Sri Sri Ravi Shankar, no, not the famous sitar player, but a famous yoga master, walks through towards the aircraft. He is dressed all in white. 'Namastes', an Indian greeting, are exchanged all around. This greeting consists of placing the hands together in front of the chest and saying namaste to another person. Namaste means 'I salute the divinity in you'. The master has a kind and open face. I briefly tune into him and sense a deep spirituality surrounding an advanced soul. He is accompanied by devotees who are also dressed in white. One of our group says that at least one devotee is wearing a special toe ring, called a toe stopper, which also suppresses sexuality. That is fine. These men are dealing with other issues in their reality. I am not criticising their decision. I am merely observing the fact that there is an element of their humanity that they will have to deal with eventually, whether it is this lifetime or another one.

In the West we hear a lot about 'Delhi belly' stomach upsets being a danger when westerners first arrive here. Many people suffer from respiratory infections, which has been my experience. Perhaps I am particularly vulnerable due to my weak lungs.

In Varanasi there is a deer park. Buddha had a reincarnation as a deer, it is believed. In addition he was an incarnation of Vishnu, the Hindu god, and is therefore a revered figure for Hindus. Varanasi is recognised as a centre of pilgrimage for Hindus; Sarnat fulfils the same purpose for Buddhists.

Wikipedia has this to say about Varanasi (Benares):

> ***Varanasi*** *(Hindustani pronunciation, also known as* ***Benares****,or* ***Banaras*** *is a city on the banks of the river Ganges in Uttar Pradesh, India, 320 kilometres (200 mi) south-east of the state capital, Lucknow, and 121 kilometres (75 mi) east of Allahabad. A major religious hub in India, it is the holiest of the seven sacred cities (Sapta Puri) in Hinduism and Jainism, and played an important role in the development of Buddhism and Ravidassia. Varanasi lies along National Highway 2, and is served by Varanasi Junction railway station and Lal Bahadur Shastri International Airport.*
>
> *Varanasi grew as an important industrial centre famous for its muslin and silk fabrics, perfumes, ivory works, and sculpture. Buddha is believed to have founded Buddhism here around 528 BCE when he gave his first sermon, "The Setting in Motion of the Wheel of Dharma", at nearby Sarnath. The city's religious importance continued to grow in the 8th century, when Adi Shankara established the worship of Shiva as an official sect of Varanasi. During the Muslim rule through the Middle Ages, the city continued as an important centre of Hindu devotion, pilgrimage, mysticism and poetry which further contributed to its reputation as a centre of cultural importance and religious education. Tulsidas wrote his epic poem on Rama's life called Ram Charit Manas in Varanasi. Several other major figures of the Bhakti movement were born in Varanasi, including Kabir and Ravidas. Guru Nanak visited Varanasi for Maha Shivaratri in 1507, a trip that played a large role in the founding of Sikhism.*

This is from Sheena's description. Buddha's preaching was a message of the middle way to nirvana after his enlightenment. By 640 AD there were 1,500 monks here living in monasteries and a 1,500-feet-high stupa. Soon after Buddhism went into decline and Muslim invaders destroyed the city. It was rediscovered when British archaeologists excavated here in 1835. The ancient ruins are fascinating, including the Dhamekh Stupa, which is believed to mark the spot where Buddha preached his famous sermon; the archaeological museum is excellent. There is also a monument dedicated to Buddha and a modern Buddhist temple with murals by a Japanese painter depicting the story of the life of Buddha.

In the early evening a boat ride on the Ganges, and then our group watched the evening aarti being enacted on two of the ghats (banks of the sacred river). Aarti is said to have descended from the Vedic concept of fire rituals and is performed and sung to develop the highest love for god. This is from Wikipedia:

> *Arti is said to have descended from the Vedic concept of fire rituals, or homa. In the traditional arti ceremony, the flower represents the earth (solidity), the water and accompanying handkerchief correspond with the water element (liquidity), the ghee or oil lamp represents the fire component (heat), the peacock fan conveys the precious quality of air (movement), and the yak-tail fan represents the subtle form of ether (space). The incense represents a purified state of mind, and one's "intelligence" is offered through the adherence to rules of timing and order of offerings. Thus, one's entire existence and all facets of material creation are symbolically offered to the Lord via the arti ceremony. The word may also refer to the traditional Hindu devotional song that is sung during the ritual.*

This was a most amazing experience for me. Seven Hindu priests dressed in red tops and white pantaloons were illuminated in the evening darkness. They performed rhythmic and sinuous movements, co-ordinating their actions as though they were one entity. The celebration was heightened with flames, smoke and music from voice and instrument. The chanting, movement and music sent me into a semi-hypnotic trance. The priests seemed unaffected by exhaustion for the length of time that this ceremony was conducted; it must have been an hour and a half. At the end it took me some time to return to planet Earth. I realise that to some extent this was pure theatre. However, it was a mighty powerful one. I was amused at the beginning of the ceremony. Some of the priests were attractive young men. They appeared most concerned that their hair was in good order as they constantly caressed it or flung it back from their faces during the preparations. Perhaps these are the 'pop stars' of their community.

I later realised that the ceremony had two inner objectives. The first was to invite and to attune the higher forces of light to the Earth plane. The second was to raise the consciousness of participants and adherents. The energy thus generated created a temporary heaven on Earth. My experience was to approach an altered state of consciousness that felt close to ecstasy. These experiences are rare for me, usually experienced only in those places of the highest consciousness.

Before and after the ceremony we made our way by rickshaw through the choking, polluted traffic-filled streets. The ride to the ghats was fun and novel. The ride back was the reverse as the pollution finally activated my asthmatic chest.

Later Sheena spoke of the goddess Lakshmi, who is the goddess of abundance. She can be invited into your life. She will leave if you are not grateful for the gifts that she unselfishly bestows. It is important thus to share those gifts with those around you.

Papa Singh told the story of his great-great grandfather who raised a detachment of troops to help the British in the uprising of 1857. The uprising had been started by the Muslim king of Delhi who was an enemy of the Sikhs. Papa Singh and has family belong to the Sikh culture and religion. The Muslims had murdered many Sikhs, including the revered ninth guru. Great-great grandfather finished up on the winning side, the British, which is probably a good thing to do in any war. He was granted many lands as a reward for aiding the British and he became, in Papa Singh's words, a 'big shot'.

Although a rich and powerful man, the great-great grandfather was unable to produce a son to inherit the properties. One day a fakir, a wandering holy man, came to his house and was granted food and good care. The fakir said to great-great grandfather, *'You have all this property and wealth and yet there is a look of unhappiness on your face. Why is that?'*

Great-great grandfather explained. The fakir took him over to the branch of a mango tree and asked him to shake it. He did so and seven mangoes fell to the floor from its branches.

'Your problem is solved,' said the fakir. *'Marry a younger woman and you will have seven sons.'*

Great-great grandfather did as was suggested. He married a younger woman and seven sons were the offspring of the union. Great-great grandfather, the two wives, sons, and daughter from the first marriage all lived happily together.

We move forward ninety years. Now Papa Singh is the owner of the properties. There is a snag, however. You remember the story of Papa's family fleeing the newly independent Pakistan. They left only with the clothes that they stood up in; from comparative poverty to riches to comparative poverty in a few generations.

We move to Khajuraho, the home of the Kama-Sutra-inspired temples which were built 900–1100 AD. Sheena has this to say. These temples are patterned according to ancient Hindu mandalas, where temple dancers offered their arts in the worship of the divine and where priests and priestesses practiced the highest form of sacred tantric sex. These were rituals symbolic of female and male elements in the universe. Sensuous posturing of the figures demonstrated the overriding interest of those that commissioned the artistic stonework.

The following is an extract from Wikipedia's account of Khajuraho:

> ***Khajuraho** is a city in the Indian state of Madhya Pradesh, located in Chhatarpur District. One of the most popular tourist destinations in India, Khajuraho has the country's largest group of medieval Hindu and Jain temples, famous for their erotic sculptures. The Khajuraho Group of Monuments has been listed as a UNESCO World Heritage Site since 1986 and is considered one of the "seven wonders" of India. The town's name, anciently "Kharjuravahaka", is derived from the Sanskrit word kharjur meaning "date palm".*

Wikipedia has this to say about tantra:

> ***Tantra** (literally "loom, weave, warp") denotes the esoteric traditions of Hinduism and Buddhism that developed in India from the middle of the 1st millennium CE onwards. The term tantra, in the Indian traditions, also means any systematic broadly applicable "text, theory, system, method, instrument, technique or practice". A key feature of these traditions is the use of mantras, and thus they are commonly referred to as **Mantramārga** ("Path of Mantra") in Hinduism or **Mantrayāna** ("Mantra Vehicle") and **Guhyamantra** ("Secret Mantra") in Buddhism.*

The Western obsession with the sexual element of tantra is not the major element. Perhaps the Western accent on that part of tantra thinking says more about the West than about tantra.

Sheena, Punam, Bill and I made an evening visit to an active temple set amid the complex of those now mostly tourist attractions. The visit was to take part in an aarti ceremony. This time the process was much more intimate. The small circular structure contained a raised area surmounted by a pedestrian access. Adherents needed to walk three-quarters of the way around the temple in order to reach the steps leading to the raised area. A priest sat, cross-legged, in front of the massive lingam in the centre.

Our small party arrived early and we sat waiting patiently for the start of the ceremony. People of all ages arrived. Most of them looked at us curiously as they found a place to sit or stand. The beginning of the ceremony was signalled by the assembly being asked to stand. Next the temple erupted in a cacophony of sounds from clashing cymbals, a drum-like instrument and a conch, the latter sounded by the priest. At certain points the whole assembly chanted and clapped. They really went for it. Unlike the Anglican celebration they were having fun as well as wearing the focussed look of the spiritually sensitive.

The sound and ritual show went on for thirty minutes. At the end all the adherents left the temple one by one, making obeisance to the lingam (representative of the male energy) by placing their forehead on its surface. Before leaving they touched the foot of the priest and placed money offerings in a bowl next to the priest. In return the priest placed a water offering (possibly this had been blessed before) into the cupped hands of the departing person and gave a sweet offering. To Bill, Sheena and I the priest gave an especially reassuring smile as though to say *'you are welcome'*. He placed a red dust dot on our third eye. We left having had a grand experience.

Next stop on our journey was Aggra. This is from Sheena's description:

> The Mughal emperor Babur established his capital at Agra in 1526. The city reached its peak between the sixteenth and seventeenth centuries, stimulated by the reign of Akbar, Jehangir and Shah Jehan. In 1648 the capital moved to Delhi. This building is still the inspiration of poets and painters, writers and photographers. Shah Jehan built the taj in memory of his wife, Mumtaz Mahal, who died giving birth to their fourteenth child. The shah wasn't great on birth control then. Twenty thousand workers from India and central Asia worked on its construction. Specialists were brought in from Europe to create exquisite

> marble screens. No cost was spared to make it the most beautiful monument the world had ever seen. White marble and red sandstone, silver and gold and jasper, moonstone and jade, lapis lazuli and coral were fashioned by 20,000 skilled workers to make the emperors dream into a reality. It took twenty-two years to complete – a symbol of eternal love where Shah Jehan lies buried, reunited at last with his beloved Mumtaz. In order to reduce damaging atmospheric pollution to the building, new industrial developments in Agra have now been banned. Only non-polluting vehicles are allowed within 500m of the taj.

We made a morning visit to the Taj Mahal, 'a teardrop on the face of eternity' according to Indian poet Rabindranath Tagore. It glows softly pink at dawn and at close of day reflects the fiery tints of the setting sun. We drove from the Sheraton hotel to the Taj Mahal in a horse and buggy cooled by the early morning breeze; awesome, awesome.

Janet, one of our party, later talked about how it was built in love and asked, '*Why do people come here?*' To which I replied, '*To see one of the most inspiring, famous buildings in the world. Perhaps they are subconsciously honouring the great love that Shah Jehan, the buildings creator, had for his favourite wife and lifelong love?*' Later it occurred to me that this was a most selfish love that almost bankrupted the country and impoverished the people. So much so that his son overthrew Shah Jehan and imprisoned him in the nearby fort. From here he could see his wonderful creation until the day he died.

I felt drawn to 'tile' the building, to create a magical space inside a circular walk around the edifice. I walked anti-clockwise chanting the ancient mantra *Aum-Ma-Ra-Oom* as I went. On the second circuit around the building the energy that I had sensed at the beginning suddenly disappeared. Initially puzzled, I came to the conclusion that whatever needed to be done was completed.

The four minarets at the corners of the square framing the Taj are not straight but lean slightly outward from the building. This is to ensure that they never fall on the mausoleum in the event of an earthquake. I was reminded of the leaning tower of Pisa, which also leans, but does so by accident rather than by design. At the conclusion of the visit there a vague feeling of dissatisfaction in my being that took some time to articulate. I came to realise that the aesthetics of the Taj were largely lost on me. I am not an artistic person. For me it was a magnificent folly, beautiful but largely useless outside artistic appreciation.

That afternoon and evening was taken up with an accident that I suffered in my hotel room caused by my own stupidity. After the doctor, called by the hotel, had sewn four stitches in my right index finger I took time to ponder on the meaning of this incident. For me there are no accidents, no bad luck and no good luck. We are creating our reality every second that we draw breath in this reality. In addition, we are learning the lessons of the past so that we can grow in character and in spirituality. The message came through from my intuition, '*Do your meditations.*' Previously, the loss of my spectacles and the stopping of my watch had reduced my interaction with the outside world. This created the opportunity for me to go within more frequently; I had not listened to the message so a more 'stinging' reminder was sent by my higher self.

I dropped into a meditation and was immediately confronted with a vision of a panel blocking the energy flow to the north of Mumbai. This work was, after all, a major reason for me to be here. Energetically I was here to assist in the facility of energy flow along the line from the Four Corners in the United States through Egypt and then into India. I had been working on this for the last year, intuitively and practically, in the places mentioned. In my meditation I simply removed the panel in order to allow more access of the energies in the direction that they needed to go. Paradoxically the energy went deeper, into the earth, rather than expanding outwards. I perceived this movement as assisting the energy movement to complete itself. This energy will create a consciousness and wisdom that will be made available to sensitive humans.

Much of the following paragraph is from Sheena's description for our next 'port of call'.

Jaipur, capital of the state of Rajasthan, is home to the Rajput warrior clans. They claimed to have originated from the sun, moon and fire according to the *Lonely Planet guide – India*. The strength of tradition here means that women have a tough time being condemned to a life of hard work and control by the men. The city was painted pink, a mark of hospitality in 1876 by the Maharajah Ram Singh to honour the visit of the then British Prince of Wales. This tradition has continued to this day. At sunset this colour of the buildings creates a warm, glowing effect. A minaret near the Tripolia Gate was erected by Iswari, who later killed himself rather than face an advancing army. Twenty-one wives and concubines committed suicide on his funeral pyre. With a little more courage on Iswari's part perhaps those twenty-one lives could have been saved. Perhaps if he had spent more time on defences and less on gathering wives and concubines, twenty-two persons may have lived longer. I know that I am making a judgement and that these events were an example of the culture of the time.

Bill and I sit in the Amber fort near Jaipur listening to Punam speak of the role of eunuchs in seventeen century life here. She explains that their role was as the guardians of the women's quarters to protect, to prevent unwanted intrusion and to be no threat to their charges. Punam likened this role with that of the eunuchs in contemporary Indian society. Today they live in their own communities. They are feared for the curses that they place on those that cross them. They will turn up, uninvited, to christenings and expect to be treated as honoured guests and entitled to food, money and gifts. There is no point in the hosts calling the police to evict the eunuchs, for the police fear them just as much. I recalled the story of boy singers with exceptional voices in seventeenth- and eighteenth-century Italy who were castrated in order to retain their beautiful voices. They were thus able to continue to entertain the hierarchy of church and state and maintain a respected place in society.

In a coach, later, on the way to Delhi airport we saw one of the eunuchs hanging around an orange juice seller's stall close to a traffic light. When the traffic came to a halt he/she, dressed in an orange sari that suited the thin frame, jumped to aggressively beg from a couple of tuk-tuks. The passenger in the first tuk-tuk refused to give, despite the aggressive clapping made by the eunuch in pursuit of some money. The passenger of the second tuk-tuk was more accommodating and gave what looked like ten rupees, a small amount. This appeared to satisfy the eunuch. She/he returned to the first tuk-tuk, berating the passenger, clapping again and showing the palm to the non-giver. Our coach moved on and I saw no more. This clapping ritual was in marked contrast to that of the Buddhist monks that we saw in Dharamsala, and which I will comment on later.

Lunch was taken two hours away in remote Simode. The hotel here was originally built for the maharajah of Jaipur. As we drove up to the entrance we passed a sign to a temple dedicated to Hanuman the monkey god, who I had mentioned previously. Three hundred and thirty steps were necessary to reach the craggy steadfast of the god. After a grand lunch I made the journey upward. The temple was locked. I found an outer wall, which had a rounded arch built into it. This location overlooked mountainous landscape with forts perched on the skyline. I stood in the arch and experienced a strong burst of energy from the stones around and to the side of me. As I looked over the landscape I dropped into meditation stance, a chi gong way of standing, which attracts positive energies to move through the body. My hands slowly dropped until the palms faced the ground. The energy radiating into my hands from the ground became so strong that the burning sensation felt as though they were facing an electric fire. I stood there enjoying the experience until a wasp appeared, buzzing around me. I took this as a sign to leave.

The festival of Holi is celebrated on the day after the full moon in early March every year. Originally a festival to celebrate good harvests and fertility of the land, Holi is now a symbolic commemoration of a legend from Hindu mythology. During Holi, the festival of colours, the advent of spring is heralded.

This explanation of the festival is from www.moxon.net:

> *Holi is an annual holiday celebrated on the full moon in March, purportedly to say goodbye to winter and hello to warmer weather. This is why Holi is mainly a northern festival, because in the south the last thing people want is for the pleasant temperatures of winter to turn into the humid tandoori oven of summer ...*
>
> *Holi is all about colour, namely colour in the hair, colour on the face, colour on your clothes, colour all over the streets and colour just about anywhere else it'll stick. The colour itself takes the form of tika powder, either thrown au naturel or added to water and squeezed from a plastic bottle; it pays to wear grotty clothes on Holi (so I simply chose randomly from my collection of sun-bleached and laundry-battered garments) because if you play with tika powder, everyone's a winner bar the clothes.*

Sheena organised the group's own Holi in our hotel. We had great fun covering each other in coloured powder, much to the amusement of fellow guests of the hotel and staff. A number of us had been sick on the tour thus far. I felt that the laughter and joyous spontaneity had improved our health a great deal.

Susan spoke of her outer work as a midwife, which she links with her inner work of helping the birth of highly evolved children. She told me the story of a difficult birth of such a child. Susan spoke to the child's soul consciousness.

'Why don't you want to come?' she asked.

'Because I am frightened. I have no father,' was the reply.

'But you have two women in this room who love you dearly,' Susan countered.

Within a few minutes the baby came in a harmonious and successful birth. Susan believes that her daughter is of the Indigo children.

These are the first wave of higher consciousness beings that are here to assist in the change to a new higher human consciousness. The daughter is soon to give birth herself. Susan believes that the granddaughter will be of the latest group of even higher consciousness children.

We go to Delhi and visit Raj Ghat. This is the last resting place of the father of the nation, Mahatma Gandhi.

We are in the park dedicated to the life and memory of Mahatma Gandhi, Sheena told the story of Gandhi-Ji's son immortalised in a film. The mahatma, as saintly as he was, as suffused with justice as he was, was sometimes lacking in compassion for his son. This resulted in a rift in relationship between the two. Gandhi was given money for his children's education. The son was not very bright so Gandhi gave the education money to a cousin. This upset and enraged the son, who left and lived away from his family. So alienated was the son that he converted to Christianity and then to the Muslim faith. He became an alcoholic. The son totally fell apart when he heard of his father's death by shooting. Within a few months of his father's death the son was dead too from alcoholic abuse. As he lay dying he was asked who his father was. When he told his questioner that he was the son of Gandhi-Ji he was not believed. For how could this old tramp be the son of the father of the nation? Gandhi's wife had beseeched her husband to be more compassionate with his son, all to no avail. I find this story so sad.

I received the intuitive impression that Gandhi had completed his mission on Earth in that particular incarnation when he was shot. There was nothing else that he could constructively do. India had gained her independence. Partition of the country was a fact. Gandhi had opposed partition but was unsuccessful. The future of the country was now in the hands of lesser mortals. Gandhi had begged Nehru to allow Jinna to be the first president of a united country in order to keep it together. When this failed it was time for Gandhi to return to source. The maniac that pulled the trigger was the unthinking mechanism.

It was time for Pat and Susan to return to their homes. I will miss them greatly. I valued their companionship and wise counsel.

We visited the Golden Temple at Amritsar. This is a fantastic building covered in gold (or a metal that resembles gold), set in a large tank of water. The whole was surrounded by a plaza of associated buildings. Where else in the world would a gold-covered building survive without being stripped bare? This is another element of the difference of India to the western linear approach to reality. Thousands of faithful Sikhs are there every day. Chanting from within the building is relayed around the perimeter. The queue to get into the temple was enormous, probably two hours in length when we arrived. We were about to leave, defeated by the crush of the faithful and the heat. Suddenly a man in white presented himself to our group. This 'angel' told us to follow him on a short cut. He took us through the normal exit despite the protestations of the guard at that point. We walked against the flow of people exiting the temple. I kept my head down in a futile attempt to appear incognito.

My turbaned head fooled no-one. Sheena had organised a local person to adorn Bill and my head with the Sikh headdress, much to the amusement of the faithful in the complex. The turban looked great on Bill, less so on me. He had the right head shape and face. My small features disappeared as the headdress 'took over'. Our time in the temple made possible by the Sikh 'angel' was wonderful. Relaxing and atmospheric it was, despite the 'wall-to-wall' crush of adherents. Afterwards we ate with the masses, sitting in rows as the free food was dished out from buckets. It was most nutritious.

Perhaps the entrance facilitated by our angel had been precipitated by one of the cosmic energies that was overseeing this trip.

A priest in the temple gave me an orange cloth wrapped around a bread offering as an exchange for the financial gift that I made.

This is taken from Sheena's description:

> *Amritsar was founded in 1577 by Guru Ram Dass. The city was sacked by Ahmed Shah Durani in 1761 and the Golden Temple was destroyed. It was rebuilt and was later roofed over with golden copper plates. (Ah, so it wasn't gold.) The temple was occupied by separatists in the 1980s attempting to create a Sikh national area. They were controversially expelled by the then Prime Minister Indira Gandhi who was later assassinated by her Sikh bodyguard. Everyone must cover their heads to enter the temple. Shoes and socks are checked by attendants. Everyone walks through water to cleanse their feet before entering. Originally a small lake in the middle of a quiet forest, the site has been a meditation retreat for wandering mendicants and sages since deep antiquity. Guru Nanak (1469–1539), the founder of the Sikh religion and a philosopher-saint, came to live and meditate by the peaceful lake. After the passing away of Guru Nanak, his disciples continued to frequent the site. Over the centuries it became the primary sacred shrine of the Sikhs. The temples architecture draws on both Hindu and Moslem architectural styles … During the reign of Maharaja Ranjit Singh (1780–1839), the Golden Temple was richly ornamented with marble sculptures, golden gilding and large quantities of precious stones. Within the sanctuary, on a jewel-studded platform lies the Adi Grantha, the sacred scripture of the Sikhs. This scripture is a collection of devotional poems, prayers and hymns composed by the ten Sikh gurus and various Hindu and Moslem saints.*
>
> *Jailanwala Bagh is the place where two thousand Sikhs were invited to celebrate Baisakhi, a big Sikh festival, and were massacred by British troops. Many Sikhs in panic had jumped into a well and drowned. This was the slaughter initiated by General Dyer. He was the commander of Nepalese Gurkha troops, not from India, so were easier to persuade to open fire on the defenceless civilians. Later Dyer was court-martialled. The feeling in India is that he was let off lightly.*

We went from the temple to a museum that is on the site of the massacre. When we reached the museum a crowd of protesters were sitting in front of the entrance, blocking it. To one side a group of policemen stood around looking relaxed. It transpired that the crowd were demonstrating against a decision to remove some of the bullet holes originating from the massacre. The whole scene was without apparent bitterness or tension. Clearly those demonstrating were aware and keen to preserve the historical evidence. Photos were taken by the locals, who were again amused by the turbans that Bill and I continued to wear. We left without entering the museum.

Late afternoon of the same day saw us at the border with Pakistan watching the ceremony of lowering the flags. It was pure theatre with khaki clad Indian soldiers goose-stepping and saluting perfectly, replicated by green clad Pakistan troops on their side. All wore exotic headgear, further enhancing the height of these elite troops. Every movement was cheered to the echoes by the audiences on both sides. Chants arose, praising Pakistan on one side immediately bringing a response praising Hindustan (India) on the other. Such nationalist fervour perhaps continues the separation and lack of trust between the two countries. Perhaps it will fade over the decades. The memories of wars between the two countries still rankle, it appears to me.

We drive to Dharamsala, or rather Mcloud Ganj, which is several hundred feet above Dharamsala in the foothills of the Himalayas. The journey is taken in four-by-four vehicles, which are very comfortable. We climb upward from the hot and dusty plain into the foothills. My struggling lungs relax in the fresh and cool air.

Again this is taken from Sheena's description:

The two towns built by the British in the 1840s as a hill station. With the exodus of the Dalai Lama and many of his countrymen after the Chinese invasion in 1960 it has become the Tibetan capital in exile with a large community of Lay people and monks. It is also the home

> *of the Dalai Lama, the spiritual head of the Tibetan Buddhists who is now headquartered at Mcleod Ganj. This latter is also known as Little Lhasa. Inside the Tibetan government compound lie the preserved Tibetan texts saved from the Cultural Revolution. There is a fascinating cultural museum containing artefacts containing amazing three-dimensional mandalas in wood and stone. The men-Tsee-Khang displays traditional Tibetan medicine demonstrated through preserved specimens and Tibetan paintings on cloth.*

We visit the Norbulingka Institute, which is a major centre for Buddhist teaching and practical work. It was named after the summer residence of the seventh Dali Lama. It was set up to ensure the continuation of the Buddhist cultural heritage. Over one hundred students learn a variety of crafts wood, metal, silk and thangka painting. The temple has a 4.5-metre-high gilded statue of the Buddha and over a thousand painted images.

I have a vision in the middle of the first night here concerning the future of Tibet, which is being decided in two places. First of all, the sacrifice of Tibetans in their home country facing up to bullying, aggression and murder from the Chinese is creating a resonance of energy. This resonance is activating the spiritual will of the people, which will reap its reward. A profound strength is being developed in the psyche of the nation. Secondly, the religious and political future is being created in Dharamsala. The latter will serve as a focus for the future re-emergence of the nation in a new and strong form. The mediaeval Tibetan society before the Chinese invasion is gone forever. A religio-democratic structure is the most probable option for the future. This is unlikely to happen in the present Dalai Lama's lifetime. His role is as catalyst and focus for the new Tibetan nation will be complete. After his passing, his bodhisattva energy will permeate the new nation. One can draw a parallel with the life and passing of Gandhi-Ji once the Indian subcontinent became newly independent.

Mahayana Buddhism ... regards the bodhisattva as a person who already has a considerable degree of enlightenment and seeks to use their wisdom to help other human beings to become liberated themselves. In this understanding of the word, the bodhisattva is an already wise person who uses skilful means to lead others to see the benefits of virtue and the cultivation of wisdom.

Janet spoke of the racial issues within the brown race. She said that Indians from the subcontinent look down on those originating in India but who emigrated from India to the Caribbean. This seems to be another form of racial discrimination. She also said that some Indians use a cream that claims to give a whiter skin. Many Bollywood stars are brown and yet appear as white on the screen. Here I am in India, a white person (actually I am patchy pink), trying to get a suntan! There is an old English saying, '*There is none so queer as folk!*'

My wife, who is from Mexico, has suffered grievously at times from overt racial abuse, particularly from out-of-control youths and children. More subtle abuse has been employed by those that are in positions of authority, or colleagues of hers. It seems to me that people who are the originators of such abuse are sad people who are unable to deal with their own internal demons and thus externalise them. My good friend Sylvester says that he was a white overseer of black slaves in a previous life. He treated them badly. In this life he has been born with black skin. He says that this is so he can appreciate the consciousness of the black race.

We went to a Buddhist monastery in Dharamsala. When we arrived, the monks were performing a clapping practice. In this, one monk, who stands, makes a presentation to a cross-legged sitting monk, who is quietly listening. At a culmination of his theological point the presenter would raise his voice, clap his hands loudly and make a forward motion with his body towards the seated figure. This was an interesting contrast to the clapping practiced by the eunuch in obtaining money, written earlier. It would be interesting to know more about the effect of clapping on the psyche of recipients and those performing clapping. Presumably the clapping creates an attentive energy in both.

This is my last full day in India. We are still in Dharamsalla. Following Pranayama practice and meditation, Sheena spoke of past lives that those present at the session had in India. Sheena saw me as a Vedic priest, bald, with a little knot of hair behind the head. I was a brahmin, the consciousness of which has been carried forward in this life. In this life I am exploring different areas of consciousness, including brahmin consciousness. Sheena saw Bill as a warrior priest. When the group was in the Golden Temple a magnificently attired Sikh dressed in deep blue came into contact with our group. He sported a long, curved knife. Although aged with a long straggly beard he exemplified the warrior spirit. Bill felt drawn to him and wished him to follow the group, which he did for some time. He also appeared in a group photograph.

Sheena saw Katherine as a princess who saw that energy as restricting, keeping her in one place. Today she is a free spirit travelling the world living her truth. Sheena saw Punam as a Buddhist nun aged seventeen or eighteen years, who had a violent and untimely death. Punam is aware of the place that she lived in that life and has experienced sadness there. She is now calm and comfortable with that lifetime energy.

Sheena saw an incarnation of Janet in 3000 BC. In this life she cleared out the temple fireplaces after ceremonies. In this life she had a fiery personality. Sheena suggested that she light a candle each morning and evening in her home in order to address her contract with fire. She should balance this by placing a small container of water next to the flame.

Katherine shared an experience that she had of attempting to sleep in a tent with the wind howling and lashing their temporary home. In an attempt to deal with the discomfort of this situation she entered a conscious state where she became the element. There was a 'whooshing' sensation in her body and the environmental conditions changed. The outside wind became calm. Katherine reminded the group of the power within our beings, and of how we are capable of so much more than we normally access.

OK, it's time for me to leave India, this country of fantastic contrasts. One has to visit it in order to experience and describe it. All other explanations are rendered meaningless unless one can taste, smell, feel the pulse of the land and its people. Even after visiting it, it is difficult to describe. Perhaps all one can do is internalise the experiences and let them out again as they return to one's third-dimensional consciousness later. The heat, the dust, the people, temples, palaces, traffic all pass through my awareness as myriad images. Will I return? I do not know. I do know that it will be some time before I complete the processing of the experiences of this trip.

I give many thanks to Sheena and Punam for making such a great trip possible. I give many thanks to Bill, Pat, Janet, Susan, Catherine, Papa-ji and Mama-ji for giving me so many interesting opportunities. Perhaps we will meet again.

Finally, this is on a lighter note. During the trip I had a dream concerning the kung fu test that I would be taking upon my return to England. I had missed three weeks of classes, which would leave me some way behind other students. In the dream I was back in the dojo and my black belt instructor spoke to me. He said, *'I will take you through the test.'* Whether he did or not I cannot recall consciously. However, upon my return I took the test successfully almost a week earlier than the instructor planned. It was almost as though I had done it before!

Life just gets more and more interesting!

Tiglath Pilesar

During the latter part of the trip to India and on the first day of my arrival back in England the words Tiglath Pilesar constantly arose in my consciousness. It filled me with puzzled frustration, so often it came in. I knew it to be the name of Mesopotamian king or kings. Intrigued, I 'tuned in' to the name to obtain more information. I accessed this energy form, for that is what it was, externally to my being rather than internally. I did this because I was not certain at this point whether the energy form was benign or not. If it had not been benign then there was the danger that an unpleasant energy could attach itself to me rather like a computer virus.

My intuition confirmed that the energy was, indeed, benign. I was told by my intuition that if I accessed this energy it would give me great strength and dynamism. This is most interesting and is an energy form that will be useful in the work ahead. I sensed that the kings who used this name adopted it because they, like me, perceived its 'strength and dynamism' and were able to use it. Interestingly, the Mesopotamian king Tiglath Pilesar III characterised his reign with many successful battles and expanded his empire greatly. Not that I would utilise this energy for martial pursuits. There again the Mesopotamian kings were living in an entirely different consciousness. I have accessed this energy consciously and it fills me with energy. This is a most precious gift from the trip.

This chapter bears the name of this 'mantra' because its energy contributed much to the information below.

Subsequent to my insights concerning the above 'mantra' or energy form, I tuned in and received the following insight. I saw the mantra connected to my work on the line of energy running from the 'Four Corners' to India through Egypt. The mantra would act as a key to unlocking the wisdom and knowledge secrets of the line.

Tiglath Pilesar

On the day that I returned from India I had the following dream. It was connected to my friend Jacques Rangasamy. This is the dream, but first two quotes.

> *The best way to make your dreams come true is to wake up.*
> **Paul Valery**

> *I did not know whether I was then a man dreaming I was a butterfly, or whether I am now a butterfly dreaming I am a man.*
> **Chuang Tse**

I was living in a different house. The only other person there that I knew was Jacques. I was due to have a one-to-one discussion with Jacques. The people living in this house were asked if someone would volunteer to dig the garden. I volunteered. As I walked to the garden tool room to collect a garden fork I passed a room from which I could hear Jacques talking to another person. I entered the tool room. The large fork that I was looking for was not there. I picked another one hanging on the wall. This was a new, green, metal one with extra prongs. I began to dig in the garden, which was already partly dug. The soil was black, full of weeds and difficult to dig. I made very little impression. To my left, two fences away, two neighbours chatted, disregarding me. Back in the house I was sitting when the owner of the house entered the room where I was and offered me a light black jacket to wear. She suggested that I may be cold. Here the dream ended.

I asked Jacques for his opinion concerning the dream. This is an extract of what he said:

Allow me to reflect on the components of your dream in turn, and then perhaps draw some general, if speculative conclusions.

I was living in a different house. A house symbolises being. This alludes to the renewal of your own being.

The only other person there that I knew was you (Jacques). I was due to have a one-to-one discussion with you. This refers to the initiatory work that we share. By the way, I am humbled to be a frame of reference for such an important dimension of your inner life.

The people living in this house were asked if someone would volunteer to dig the garden. I volunteered. This is an important and critical point, because you made the decision. Decisions in initiatory dreams always allude to a re-polarisation of your psychic energies. The garden is also the source of sustenance, and working in the garden is working with the basic life force of the universe. If you remember, the old Rosicrucian symbolic image of 'working in the vineyard of Matt' conjures up the privilege of sharing in the evolutionary work of our humanity.

As I walked to the garden tool room to collect a garden fork I passed a room from which I could hear you talking to another person. This is interesting as the representation of me is in the form of a voice. The voice alludes to a transcendental rather than a physical presence. In that case my voice would represent the teaching that I have had the responsibility and privilege of transmitting and conveying.

I entered the tool room. The large fork that I was looking for was not there. I picked another one hanging on the wall. This was a new, green, metal one with extra prongs.

The tool room that you have known has been the Rosicrucian Order and the Temple Study Group. The tool symbolises the initiatory technique that translates spirit energies into working propositions in life. The symbolism is quite clear, inasmuch as for the new task you have set yourself, new techniques will be issued to you.

I began to dig in the garden, which was already partly dug. You will be continuing work that has already started. Or it might be an indication that you're sharing work on a much larger scale.

The soil was black, full of weeds and difficult to dig. I made very little impression. The black soil is an image borrowed from alchemy. The word in itself comes from al-kemit, an Arabic word meaning "Black earth'. It alludes to the soil of Egypt after the annual flood of the Nile when everywhere is covered by a black slime, from which new life-sustaining growth will emerge ... The weeds and gardening difficulties you experienced suggest that you have joined the initiatory work at the beginning of a new cycle ... which always offers difficulties. The weeds probably allude to unwholesome ideas and concepts that need to be cleared before healthy growth can spring forth.

To my left, two fences away, two neighbours chatted disregarding me. I am not sure what this detail means. It could be another existential dimension, where disincarnated beings exist. That may explain their apparent lack of interest in you, because you cannot reach each other across the existential divide. They may well be ancestors of yours.

Back in the house I was sitting when the owner of the house entered the room where I was and offered me a light black jacket to wear. She suggested that I may be cold. This is absolutely fantastic, for the owner of the house is the great mother. She displays caring towards you and gives you a jacket that bears the colour black. The representation of the great mother that we have studied and worshipped is the Black Madonna. To me, it signals that the great mother has extended her arms to you as a son, hence the colour of the jacket that would bind you to her. She is anxious to build up the warmth in you, suggesting her direct intervention in your energetic constitution to transform it to the requisite calibre for the work you are doing for her.

It is a great dream, and timely too in these days of mass transition and transformation. You have worked hard and conscientiously, and you have been accepted. Many have been called but few have been accepted, as the scriptures say. You should be honoured and privileged.

This is the end of Jacques' perspective on the dream.

Soon after the above dream another one presented itself. I was in a large store selling many different things. The structure of this store was different from any other in this third-dimensional reality. The walls were constructed of pale stone or concrete blocks. The floor was constructed of a light-coloured material. The store was full of Eastern people. From the entrance I walked through the store to meet companions at the exit. The store was divided into small rooms and the way of walking was meandering. In one room two women were seated and talking. There was nothing else in this room. Off to one side, as I walked, small rooms displayed goods in glass cases. A potential customer stood in the room. I reached the end room without seeing the exit and waited for my companions.

After a period of time they did not arrive, so I began the return journey. After a time I needed the toilet, which was back at the exit. From the exit I made a second return journey and this time reached the entrance after seeing a young western woman holding a visa credit card. At the entrance I met a Chinese man, who watched me as I reviewed an electronic screen on the wall. On the screen I had entered some answers to questions that had appeared there. While I had been walking in the store someone had defaced the screen by drawing the figure of a woman there. The figure did not obscure my answers. The figures on the screen began to break up. The Chinese man copied my answers from the screen onto a blackboard before they completely disappeared. Here the dream ended. I sensed that at least one of my companions was there, as well as the Chinese man.

This is friend Suzanne's perspectives on my dreams:

> *As for your dream, I just picked up a couple of things consciously by the words you used.*
>
> *When you said MEANDERING, that is a term I use and I feel many humans walking this Earth are doing this these days; it is not like being lost, but wandering with a purpose. There is a saying,* 'Not all who wander are lost.'
>
> *The two women in the room ... I feel they are also your companions.*
>
> *The drawing of the woman on the screen, I immediately thought of the Goddess. In any event, nothing can hide the truth no matter what.*
>
> *It would appear the Chinese man would indeed be a companion.*

If we are fortunate we can interpret our own dreams. The following was such an occurrence.

I was standing at the end of a runway preparing to run and do the triple jump athletic event. I had the correct shoes on my feet. Bizarrely, I was carrying a duvet tied around my shoulders. I started my run. After a few strides I realised that the duvet was still tied to me and that it would affect my performance. I struggled to remove it. I was free of it before I reached the take-off board. However, I was unable to accelerate to top speed. I completed the three phases of the jump but without a satisfactory distance; the watching crowd 'oooahd' in disappointment.

I interpreted the dream in the following way. I saw the duvet as a symbol of my lack of 'awakeness' and my slowness to throw off my dream state. This results in my inability to 'take-off' in my inner and outer life as much as is possible.

Paramahansa Yogananda said that we are living in a dream, and when we dream we are dreaming inside a dream. For me, dreaming is another way of fulfilling our reality. We live certain aspects and experience certain things in a dream, which means that we no longer need to fulfil them in three-dimensional reality. It may be that dreams are also a way of filtering experiences out of our unconscious that we no longer need. This is a clearing-out process if you like. For us, watching films, plays, listening to the radio can be another way of experiencing reality vicariously. If we are smart enough, learning from other peoples' experiences can assist us in negating the need to go through those experiences. This is one of the marvels of the communication age. We have the opportunity to access an enormous range of experiences that was denied to our forebears.

So what is the difference between dreams and visions? For me, the latter is part of our everyday consciousness, albeit an altered state version. The former is part of the sleeping state. Neither is part of the objective consciousness controlled state. It could be argued, however, that visions are frequently started by an objective consciousness intention.

The following is an example of a vision begun from such an intention. During a Metamorphic healing session with Louise, she spoke of a contact that she had with dolphins while she was in a meditative state. She spoke of their current work, in which their sonar activities were creating channel openings for the influx of cosmic energies and knowledge to the Earth plane. That evening, In Louise's absence, I suggested to a group of fellow meditators that we explore this area of work as we meditated. As soon as we entered a meditative state I perceived myself in the presence of a number of dolphins swimming around in tight circles. Initially, I thought the room that I was meditating in had filled with water, with the dolphins also. I quickly realised that I had entered the domain of the dolphins. I also realised that this domain was a psychic one because the dolphins were much fatter than in third-dimensional existence. I perceived their etheric bodies. One of the dolphins swam closer to me and fixed me with an eye as it positioned itself to me side on. This dolphin began to communicate with me mentally. It spoke of the communication work that Louise had alluded to earlier.

It communicated that, indeed, their sonar communications were being used to open channels of knowledge, wisdom and inspirational experiences for beings on Earth. Specifically, communication was strong with the area of the cosmos around Ursa Major, because the latter was a region with particularly strong communication abilities. These abilities were being communicated to babies and young beings on Earth. These beings, both human and non-human, were the future in a higher energetic environment that was developing even now. These young beings were the ones that would take new civilisations forward. Many older beings were fixed in patterns of the past and could not change to cope with the new vibrations. Indeed, the dolphin continued, even those of a high spiritual disposition living on the planet now would struggle as the energies continued to increase. It is probable that most beings would be leaving due to the energy changes that would continue to rise. This completed the information that was imparted to me and I came out of the meditative state.

This information was presented to me in a logical progression. This is not the way that dreams work in many occasions. The time frame in a dream is usually of a different order quite often for me. In addition, the dream does not always progress in a logical sequence. Although on some occasions it does appear to do so.

Later I had a similar experience with the name 'bodhisattva', which is the name of a person or energy form for those that have entered Buddha consciousness but has elected to stay on the Earth to help humanity. I tuned in to my guidance and asked why I was constantly receiving this name. This is what guidance came back with.

You remember that you were told that the final raising of consciousness on Earth would result in a separation between those that had awakened, or partially awakened, or wanted to awake on the one hand, and those that were still asleep in material consciousness on the other. There will be a gentle separation of these two worlds. There will be no mass deaths, no apocalyptic Earth changes, just this gentle moving apart.

In order to assist material consciousness humanity to awake, bodhisattva beings will stay with this material reality. In order to help such beings, others in this 'web of consciousness' will also stay. These beings may be individuals or groups.

I replied. *Yeah, right. Are you saying that groups, as individuals or as a group, that I have been involved with will stay to help? We have been working pretty hard in order that that should not be the case. What about free will? This is a free-will universe, you know. We could say 'not on your nellie', we won't stay.*

The reply came immediately. *You are correct. You are living in a free-will universe and you may say 'not on your nellie', as you so colourfully put it. However, these decisions were not and have not been taken at the level of objective consciousness. Some of these decisions were taken long before the beings concerned entered into a physical body. There is no final decision on who will stay or who will go. Rightly you will be surprised who will stay and who will go. Consciousness is changing so fast that no being is finally sure who will stay in material consciousness and who will go. We are not saying that you will stay. We are giving you an update on the state of 'the game' right now. We would not say if you are staying even if we knew, for this could interfere with your work on yourself, your work in the community of beings, and your work in the group.*

I continued with the comment, *Thanks for the info but put me on the good ship' light body' consciousness. I really haven't been running around the planet in order to do more of the same ad infinitum.*

Not to be outdone guidance finished with, *remember that this would be an opportunity for service for those that stay.*

By this time I was having some fun with this conversation. I continued, *So having done all this work with the intention of leaving this less than perfect reality, some unfortunate beings are to be told 'Sorry, it's time for plan B. You are going to have to sweat some more on Planet Unfortunate.' I will make a deal with you. You come and interact with this reality and I will change places with you, sit on ethereal consciousness and give out advice and wise words when you screw up.*

I had no reply from that. The conversation finished, which is not surprising as I was talking, probably, to another aspect of myself. I feel with the last comment that I have strayed into ego-consciousness.

There is occasion when an intuitive hint can open out to much more information. At the beginning of a meditation with friends George and Jemima, I was guided to suggest meditating on past influences *as far back as was necessary.* The three of us then went into a quiet meditation, working with our individual insights. At the end of the meditation George spoke of his experiences. He was taken back to a time on the Earth before Homo Sapiens lived here. The Earth was pristine. George saw the predecessors to present humanity. He saw Australopithecus, Neanderthal and other such beings. He was told that these were intelligent but had not been imbued with a living soul by the universal forces. He was also told that man was the first being to have this soul consciousness.

My experience was entirely different. I was presented with an initial image, as though from a pen print, of a man dressed in the clothes of the dark ages. He wore the tight leg hose of the time, a short jacket and a hood over his head. Immediately afterwards I was presented with a more substantial, almost living, image. I was seated in what appeared to be a room in a loft or roof-space. In front of me and facing away from me examining a scroll was a monk. I knew this monk to be the thirteenth-century mystic and magician Roger Bacon. The scroll that he was examining had Egyptian hieroglyphics on it. The colour of one of the symbols was vibrant red and blue as though newly placed on the scroll. The gaze of this monk was intense, as though he was trying to understand the images. He was having great difficulty. As I perceived this image I was given background information concerning this scene. I, in that lifetime, was a travelling mendicant monk. My undercover role was to, secretly, carry magical and alchemical scrolls between those practicing magic of the ancients. My travelling role rendered me ideally suited to this secret role. Of course, this was unknown to the church and was incompatible with its teachings.

The scroll carried the arcane knowledge of how to turn water into wine. This was practiced by the Master Jesus. This mission was a failure. The scroll could not be interpreted by Roger Bacon. The background voice told me that the level of consciousness of those present was not high enough to penetrate the high vibration of the information guarded by the symbols. The whole network of information of sharing was shut down. When in the company of other monks, I 'let the cat out of the bag' concerning the secret network. The church authorities reacted predictably and I was banished. The final information that I was given was to the effect that I am now working on turning my consciousness 'from water into wine'. This last sentence was the creative impulse for the vision; for the times are now appropriate when this knowledge can be used for transmuting the human consciousness.

Adventures on Greek Islands

My friends Mary and Joan holiday and perform spiritual work in various parts of sun-kissed Greece. For them it is a paradise. For me it is less so, partly because I travelled in the height of the holiday seasons with thousands of other British sun seekers. Nevertheless, there have been some adventures that are worthy of reporting. The following are those stories.

KOS

A few nights before travelling to Kos with wife Jaqueline and sister-in-law, Coti, I had an unusual dream. In this dream three companions and I were sucked into another dimension by an upward-pointing pipe-shaped mechanism. After a number of adventures that I, subsequently, couldn't recall, my companions and I found ourselves in a bare, windowless room. I was wondering how we would return to this dimension. As soon as the thought was made a circular opening appeared in one of the walls. A white horse's head appeared. It sucked inward through its mouth and we were immediately transported back to this reality. I later intuited that my three companions were other aspects of myself. Thus my physical, mental, emotional and spiritual realities were the recipients of this experience.

I explained my dream to Jaqueline and Coti at our first evening meal in the Kos hotel. At the end of the explanation I made the intuitive leap of awareness that the dimensional journey in the dream was linked to an inter-dimensional portal in Kos, namely the Asklepion. This place is said to be the world's first hospital. This may be true for Western civilisation. Further research may discover more ancient hospitals in China and Egypt. The Asklepion is where Hippocrates, author of the Hippocratic Oath, practiced his healing craft.

Before my first Asklepion visit I 'tuned in' to my intuitive force and asked for personal healing at this high energy portal. My request was for further remission of an asthma condition and painful shoulders. I booked to go on a tour of the island mainly because it included a visit to the Asklepion. I had little time here on this visit due to the needs of the tour to move on. After I listened to the historical explanation of this magical place by our trusty guide, I had only twenty-five minutes to explore. The one physical experience for me was of a strong pressure in my head as I walked around. This lasted but a few seconds and then disappeared. As we left I wondered if the work that I needed to do there had been completed or if another visit was required.

I find it fascinating that, when the work of the spirit is done consciously and effectively, the universe conspires to organise arrangements around it harmoniously in order to create a satisfactory conclusion. On the last day of our Kos visit the previously poor weather cleared. This allowed me to return to the Asklepion, which I felt pulled to do. Each link of my travels to the Asklepion from our hotel went perfectly. Sometimes my connection was made within a few minutes of bus departure time. The final part of my journey to the sacred site consisted of a four-kilometre trek through town and country, culminating in a climb up to the hillside site. Along the way local people pointed me in the correct direction. It was quite like old times for me, trekking to ancient sites of the spirit under the hot sun with backpack on my back. I felt happy, content and fulfilled. I had barely 45 minutes at the site before the return journey needed to begin.

I entered the sacred pile after persuading the pay booth person that I was indeed a pensioner and was entitled to the reduced entry fee. Walking in I received the intuitive impulse to tile (walk in a circle around the site with a spiritual motive, thus creating an energetic standing wave). I felt impelled to invoke the sacred chant Aum-Ra-Ma-Oom internally. This internal chant ensured that no disturbance was made to 'man nor beast' on my perambulations. The three physical levels of the Asklepion caused me to walk in the shape of a figure eight with an extra circle added on to the vertical. As I left the site I sensed that the vibrations of this healing place were being absorbed through my pores into the physical body. I also sensed that the energies thus gained would remain with me and could be called up and visualised at will. After this work was done I left to return to Kos town for shopping duties for wife Jaqueline, and then to the return bus to Kardomena. The latter was the small town nearest our hotel.

Much later the realisation dawned on me that my visit and internal work had caused an inflow of energy to this sacred place. This energy woke up the old power vibrations which would be 'amped up' by newer ones.

Spiritual duties complete and family members duly rested, we returned to England. Upon our return several days later I was feeling 'out of time' and out of synchronicity with the energy of my homeland. I put this down to the powerful energies of Kos and the Asklepion; I also sensed that this magical island of Kos was operating in a slightly different time frame to the one here in England. Those of a sensitive nature would be affected by it. Jaqueline and Coti both felt tired and 'not in sync' when they returned.

My puzzlement and continuing feeling of being in another time pushed me to ask for guidance concerning the reasons after five days with no change in my out-of-time sensations. This is what I received:

As the energy of the planet changes many physical locations will have their vibrations raised before others. This is particularly so in the region of energy portals and other high spiritual places. Kos is one of these places. I will give you more information concerning the effects of the 'tiling' that you felt drawn to do at the Asklepion and other places for there are a number of effects. You already know that one purpose is to raise or reactivate the energies in certain locations. In addition, 'tiling' has the effect of creating an energetic blocking process. In this way those high energy locations that have been hijacked for nefarious purposes by those of the dark persuasion are no longer available to them.

This was the case and the purpose of for your 'tiling' of the Washington Monument. The cosmic forces worked hard on your awareness to persuade you to do that particular work. You will remember that your camera was removed from your backpack and placed on the monument boundary wall after you had left this area. In this way you were encouraged to return in order to reclaim it and become aware of the work that was needed to be done.

The other function of 'tiling' is to create an energetic vortex as a gift to the 'tiler' and assist in the development of his or her consciousness. This was the case with the 'tiling' done at the Asklepion. You are feeling the effects as your consciousness has been altered and your being works on the integration of the changes. The whole island is a few micro-seconds out of time with Cheltenham (my home town). It is in advance of Cheltenham in this respect. This is why Jaqueline and Coti have been affected also. In Jaqueline's case this change has reawakened her interest in the tarot and her cultural links with the Mexican 'day of the dead'.

It was mentioned before that 'tiling' work is important for the local place, for Gaia and for the 'tiler'. You will recall how sick you felt before visiting the mountain-top site of Monte Alban in Oxaca. The reason was that you were being prepared for this tiling work by cosmic forces.

On another matter during Coti's month-long visit to England from Mexico she had two night-time psychic experiences. In the first one she woke up to find the figure of a man standing in the doorway of the bedroom. She returned to sleep without any further issue. Just before the Kos visit a similar apparition appeared next to the window. He left and was replaced by another male figure. Neither experiences were threatening and, indeed, were perceived as being benign by Coti.

This is from greeka.com:

> *Kos, Greece is an island part of the Dodecanese. It is the third largest of the Greek Islands of the group and the second most popular and touristy island after Rhodes. It is located between Kalymnos and Nysiros. It is very well organised and has everything in terms of tourism infrastructures. The various charms and beauties of the Greek Island are not visible at the first sight but, after a while, picturesque villages and the fine beaches amaze all visitors.*

I will finish on another note. Those that have read our previous books will be aware of my disenchantment with organised religion. This is from *The World As You Dream It* by John Perkins.

> *I have spent many hours in the Catholic Church. It is a difficult religion. The priests are very confused about their beliefs. They talk about them all the time, yet have difficulty using them. Yes, from all I've heard, Christ was a great Shaman. He healed people, animals and plants. He healed rocks, rivers, minerals and the sky.*

SKIATHOS and more...

The following year I visited the above island where a family wedding was taking place. Before the ceremony I mused on the process of witnessing. The following is what came to me.

> *Witnessing is a powerful tool. It is an active, not passive principal. A witness, pure in intent, brings his or her energy to the event without colouring it with judgement or interference. The process of witnessing feeds and sustains the witnessed event. It nurtures it. Witnessing provides comfort and support to those actively involved in the event. It is an entirely positive activity if the witnessing is carried out with sympathy, compassion and an open heart. A TV camera vision of a horrific event is also witnessing as well as recording. This is a more*

diffused form as it is not perceived with the human eye. Witnessing, properly completed, can remove the need for judgement.

One of the people attending the wedding told me the following uproarious story.

A friend's grandmother decided to lose weight without asking for advice on methods that would suit a person somewhat advanced in age. She decided that the best way was to heat up her body. In order to achieve this objective she went to bed wrapped in three bin liners. The upshot of this bizarre decision was that she ended up in hospital for three days with severe dehydration.

For the second attempt she bought an exercise bike. One day her son received an emergency telephone call complaining that she had trapped her foot between the pedal and its shank. Aforesaid son raced from work to release the trapped lady. Thereafter said exercise bike was disposed of.

For the third attempt, Grandmother decided to go walking in the snow and cold in early January. Again, the long-suffering son received a phone call from Gran, who had locked the door of her house and, upon her return from walking, couldn't find her key. She moaned that she was freezing on the doorstep. Son again rushed over to the back door in order to aid the stricken woman. When he reached her home Grandma was nowhere to be seen. Son John, for that was his name, spent the next half an hour attempting to pick the lock, all to no avail. He took a break and peered through the window of the house. He was staggered to see Grandma contentedly sitting in a chair drinking a cup of tea. She had found her key and entered through the front door!

The comments of son John are, no doubt, unprintable after this latest escapade. One wonders if Grandma continued with further adventures along the exercise path.

Alex, the Afghan bar waiter in our hotel, has been in Greece for three and a half years. He is a political refugee. He is a slim, lithe young man with a ready appealing smile. When he arrived in Greece he was put in prison for a month and a half. Upon agreeing to be finger printed he was released with no government support. He is now stuck in Greece with residential status but no prospect of receiving nationality status. He cannot travel to any other country. One prison has been exchanged for a larger one. One of the frustrations is that he is an interpreter by profession and can only get seasonal work as a barman. He is bitter about his lot in life. When I asked him about returning to Afghanistan he said that he could never go back.

I asked him if he believed in magic. He said that he did. I told him that I would work magically on his situation.

You must work on it also, I continued.

I then pointed to his head and my heart as though to drive the necessity of joint working into his psyche. I then left the bar, resolving to work on his difficulties at a future date as circumstance allowed it.

The next day, after my talk with Alex I received an intuitive message. I was told that there was a bureaucratic system that could help Alex expand the number of countries that he could travel to and work in. As I told Alex this, more information was added through my intuitive faculty. I repeated this 'channelled' information. I said that it may be possible to bypass the Greek government, which other problems on its mind currently with a financial crisis. An appeal to the European Union representative in Athens could be beneficial to him. Alternatively, it may be possible to find out more information on the internet.

After returning home I told my friends Mary and Joan the story and we meditated on it. In the meditation I received the information that Alex had become stuck in Skiathos because he had a previous life on the island. No doubt there is some recompense or closure to be made as a result of this previous life. Mary was shown a curved pillar of light coming down from the cosmic realms and covering Alex. We took this as a positive sign for the young man.

Two of the wedding celebrants shared the hotel that I was in and had rooms on another floor. The room cleaner on that floor, a slim young woman, had a ready smile and a positive word for the two British ladies. She is an Albanian living with her husband and small child. The two parents struggle to make ends meet in their poorly paid professions. The husband works in a local popular restaurant. There is no work for them in the winter. So they must make enough money in their summer employment to see them through to the next season. It seems such a far cry from the welfare protection of the UK. The two ladies resolved to give the Albanian cleaner a handsome tip at the end of their stay.

Senior family member, Ivy, one of the two ladies mentioned above, hurt her leg and needed medical attention during her stay. A pleasant doctor arrived and dressed Ivy's damaged leg. At the end of the treatment and after the good doctor had departed a strange unexplained incident happened in Ivy's room. The electric light, which had been switched off, was switched on by an unseen hand.

As Ivy told me the strange story she explained that she thought that the unseen hand was that of my mother who had passed into the higher realms some two and a half years before. Ivy thought that my mother was overseeing her treatment. I 'tuned into' her words and picked up the word 'grandmother'. I asked Ivy if her grandmother, also deceased, was taking care of her, or was she playing an overseeing role in her life. Ivy confirmed that, indeed, was the case.

Wedding successfully negotiated, we made our way homeward. I assumed that I was now completely chilled out and relaxed. This was the case until, in my car, we reached the exit barrier of the airport car park. The barrier guard was reluctant to let us pass as he could not find our booking on his computer. This booking had been an ongoing saga since I had made it and paid for it three months before. I found myself raving at him and his company's incompetence. Perhaps because of my aggression in the moment he let us drive out and away. We drove onto the motorway towards our home destination. I calmed again. Within minutes a large four-by-four vehicle towing a caravan cut dangerously in front of me, forcing me to slow the car dramatically. My reaction was immediate and not calm I drove alongside this vehicle and cut inside, doing to him what he had done to me. As I accelerated away from him he flashed his lights. My reaction was immediate and unthinking. My hand moved towards the rear-view mirror in a two-fingered insulting salute. The family member sitting next to me looked piercingly at me. She said nothing but I picked up the mental vibe that she was thinking that she had seen something in me she hadn't seen before. Usually I am calm and laid back.

It is commonly recognised that we will behave in the comfort and security of our car in a way that we wouldn't dare when face to face with another person. Well so much for my chilled out, post-holiday, disposition!

After telling the following story to a fellow course member of the Temple Study Group, of which I am a member, the following day she then told me this.

A friend of hers was about to drive into a parking place in a busy inner-city area. Just then another car did so. The driver of the other car appeared to raise two fingers in her direction, in what appeared to be the aforesaid sign of opprobrium. The slighted friend responded by doing the same with interest. She drove on a little and found another parking place nearby.

As the slighted woman entered a lift a little later she was joined by the man who had beat her to the parking place. He leaned over to her and said, *'Madam, I was trying to tell you that there were two parking places!'*

One of the objects of the Temple Study Group course mentioned above was to work with the energy of the ancestors. My good friend Margaret woke one morning to find that the door of her bedroom had been opened and a woman with an old fashioned hat was staring at her. Margaret screamed for no reason that she could explain except that the vision was such a surprise. The scream was so loud that another course member sleeping elsewhere was woken up by it. The apparition, if that is what it was, disappeared and Margaret attempted, with some difficulty, to return to sleep.

Margaret was convinced that she was not asleep during this strange visitation. Did she see a ghost of her ancestors? Was she imagining the whole thing? Is there some other explanation?

This is from Greeka.com:

> *Skiathos, Greece is a very green island covered by a thick pine forest and considered as a protected environment. It is located between Skopelos and Volosa town. The Greek island of Skiathos is very popular and can get really crowded during July and August by people attracted by the wonderful long and golden beaches of the island which are boarded by trees and have crystal clear waters.*

Cheltenham

Cheltenham first became famous in 1716 when a spring with healing waters was discovered on the site of what is now the Ladies College; a visit of King George III in 1788 confirmed its position as a fashionable spa town.

Friend Julia told me that she had been encouraged to move to live in Cheltenham after her marriage to Ken in 2010. Once Ken's house had been sold in Leeds the couple did indeed move to Cheltenham. Julia's discarnate guidance was absolutely delighted at the couple's move to the city and told Julia so.

Some-time later guidance visited Julia again concerning the subject of Cheltenham. She was informed that the city was the grail cup of this country. This was a bald statement that could mean one of a number of things.

Later Julia developed the theme when explaining the story thus far to me. She said that if you looked down on Cheltenham from one of the high spots around the valley in which Cheltenham nestles then the bowl and the surrounding hills do, indeed, take the shape of a goblet.

I asked Julia to let me know of any further insights that she received on the phenomenon.

The next day I received the following email from Julia.

Concerning the energy that gave you a headache at Lansdown, I was told that this is stuck negative energy and that it was possible to remove it at your sound and healing evening with one of your Rosicrucian chants.

I was also told that Cheltenham would become a sacred place where people would come for 'healing and refreshment.'

They suggested that we could have a meditation where we look down on Cheltenham from a hill or high point and see it as in a deep bowl and that we fill this bowl with the Christ light as in a grail cup.

The 'headache at Lansdown' referred to by Julia happened to me when I was dropping leaflets at two blocks of Georgian flats that partially enclose a park area. During the leaflet drop their began a severe headache that disappeared as soon as I moved away from the area. I sought guidance from my internal resources. I received the impressions that there was a great deal of suppressed energy in the area. There I 'left it' until Julia's above intervention.

Since then Julia received further information about the stuck energy and she was told that it had been caused by witchcraft 'of the worst kind.' Those were a spirit's words, not hers.

She had a feeling they might ask me to go there to eradicate it. If they did, Julia and Ken volunteered to come along. I agreed that they should be there as Julia was the 'lead crazy' on this one. She was receiving the majority of the insights.

The following night I received a download from guidance concerning Julia's point reference Cheltenham as a centre for people's 'rest and refreshment'. I was informed that the waters of Cheltenham would become, once more, a focus for this healing. In the eighteenth century, Cheltenham, like Bath and other centres, was a spa town where mostly wealthy people would come. They would 'take the waters' as a method of healing.

I can't quite get whether the negative energies came and shut the spa healing down or whether these energies were always here and the spa movement thrived in spite of these bad energies. I was further told that we can use the fountain in Montpellier (centre of Cheltenham) as a focus for positive meditation and healing and encouragement of this revitalized healing movement. A mediation group has worked on healing Cheltenham using the fountain as a centre in the past.

This work is in addition to the healing of the negative energies around the flats.

A further email from Julia said:

> *We'll be very happy to come with you re: Lansdown and I was also told that once this area was cleared the people living there would feel much healthier and 'uplifted'. So it looks as though we'll be doing them a big favour. It's funny, Clive, but Kenny and I used to cut through there on our way to town and I never liked the feeling of the place as we passed through. Now we walk to town via the Lansdown Road via Montpelier and I much prefer that.*
>
> *It would be lovely to involve Mary and Joan (two of our meditation friends) as we hold them in high esteem and I'm sure they would add a great deal to what we are trying to achieve.*
>
> *I feel we are being given a great opportunity here to enhance the whole atmosphere of Cheltenham in preparation for the New Age work that is going to go on here.*
>
> *And further, Spirit seems keen for the three of us to go to Lansdown to do a clearing. This could also include friends Mary and Joan, if they wish. It was said that you have a very old and wise Egyptian guide called Alexander who is very successful in helping to clear 'blocked' spaces. It was also said that Cheltenham will become one of the focal points for the new energies, but at the moment is not quite ready to receive it.*
>
> *Plenty for you to think about, Clive! I also tried going on to different websites when I fed in 'History of Witchcraft in Cheltenham'. I feel the period of this happening at Lansdown was the late 1700s but there is quite a lot to read through. However, you may find it interesting.*

The late 1700s for witchcraft involvement would link with the spa era in the town. Perhaps witchcraft did play a part in the decline of the spa movement in Cheltenham.

So, thusly it seemed at the time, the healing of the Lansdown energies was the first priority. Then when the energies lightened we could work on increasing the light through the waters. This would facilitate the town moving towards its destiny of 'healing and refreshment'. There is also the further, perhaps deeper, work connected to the grail cup of England ideal. This may become the more important element as an aid to the evolving consciousness of this 'sceptred isle'.

It is ironic that the original reason that I visited this area was to drop leaflets for a chi gong class that I had planned to start in the Leckhampton area. I had not planned to drop leaflets in that area originally. However, it was friend and neighbour Demelza who suggested it as there was a reasonably large population of younger people who may be interested.

The class did not take off and I was consequently disappointed at this turn of events. Could it be that I was inspired with the Leckhampton class idea in order to bring me to this troubled district? If this was the case then the proposed class was the 'sprat to catch a mackerel'; I being the sprat and the healing need being the mackerel. As Shakespeare once said, 'There are more things in heaven and Earth than are dreamt of in your philosophy, Horatio'. The quote may not be strictly accurate but you get the drift.

On the spur of the moment I decided to visit the area of the Lansdown flats before our intense inner work on the area began. I 'tiled' the area, working anti-clockwise walking around the outside. As I write this I receive an echo of the headache that started this quest off. I take it that the negativity is still in place right now.

I wrote the following concerning tiling in our book *'We're Still Not Alone'*.

Tiling is an old mystic idea. Simply walking around a building, room or area can change the energy inside, for better or worse, retaining and focussing internal energy, keeping out discordant external energies, funnelling in positive ones. The conscious attitude of the tiler is also significant. By using sound, group energy and constant repetition, a standing wave of energy can be built up. The human element is key.

On this occasion I had chanted a protection rune rather than my normal Rosicrucian one. Perhaps I needed this support, given the nature of the resident energies.

Again I felt drawn to work in the area again fairly quickly. I emailed the other two 'spiritual musketeers', suggesting that we work in Lansdown the next day. They both readily agreed.

Before setting out to pick-up Julia and Ken the next day, I did a short meditation. I was immediately taken to a point above the central green area overlooking it. I was shown a top-left to bottom-right and top-right to bottom-left cross dissecting the afflicted area. The ends of the cross finished at the circle of energy that I had created the day before in my tiling.

Puzzled by this unexplained vision I asked Julia for guidance once when I arrived in their flat. She said that I had set up a protection ring before our current work. We drove to the area of our work. Julia's guidance told her that we were to 'tile' the green area only. Ken was to walk clockwise. Julia and I were to 'tile' anti-clockwise. As we walked we were to chant Aum-Ra-Ma-Oom. I had used this powerful mantra on many occasions before. Guidance also informed us that there was a point on the walk where we were to walk past each other. This crossover point was a powerful part of this ceremony of clearing the negative energies.

We began our walk as advised. Julia chanted the mantra out loud as we walked taking care to lower her voice as we passed other people. We didn't want to frighten the good burghers of Lansdown, I, less courageously, repeated the chant silently. We completed the tiling and re-assembled at our start point. There were two points on the walk, stone blocks in the ground, that I thought were significant in some way for our work. On the second one I wanted Julia to put her stick on one of them. She duly did so without me asking. I haven't got a clue why I wanted her to do this.

Once we had joined forces again Julia sensed a lightening of the resident energies. I felt that, once we had come together again, we had drawn a noose around the new energies, which were now securely in place.

One unexpected insight came to me as we pondered on this work before leaving. I was told by guidance that this tiling and healing linked to one I had done at the Washington Monument several years before. The current healing had completed the Washington one.

We then departed back to Julia and Ken's flat for tea and biscuits, much deserved in our view and much appreciated once consumed. As we talked over the repast Julia was guided to say that Ken and I had a life together in the Confederate Army during the American Civil War. Julia also had been connected to Ken. They had a relationship, which resulted in a child being the offspring of their union. Unfortunately, the story did not have a happy ending. Julia was a black slave in that life but Ken was white.

In those less tolerant times they were forced apart. Happily in this life they have a most successful and happy life together.

We parted with the agreement to meet at our usual sound healing session the following Friday. Julia's guidance informed her and she us that a chant for the new energies in Lansdown at that meeting would finish the work. Finally, Julia was reminded that the meditation filling the grail cup that is Cheltenham with the Christ light could be done at our sound group healing.

The day after the clearing work I received an email from Julia that contained the following:

I thought you might be interested to hear further information that I received re the clearing on Lansdown.

When I went to bed I had a clear vision of a rather old fashioned lady. She had a thin white face and thin lips and was wearing an old fashioned white bonnet. I asked my guide who she was and she said it was Alice who was hung on the tree on Lansdown where we did the clearing. Apparently she was a good woman who practiced white magic helping people with her herbs and healing potions. She was only 46 yrs of age when she lost her life. The people who were practising black magic made an example of her by hanging her as she was against their practices. My guide said she wanted to give us heartfelt thanks as she was being held back by the 'stuck' energies but she now felt great relief in being released from the trauma and would now be able to progress and move on in spirit. I also got her surname which was Truman. I said 'how on Earth did I get that?' My guide said it was because I had access to the Akashic records. Ah well – crazier than I thought!!!

And still later another message from Julia.

There have been further developments which I thought I ought to pass on to you.

When we were having our meditation tonight, the lady Alice I told you about came through to thank us for helping her. She said 'You are such beautiful souls – thank you so much.' Apparently Ken and I met up with her in Spirit last night – she took a real shine to Ken!!!! You are meeting her tonight I'm told.

It transpires that the reason she was so traumatised is because the black magic people bound her ankles together and tied her to the tree upside down. They beat her with sticks and set fire to her hair and she was hanging there for five days before she died – poor soul!

She had three brothers and two sisters. The sisters stayed away while the brothers came to help her and brought some water for her. But when the black magic people found out the rounded up her sisters and brothers and stoned them to death.

The brothers and sisters have since reincarnated but Alice has been held back by the trauma. That's why she is so grateful. I'm told she is now receiving counselling from all three of us, so that she will then be able to move on. She has made it clear that she would like the opportunity of carrying on with her healing work in her next reincarnation.

I have one last addition to this saga (it might not be the last, who knows!).

I was told that when we met Alice in our sleep state I asked her if she had any particular close friends from that lifetime and she said she had a really lovely neighbour called Fanny and they had struck up a close friendship. So, with the help of guides they have been reunited and this has made Alice very happy. Fanny was very badly affected by what happened to her friend and suffered severe asthma attacks as a result for the rest of her life. She has since successfully reincarnated but was very happy to be reunited with her dear friend and we feel that she will be very helpful in helping to restore Alice's confidence. Fanny's surname at that time was Byrne, so I'm sure that anyone who is good at tracing old census forms would be able to verify this story.

I'm told that you met up with Alice last night and that it was a very successful meeting. You were quite cheeky and very relaxed with her and she loved it!!!

I'm sure she'll do well now.

I've also been given to understand that the reason Kuthumi (hope I've spelt that right) was with us on the clearing was because of his interest in the animals. The black magic people had made some very cruel animal sacrifices on that green so he wanted to make sure that they were eradicated.

You were also right about souls disintegrating as Spirit told me that this has happened to the eight people involved in these atrocities.

I sent this to Julia:

I have been pondering over the walking ceremony that we did at the green last week.

I wonder why your guidance asked that you and I walk anti-clockwise and Ken clockwise. Normally, when walking on my own, I do three circuits anti-clockwise. This builds a standing wave of energy for the cosmic forces to work on. There has been one variation to this. When working at the Washington Monument I completed a spiral of walking eventually touching the monument at the end.

If you feel it appropriate I would welcome some input on this.

Julia replied:

When I asked about this, what I was given was... That was all that was needed. You did exactly what was asked. 'There was a very powerful presence working with you from within the White Brotherhood and they were able to work very succinctly with this ritual.'

There are Angels in the Detail

This was dictated to me by Spirit and when I asked the source they said it was 'Kuthumi'.

OK, good people. I hope you enjoyed the story of Alice Truman. It was so good working with Julia and Ken. They are such beautiful souls. It is time to move on.

Eccentrics

Stories concerning those not in the 'mainstream'.

It is a long-standing tradition in England that when one reaches a mature age, elements of eccentricity begin to permeate many individuals. I say this because England is the culture with which I am familiar. No doubt the same is true in many other cultures. These changed behaviour patterns are viewed with humour by much of the population. Bizarre, strange and unusual behaviour is accepted from those of a certain age. Part of these changed behaviours can be traced to freedom created by the opportunity to release responsibilities and duties of young and middle age. Employment has been dispensed with. Children have flown the nest. The straitjacket of mundane expectations has been lifted. Perhaps financial resources are available to pursue personal interests and traits long buried in the pursuit of duty. In addition, there is a long-standing tradition of eccentricity among those with inherited money. These are people who never need to pursue the mundane life and are therefore free to express their personalities. Such freedom is a heady brew. Two of the following stories are about people from this group with inherited money. There is a further reason, in my view, for this sometimes quite sudden change in behaviour. There is the change in personal psyche characteristics that is a normal part of the human condition. Around the age of fifty a spontaneous merging of elements of personality can occur, making one a more rounded, balanced person. In this change one questions, reviews and institutes changes in the way the purpose of life is pursued.

Many eccentrics are obsessed or closely interested in their pursuits. I include myself in this category. In addition eccentrics don't care much for the opinion of others when considering their pursuits.

Science has a more 'illness-related' view of eccentricity, which is only partly true in my view.

It seems to me that eccentric behaviour is less evident in younger people. I believe that there is another reason for older people that are of an eccentric disposition to become more so as the years roll by. My experience is that as people become older they care less about what people think about them. Therefore they are less constrained by social norms. They thus feel increasingly able to express themselves in the way that they wish. There are many examples of eccentrics. The following are a few examples from my experience and those of my acquaintance. Eccentric people are less in the mainstream of thought and therefore are more likely to disagree with the existing social paradigms. Therefore, they are less controllable by those that would rule us.

The party was in full swing. Food, drink and conversation were fuelling the enjoyment of the people sat on the wooden decking on a balmy evening. Into this conviviality a shambling figure loomed from the darkness outside. Unshaven was this fifty-something figure, no laces in his ancient suede boots, Hawaiian shirt half hung out of his trousers with midriff in plain view. This was topped off by a jacket that had a number of contacts with wet paint in the past. Mine host introduced Luke to all assembled. An initial reaction would be to feel sorry for this tramp-like figure. Doubts about his true antecedents surfaced in me when Luke spoke in response to the number of 'Good evenings' spoken in his direction. He replied in a mellifluous voice with charm, poise and ease of movement with a voice that was cut glass and out of the top bracket of society. Luke settled himself and proceeded to charm all present with his relaxed conviviality. After a little while mine host whispered in my ear.

'He is a member of the ... family,' mentioning the name of a long established industrial dynasty that was fabulously wealthy. Luke was something of a black sheep, having fallen out with the hierarchy in the dynasty, but nevertheless was sufficiently well funded to live the bohemian existence that he loved. He was also very generous to those around him; a man with a kind heart. Unfortunately, his kindness is, at times, taken advantage of by those that are not of such a generous disposition. A pleasant few hours were spent in his company. We all laughed a lot around him.

Morris is a nondescript man living in an unremarkable house on the Isle of Man. There is nothing obvious in his life to cause comment. There is one feature, however, that is known only to close family and friends: that is he is rich in monetary terms. The only outward demonstration of his wealth passes most people by, unrecognised. He uses a large bar of gold as a doorstop. He views this as being highly amusing because most people do not know what a bar of gold looks like. There has been no attempt to steal it. Do you know what a bar of gold looks like, in the flesh so to speak? Henry, who is mentioned later in this chapter, says that such bars are extremely heavy. When Henry visited a gold mine in South Africa the members of the visiting party were invited to pick up such a bar with one hand. If anyone was successful in picking it up then they could take it away was the offer. What an incredible invitation. Everyone tried but no-one could pick the valuable piece up single handed. So keep your eye on doorsteps when visiting others. Pay particularly attention when paying a call on those that may have a twinkle in their eye as you examine their doorstop!

Friend Mary tells the story of a woman of her acquaintance who lived in a houseboat and regularly walked her dog on the adjacent footpath and fields. There is nothing unusual in that, you may say. However, on her regular forays she would wear, strapped to her back, a pair of angel wings. These were large and consisted of white feathers attached to a metal frame. Apart from this strange behaviour everything else about her life was apparently mundane. None of the other people that she met on her walks ever made any comment about the odd appendage strapped to her back. One could say that those around her were exhibiting a typical English trait. This was the English national character of never making a fuss, whatever the circumstances. In this country there is also the attribute of allowing other people to be what they want to be, decency allowing, as mentioned in the introduction to this chapter. No-one knows, apart from the woman herself, why she wears the wings. Perhaps she talks to the angels on her walks.

My friend Margaret White paid a visit to another member of the Temple Study Group, who took her to the theatre to see a comedy. When Margaret returned home I asked her if she had enjoyed the play. '*Yes it was fine,*' she said. '*The only problem was that I laughed in all the places that the rest of the audience didn't. They laughed in places that I didn't.*'

'*That's absolutely fine, Margaret,*' I replied. '*You are a 'crazy', an eccentric. This is the type of things that eccentrics do.*' She appeared to be content with my comment. At one of our regular Temple Study Group (TSG) meetings, Henry, a man of dry humour, made this comment to Jacques, our esteemed group coordinator, at the end of a particularly valuable esoteric discourse.

'Listening to you, Jacques, is like smoking a "spliff". One feels elevated beyond everyday mundane worries. One feels lighter and at peace with the world!'

Once the laughter died down Jacques replied that that was one of the better compliments that he had received.

John, a fellow member of the TSG, talks of his time growing up in a mining community. His father and uncle both worked at the narrow coalface hacking away at the seam. It was necessary to lie on one's side to perform this backbreaking task. Money in the 1950s was in short supply in the Yorkshire coalfields. An evening meal often consisted of potato and turnip, little else. Life was tough, money available for rent at the end of the week was often insufficient. John speaks of the doctor that served this community, Dr Wainwright. The good doctor would stride into the waiting room to cast his eye over those that were waiting to see him. The genuinely sick and the workshy were all mixed together. The young John was once seated there among the not-so-merry throng of coughers and wheezers when Dr Wainwright arrived. Quickly scanning the well-known faces the doctor picked on one man by pointing his finger at him. *'What are you doing here?'* The imposing figure of the medical man demanded in a loud voice in front of the packed room. *'It's me leg, Doctor,'* the unfortunate man replied. *'There is absolutely nothing wrong with your leg,'* shouted back Dr Wainwright not bothering with the formality of an examination. *'Get back to work.'* With that the disconsolate miner slunk out of the room. I doubt if a modern general practitioner would get away with such a lightning diagnosis in current more patient-focussed times.

On one occasion a triumphant miner turned up at the pit office with a sick note completed by the aforesaid doctor. The man was disgusted when the sick note was rejected; on it the doctor had written 'drunkitis' in the line reserved for ailment description. Another sick claimant arrived at the office triumphantly waving a sick note. This too was rejected as being invalid.

'It says here that you are suffering from "malingeritis",' quoted the pithead clerk.

'If that is what the doctor says I am suffering from then that is what it is,' blustered the claimant. He clearly didn't understand the joke.

Before newspapers became totally the possession of industrial magnates intent on concentrating their editorial policy on narrow lines of ideas, there was room for writers of independently creative mind. HL Mencken was such a one. He wrote uncompromising and challenging articles in the US before World War II that upset many people. In order to minimize the time he spent replying to critical letters he had mimeographed thousands of a standard letter. This was before the age of the photocopier. These were sent out in reply. This is what he wrote. *'I am sitting in the smallest room in the house. I have your letter before me. Soon it will be behind me. Yours, HL Mencken.'*

A friend told me some stories concerning Mavis. A person of domineering personality, she would persuade friends to sit in her bathroom at Christmas singing carols. If this was not bizarre enough, Mavis would bathe naked during this social event. How the friends were persuaded to join in this bizarre ritual is difficult to imagine. One of Mavis's prime items of dress was a pair of Wellington boots. These are rubber boots that are tall enough to reach above the knees. This item of very wet weather apparel would be worn by Mavis on many occasions. Mavis is very fond of classical music concerts. She loved to reserve seats at the front of the auditorium. Invariably arriving late, she would clump her way to the front in her rubber boots, spread her not-inconsiderable bulk over her seat and as much of those seats adjacent to her as she could get away with, and promptly fall asleep. Quite what she enjoyed on these occasions is open to question.

One time it was necessary for her to visit a medical specialist at his surgery. She arrived, with my friend, in one of her usual ancient, voluminous dresses wrapped around her bulk. The whole was topped off by the usual rubber boots. Flopping down on the specialists couch she announced that she was ready for the consultation. The professional person, apparently not used to such a strange apparition, looked over to my friend with a pained, quizzical look on his face. My friend looked back at him. The moment was timeless. Let us say that mutual eyebrows were raised metaphorically! On one famous occasion Mavis was concerned about the possibility of having cancer of the breast in her seventy-year-old body. As she discussed this possibility with my friend she, without further warning, undressed the top part of her body and exposed herself in order to demonstrate her worries. She thrust the most wrinkly and flaccid breast in the direction of my friend to demonstrate her point. My friend later said that it was one of the most revolting sights that she had ever seen. On one occasion Mavis asked my friend to accompany her to a tattooist. My friend baulked at the indignity of watching Mavis having a tattoo on her not-inconsiderably sized rump and declined to go.

My wife, Jaqueline, is not the person most interested in the world of the psyche. So, I was heartened one day when she announced that she would be using her psychic powers. This announcement occurred, one day, when she was experiencing one of her most uncomfortable, but sadly usual, menstruations. I was most heartened by this turnaround in her views of, what many people call, the paranormal. Our subsequent conversation went like this.

'That is wonderful, Jaqueline,' I replied. 'What are you planning to concentrate on? Will it be developing your intuition? Or perhaps you will develop a skill with the tarot cards. Could it be that you will train in past life regression?'

'It will be none of these,' she replied. *'I am planning to give you my menstruation periods!'*

'That's OK, Jaqueline,' I finished the discussion. *'Are you planning to give me the female equipment to go with it?'*

This comment ended the conversation. The difficulty of transferring the relevant female body parts was obviously too big a potential task.

In a previous book we wrote concerning a strange use by Mexican women of their menses in times past. Mystics are aware that menses contain great psychic power. The Mexican women would mix the menses in the food of their men in order to exert psychological power over their menfolk. It is alleged that this substance was so powerful that, if the women overdid it, the men would become zombie like in their behaviour. You need to know this before the next story.

Inevitably menopause began in Jaqueline's body as the years flew by. As she mused on her failing menses, Jaqueline ruminated out loud that maybe she ought to freeze some of the last drops.

'Whatever for?' I made this puzzled response.

She replied, *'So that I have one last potential control over you!'* There was laughter in her voice as she spoke, I was relieved to hear.

Jaqueline has two cacti which she lovingly takes care of, partly, I suspect, as they originate in her beloved Mexico. As the winter grips this part of the country they are transported from the kitchen to the warmer living room. *'This is to help them to survive,'* I commented one day. *'Yes,'* she replied. *'They are also happy to be in company,'* she added: shadows of Prince Charles talking to his plants. This is an idea of which I heartily approve.

As a young woman, Jaqueline started to learn fortune telling using playing cards. One day she was asked by an acquaintance to read the cards for her. Jaqueline sensed that the woman would lose something of value. Two weeks later the son of the woman disappeared for some time. The woman blamed Jaqueline for the disappearance which, of course, was not the case. Jaqueline then abandoned fortune telling as too much hassle for her. One night she was sleeping at my mother's home. She was woken by the weight of a cat jumping on her torso.

'Oh, go away, Harry,' she said sleepily to the cat that had landed on her. She recognised the purr and the weight of the family animal. It wasn't until the following morning that she remembered the incident with a start. Harry, much beloved in the household had, in fact, died some months previously.

Winston Churchill was hosting a dinner for Commonwealth leaders. The chef de protocol quietly went up to Winston during the feast. The chef told the great man that one of the guests had slipped a solid silver salt shaker into his pocket. Churchill did nothing until the meal had finished. He then sidled up to the offender, produced the matching pepper shaker from his pocket and said, *'Perhaps we had both better return these before we are discovered.'*

Many years ago I lived next to an elderly man of Polish nationality. He was a gentle soul and a kind and considerate neighbour. I discovered that he arrived in our country after World War 2 and had settled in my home town. He had the most acquisitive nature. The front and rear gardens of his house were piled high with planks, building materials and bric a brac of all sorts. None of which seemed to be moved or utilised during the years of our neighbourliness. On rubbish collection bin days he would peer into the rubbish bins of all those people that lived in our cul de sac. He would regularly remove items from the bins and add to the piles on his property. Various neighbours would complain among themselves about this bizarre behaviour. However no-one would complain directly to him perhaps because of his inoffensive nature. Only once was I allowed to set foot in his house, in his kitchen, which was sparse and filled with ancient furniture. It looked like something out of the 1930's.

Eventually I discovered that he had been in the Polish army during World War 2 and had been a prisoner of both the Russians and Germans. Perhaps the privations suffered by him resulted in his obsessive collection of mundane and moribund objects. One final interesting fact about this man was that he kept a hedgehog for a pet. He would walk up and down the cul de sac closely followed by the hedgehog.

My friend Mary was walking down a street in London with her friend Eduardo; the name is changed to protect the innocent! Now Eduardo is a monk, very obviously so as he wears a monkish habit. The pair were stopped as they walked by a woman handing out religious tracts.

'Do you believe in God?' The woman asks Eduardo.

Very politely and patiently Eduardo replies, *'Well, actually I do!'*

Doh!

He takes a tract from the woman and the pair march on to the next little adventure. Outside another shop an Iranian woman halts the pair in order to describe the plight of women in Iran. After an initial description the woman asks Eduardo if she can call on him.

'Actually, no. I live in a male-only community with one other man,' replies our friendly monk. Suitably abashed the woman retires and the two walk on. It is almost as though the monkish attire is invisible to certain members of the populace. The visit finishes with the pair embracing with a fairly long hug before Mary leaves for home. As the hug is underway Mary realises that this must be a most bizarre sight as a monk conducts a long embrace with a woman in the street in front of the citizenry of the metropolis.

Henry, one of the long-standing and honoured members of the Temple Study Group, a group of mystical friends, passed to the great initiation beyond the physical. Friends and family were devastated at the loss of this humorous and kindly man. One night about 3am I was wandering around our flat unable to sleep. Suddenly an image of Henry came into my consciousness. He was sitting, very relaxed, one leg crossed over the other smoking the heavenly version of a 'spliff'. During this last incarnation this particular weed he used as a relaxant. His body shape was now slimmer than in the latter part of his physical life. The message was for all those grieving for him to cease doing so, for he was fine. Another of Henry's relaxing pastimes was to garden in the nude. Fortunately, he and his wife lived in a remote spot with no neighbours to be 'surprised' at his natural state.

Finally, friend George told me of two eccentrics with whom he is acquainted. One, a philosophy professor at Oxford University, would conduct tutorials, one-to-one teaching sessions in his university rooms, with a curtain between him and the, no doubt, nonplussed students. He obviously had decided, as far as these sessions were concerned that the professor/student relationship was not to be a personal one. Perhaps the professor's intention was to drive the students' attention into the material being considered in the session. Thus the personality element of the meeting could be considerably reduced. Another professor at a different university would teach sitting beneath his desk, well out of sight of his students! Perhaps he was of the view that teaching was a fine profession if it wasn't for the students!

Healing

Musings on alternative elements of healing

Every human on the planet has the ability to heal themselves, others, our friends in the animal kingdom as well as dissonant energies in the environment. It is one of the gifts of the gods when we were created. Some people are more aware of this gift than others. Some have worked at developing this talent more than others. Nevertheless, we are all capable of performing healing. It is one of our inalienable rights that those that wish to rule us have attempted to steal from us. When we gather together in groups the healing power is increased many times.

There is nothing in this third-dimensional reality that cannot be healed given the right intentions of healers and those seeking and open to healing. All that is necessary is right intention, a good heart, an environment that is conducive and the cooperation of the universe. The method is secondary. There are very powerful modalities of healing. Try one that suits you. They all have value. I have written before of a friend who is a very skilled Reiki healer, of which more following. The most important point about her is her focussed compassion and self-belief. These are the creative forces behind her healing power. Give healing a try. You may be amazed at the results.

I have had the good fortune of giving and receiving healing through the medium of Reiki. In its present form this spiritual healing mode began in Japan in the nineteenth century. There are those that claim it is much more ancient than that and originated in Earth's deepest past. Some claim that this technique was taught in ancient Lemuria to all that wished to partake in its genius. Thus the

Japanese emergence was a re-discovery of Reiki as a gift to Earth and its inhabitants sorely in need of it.

I employ a system where the person receiving the treatment sits in a chair, although many practitioners encourage their clients to lie down on a bench-type healing table. Reiki can be a 'hands-on' system but, personally, I do not touch those receiving the healing in the normal course of events. Occasionally I may place my hands gently on the recipient's shoulder if I am encouraged to do so by the spiritual forces. I do not believe touch to be entirely necessary as the energies transmitted do so through the atmosphere and the recipient's aura as well as through matter. However, I am not against the use of touch. We all have our own methods.

One time I was giving healing to a neighbour's mother. The next day the neighbour told the story of a problem she was having with her television. A satellite company had been attempting to send a signal to her TV in order to activate certain satellite channels. For more than twenty-four hours the signal had been sent on a number of occasions without success. After the Reiki healing the additional channels worked with no problem and without further intervention from the TV satellite company. This, obviously, had not been the purpose of the healing session. We, those that had been present at the healing, were amazed at this unexpected happening. So can such healing work on supposedly inanimate objects or is there another explanation? During the course of healings on Jeanne, the neighbour's mum, I was inspired to include the chi gong routine called 'bone marrow clearing'. The purpose of this routine is to speed up the healthy production of blood in the bone marrow. I felt drawn to request that she perform the routine every day that she had sufficient energy. A few weeks later Jeanne recounted a comment made to her by a specialist doctor. He said, '*I am concerned that one of the drugs we are giving you will severely affect your blood-making capacity in the bone marrow. We will need to monitor it!*' So sometimes healing can anticipate the healing needs of the body as well as treat existing conditions.

During a subsequent healing session with Jeanne there was a break for relaxation. Jeanne said to me, *'My father turned up and spoke to me during that meditation.'* (The father had long since passed to the higher realms.)

I asked, *'Has he spoken to you before, since passing?'*

'Nope,' replied Jan.

'What did he say?' Jeanne really had my interest by this time.

'That girl (referring to Jeanne's daughter, Demelza, sweating and pushing the lawnmower outside) *is cutting the lawn all wrong!'* So humour is a factor in the higher realms as well as in this mundane reality.

After the above television event my refrigerator broke down. It came into my consciousness to perform a Reiki healing on the ailing machine. I did so, and the machine resumed normal working and was still doing so weeks later. Later still I could not start my car one day. Various attempts at generating assistance were somehow blocked. Mystified I sat in the driver's seat wondering about this issue until the thought came into his head to try Reiki. This I did. The car started first time after this intervention! Thus healing mechanical items is no less successful than healing people. One time I was asked to perform a healing on the dog of a friend. The animal was lying on one side as I approached it. I was in some trepidation as I had never worked on any biological being other than a human. For some minutes I worked in my accustomed fashion, at the end of which I stood up, looking down at the dog. The latter's response was to look up at me as though to ask *'Have you finished?'* Incredibly, the dog then turned over and presented its other side to the astonished healer and assembled family. Who said animals are dumb?

Another story concerns Demelza, my neighbour mentioned above. One evening Demelza and I were discussing the vegetable garden, which the latter lovingly tends and which is adjacent to the block of flats where we both live.

'Could I ask a special favour concerning the leeks, which are struggling to establish themselves?' Demelza said.

I thought, *she must be asking me to perform a healing, perhaps a Reiki session on the drooping vegetables.* My ego started to expand.

Demelza continued. *'In the north of the country, in such a situation, men are asked to urinate on this crop in order to give them a boost!'*

I laughed out loud, closely followed by Demelza as the bizarre image of such a treatment to the suffering vegetables hit home. I did agree to this strange proposal; my amusement fuelling the agreement. In fact, I never needed to perform this, to me, bizarre ritual. Still, what do I know? Perhaps there are chemicals in the urine that are beneficial to such vegetables.

This story reminded me of the strange healing process of drinking one's own urine. I knew someone who indulged in this practice and was an enthusiast of its benefits. Fortunately, she did not do so in my presence. My social conditioning gives me the feeling of abhorrence concerning this practice. Is this a response through my buttoned-up, slightly repressed psyche?

As I said in the introduction, it is my view that the healing mode or mechanism is of no greater importance than the sensitivity of the healer. All humans possess the ability to heal. Most do not bother to develop abilities in this direction, although the trend is for more people to do so as allopathic methods are not always successful. Such healing can be of a very simple process. If asked to help by a distressed or sick person by simply sending them love and compassion, then much can be achieved. Nothing needs to be said. There need be no complicated training or ceremony. Keep it simple and practice on yourself. You can 'programme' yourself into better health.

Ram Dass, the lecturer and follower of Eastern mysticism, said that he worked with people about to die in India. He did this by simply sitting next to them and working on himself. Oftentimes the people dying would be very distressed and uncomfortable. Ram Dass said that as he worked on himself the sick person would gradually become more relaxed and would cease from fighting their approaching passing into another realm. We are, after all, conscious beings whose consciousness is as large as the universe. This is an amazing view but gives one a great sense of freedom. So if we are working on ourselves in a positive way we are working on the whole universe. Thus we are also working on all other beings in the universe. This is the most profound truth. If this was taught in the schools, universities and medical schools, can you imagine the society that could flow from this approach?

Readers may recall the story of a healing which I was involved with in one of our previous books. Many phenomena manifested during and after the healings in those events. One of which was the blowing of fuses in electrical equipment, bizarrely not replicated by fuse box switches during healing sessions. So this is another example of how the healing energies can have a profound effect on supposedly inanimate objects.

So, do we need outside intervention for our healing?

There are those that claim laughter is great for healing. Indeed claims have been made for recovery from serious illness facilitated by laughter. I always feel better after a good belly laugh. This potential healing seems to be ignored by western medicine. Perhaps laughter can release endorphins. Endorphins are chemicals produced naturally by the nervous system to cope with pain or stress. They are often called "feel-good" chemicals because they can act as a pain reliever and happiness booster. This certainly will assist our general demeanour which must play an important part in our overall health. It seems to me that many humans become conditioned and affected by bad news put out by media and other sources.

When travelling in the southern desert states of US I was always pleased to breakfast in roadside cafes. Locals would enter with a cheery "good morning, how are you?" To be met with "I'm good, how are you?" These simple conversations always cheered me on my often solitary travels across this vast country. Upon leaving I invariably felt lifted in spirits as a result of the bonhomie. I am convinced that this contributed to my good health on these trips.

The setting was pleasant, the company convivial. The people

gathered around the pub table enjoyed each other's conversation and company. The subject under discussion turned to healing.

'We have had great success healing cancer and other serious illnesses,' said a friend of the work that he and his partner were doing in Switzerland and Germany. *'It is essential that the people we treat pay so that they value the work that is being done. It must be a significant amount.'*

Demelza spoke of the work that I was doing with her mum, Jeanne, who had liver cancer. The above friend offered his services to work on Jeanne. Dermelza, however, said that Jeanne was perfectly happy working with me. The friend attempted to persuade me to charge significant amounts of money for my services. Although I could see the argument that people appreciate that which they pay for in some measure, I baulked at making a large charge. It is not in my nature and I am not on the breadline. As a teacher of chi gong and tai chi I had charged my clients. This had been a business for me but the healing wasn't one.

'It is important to work intensely,' continued the friend. I could certainly see intensity as a powerful way of imparting healing to those that have a serious condition. I decided to work on the ideas that the friend had been advocating through my meditations. This I did, asking guidance in order to proceed with Jeanne's healing in a more effective manner. The following is the message that I received.

The presence of Demelza was significant at the meeting in the pub. This was not only because without her the discussion of her mum's health would not have gained significance, but because of her profession as a lawyer and thus the contractual nature of such a role.

In your dimension of reality the healer/healed relationship could be perceived as a contractual one. The two parties enter into an agreement for a planned outcome. In our reality the healing relationship is much more one of a cycle of energy passing between the healer (from cosmic sources) to the recipient and a payment of some sort completing the reciprocal arrangement back to the healer. This arrangement is perfect for your friend and his partner because this is their livelihood. You on the other hand require a different cyclical arrangement. Have we not always taken care of your material needs? (I had to agree that this was true.) In order to create a perfect cyclical arrangement for your healing work you will need to find a process whereby the recipient of your healing makes a payment, but this payment must not be to you. If you take the money from this transaction then the cycle of energy will be interfered with. The recipient of your healing should, themselves, decide the amount to be given, but you decide the needy receiver of the money.

So this was the message that I received. I had already decided to work in a more concentrated manner, so the above message gave me the other part of the revised healing arrangement. I quickly decided that the recipient of the money should be a family in Mexico, two of whose members had been outrageously imprisoned for a murder that they did not commit.

The following weekend I rang Jeanne, advising her that I believed our weekend sessions were 'sticking plaster' sessions which made her feel good about herself but was not reaching the root of her health issue. I proposed that she return to Cheltenham to allow us to work together twice a day for seven days. I also proposed that she paid a donation to Jaqueline that would be passed to the suffering Mexican family for essential costs.

After talking the idea over with her family Jeanne rang the next day agreeing to my proposal and asking to begin the healing at the beginning of the next week. So this work was begun and continued for some months. We worked together for the whole week proposed earlier. Jeanne then returned to her Oxford home with the promise of absent healing from me during the interim two weeks. She took with her an audio recorder with details of two of the healing modalities that we worked with. Thus she could progress her own healing.

Jeanne continued to take her chemotherapy medication during our work together. She was of the view that the conventional allopathic medicine would work side by side with the alternative methods that

I employed. We agreed that she would return for a further weekend of work at the end of the two weeks. One further twist to the cycle of energy occurred when Jaqueline told her mother about the healing arrangement. The latter said that she would add her healing energy and that she would ask the woman wrongly imprisoned to pray also. Both mexican women, Jaqueline's mother and the wrongly imprisoned woman, are powerful manipulators of energy. Thus prayer and healing energy is returning to Jeanne in response to the money energy transferred to Mexico.

Later the woman and her two sons were convicted of the murder and given seventy years each in prison. The injustice of it burned me up for days. I was upset until a friend told me that this was my reaction and that I was being confronted with this situation by the cosmic as a test. There was no way that I could judge the true reason karmically for this apparent unjustified incarceration. After this advice I calmed down and worked on ways that I could practically assist the family without undue interference.

When speaking with the above friend further on the matter of Jeanne's healing I told him of her enthusiasm to follow a twin track approach to her healing. She would continue with the chemotherapy and, at the same time, work with me with meditation, Reiki and chi gong modalities. When he heard that she would continue with the chemo he said, '*You will lose her*.' I was aghast at this bald statement.

'*Why?*' I asked.

'*Because the chemo is breaking down her immune system and what you are doing is attempting to build the immune system up. The two systems are working against each other*.' I argued that she believed and was motivated by the belief that both systems were developing her healing. Jeanne passed to the higher realms early after a most enjoyable Christmas with her family and a visit from her brother, who lives in Canada. She passed quietly after her ferocious battle with the 'big C'. She told the nurse looking after her that she was ready to die one morning and she passed to the higher realms within hours.

Her daughter, Demelza, subsequently told me that the healing given to her during our sessions had improved the quality of life during her final months. It had also given her a sense of personal empowerment in her self-healing. It did improve the quality of her life. Demelza, although tearful at times, did not feel separated from her mum. Memories of the experiences they shared were always available and a sense of proximity remained after the passing for Demelza. I tuned in after the passing to my guidance. I was shown, much to my surprise, winged cherubs flying in the higher realms. Jeanne had always had a great affinity to babies. I took this as a sign that she was being well looked after.

During a Reiki healing that I gave to Audrey one time, Faye saw purple rays descending to my body. This is interesting as Reiki healing is an attunement process attracted to and moving through the healer into the aura and body of the recipient.

As part of my preparation for a healing session I usually play my Tibetan bowl. It really is a musical instrument that has a spiritual perspective. People that are in the room during the playing invariably comment that they feel the vibrations being raised. One of the most amazing elements for me as a result of this instrument is that the bowl rarely produces the same sounds. Sometimes it sounds loud. At other times it is quiet. Sometimes the sound is soft, sometimes strong. Often, in the middle of the playing, the note will change from high note to low for no apparent external reason. As I stand and play often there is the vision of Tibetan monks sat in meditation, enjoying the sacred vibrations of the bowl. A friend says that these sacred instruments can be hundreds of years old. They are frequently made for particular individuals.

The tone of a singing bowl improves with age it is alleged. This is certainly true of my bowl; the sound of which has deepened and strengthened over the 30 years of its use by me. I use my bowl either by striking it on the outside with a wooden piece or I rub the rim of the bowl continuously around it which creates the most extraordinary vibrating sound. Besides its use in healing I also use it as a means of enhancing meditation practice.

There are times when an insight will help someone heal themselves. My great friendship with Audrey and our like-minded approach to reality ensures fertile ground for mutual assistance. One time Audrey was suffering from the sudden onset of a pain in her side for no apparent cause. As she told me about the condition I had an insight that the painful condition emanated from a non-physical cause. '*I sense intuitively that your discomfort has an origin in your past. Someone or a number of persons have given you mental or emotional hurt. This has now filtered through to a physical condition,*' I told her.

She replied that she would meditate on my words. A little later she called me to say that she had a message from her guidance on this matter. '*You must stop bending over backwards,*' it told her. In other words, do not be so accommodating of other peoples' needs to her detriment.

I wonder if negative emotions can be responsible for illness as well as lowering our spirit. Some psychologists believe that depression is suppressed anger. Freud claimed that depression was anger directed inward to one's own self.

We wrote this in our first book '*So You Think We're Alone*'.

> *One evening, while all were squashed in the van, Birch was feeling particularly negative. He had insect bites on his body and swollen arm from a particularly voracious insect; 'Montezuma's revenge', and he felt sorry for himself. This was not a good time. Birch must have been complaining, for Cynthia's voice suddenly cut in, upbraiding him for being negative and encouraged him to be more positive. Birch took the advice and, guess what? The difference in his attitude made him feel much better. Sometimes a true friend is someone* who sees a bigger picture around us and then lets the rest of us in on the secret.

Some authorities claim that the placebo effect is important in the use of anti-depressants. It is not that the drugs don't work but indicates how important the mind is in healing. Meditation which is a mindful activity is also claimed to be most beneficial in healing.

A placebo can be described as a substance that has no healing effect or as a measure to placate someone. The medical fraternity use placebo as a control in testing new drugs.

MRI scans taken of people on Prozac show the same changes when they were given placebo but thought that it was Prozac. A similar observation was made with people suffering from Parkinsons disease.

So structured healing idea is in opposition to the Reiki idea of channelling energy to the person through chakras or energy interfaces of the body and allowing the body consciousness to direct the healing where it is most needed. 'You pays yer money and takes yer choice!'

It could be argued that the mind, must see the body being healed; it must hold the image of the body being completely healed and healthy, with nothing wrong at all. And it must know for certain that this healing is either taking place now or will some time later. Do you accept an instantaneous healing or does your belief pattern need more time? This knowing is essential, but still is not enough.

Next the emotional body must become involved. One must feel the emotion of what it will be like to be completely healthy, no more illness. You must actually feel the emotion and not just have your mind thinking it is feeling the emotion. This is a difficult part, but without the emotional body involved, nothing will happen.

One morning I am relaxing in the garden enjoying working through chi gong and tai chi routines. As I relax into the moves I hear the click-click of high heels on the path nearby. I look round to see the smiling face of neighbour Demelza. *'My car won't start. Will you Reiki it for me.'* She turns and disappears before my words, *'I will do my best,'* are out of my mouth. Relaxing exercises finished I move over to the non-starting vehicle and go through my Reiki routine. As I proceed I receive the strong message, *'Demelza should rest more or her health will break down.'* This was quite a surprise for me as my thoughts were on the car. I finish and wait for Demelza's return. Upon her return she tries to start the car but the battery sounded flat. So the Reiki did not cure that then. However, the message to rest more and take a break from work and family pressures resonated with Demelza. She decided to holiday and immediately felt better physically once the decision was taken. So, perhaps the car fault and my involvement physically had more to do with Demelza taking care of herself as much as it did about taking care of the car.

I have written elsewhere that I believe in the holographic nature of humanity. In every cell of our body is contained the sum and potential of the whole body. Stem cell research, within allopathic medicine, is inching gradually to that realisation. Such cells can be encouraged to grow many other types of cells within the body. The following two stories take this idea further.

Brain scientist Karl Pribram suggests that the entire human body is like a hologram, every part of it storing memory; this is not so different from the ninja concept of tai sabaki, the truth of the body. In Pribram's experiments, rats were taught to run mazes. Then they had the memory centres of their brains removed. Remarkably, however, they could still remember their way around the maze. Their bodies remembered. It is the body, not the brain, that remembers.

When a PhD student was referred to Professor John Lober at Sheffield University he examined the student and found he had an IQ of 126 (which is pretty good). He also had a first-class mathematics degree. In his intellectual and physical appearance he was first rate. A brain scan revealed he had no brain. His cranium was filled with cerebrospinal fluid and his cortex was one millimeter thick. A normal thickness is four point five centimeters. So where was all that intelligence located?

So does disharmony cause disease? It could be argued that if we return to a life of balance, healing follows. When something or someone is aligned with its own inner or outer nature as well as the natural world, a state of harmony is created. This is a state of balance that can be achieved through our own efforts, those of healers that we are drawn to work with and healing effects that reach us from the cosmic realms.

As we increase in awareness, new forms of healing present themselves to us. Recently I have been working with my personal Merkabah. One way of looking at the Mekabah is as an energy form surrounding our bodies as two tetrahedra joined together. One of the figures points up and one points down, making the Merkabah. Early one morning I was consciously working with my Merkabah, visualising its structure and its rotational movement. In this instance the movement was anti-clockwise. Immediately I was confronted with an image of a large metal chute, pointing downwards, out of which flowed a bubbling, viscous brown liquid the colour of gravy. After a period of reflection on this image I took it to mean that certain physical or psychic impurities were being rejected from my being. A further realisation was that it was the rotating Merkabah that had created this healing effect.

There is one downside to this healing. Generally speaking, once we begin the process of surfacing the inharmonious elements of energy, then the likelihood is that we will feel quite poorly. Until they are cleared our bodies will reflect the impurities in them. My own experience is of feeling as though I have been dragged through a hedge backwards for some considerable time until the impurities are cleared.

I worked with this Merkabah energy format for some time and then moved on to other projects. However the universe had not finishes with me in this regard. I was prompted to work with friend Sean some time later creating a revised Merkabah form that grew out of our joint meditations. In this revised version we perceived the Merkabah as globular structure that resonated at a particular vibratory rate. The genius nature of this form was that we perceived that each person has a unique Merkabah all vibrating at different rates. One of the mind blowing pieces of information that we were given by the universal forces in our meditations was that each Merkabah was as large as the universe itself. The reason that billions or trillions of Merkabahs can exist concurrently is because of their differing vibrational rates.

In addition we were told that each Merkabah is tied to the human body. How that changes when we pass over to other realms of existence is unknown to us at this time. This globular Merkabah is tied to each human through lines of force. Each time we meet to work with the Merkabah, we re-inforce it's nature as part of our attunement. Sean and I have been blessed with this opportunity to work on, what we consider a sacred task. The energy perceived when in these attunements is phenomenal. One time we were given an extra blessing with the arrival of what we were told as the Jesus energy. These are ongoing meditations which change and develop over time. I believe that I have been prompted to give this information at this time to others who are looking for a spiritual attunement with Merkabah. This is our and the spiritual universes present to spiritually awake individuals. Treat this with respect and humility. It is a great gift.

In *How Your Mind Can Heal Your Body,* by David Hamilton, the author works in a similar way to my perspective of healing. He writes of a quantum field healing visualisation. In this process the person wishing to heal themselves visualises the body part or organ, then imagines going inside to perceive the bones, muscle, flesh tendons and joints. The visualising person then goes inside to the cells. The cells, DNA and atoms are perceived as far down the scale as the subatomic particles – protons, neutrons, electrons and others. These particles are part of a quantum field. Then the healer works with a further visualisation and mental affirmation technique to complete the healing. For me this is interesting but I feel it is not necessary to go into such scientific detail. I stop at the level of the cell and the DNA.

Mary Fitzgerald heard of a woman, aged forty, who had died as a result of a motorcycle accident. She had a successful career as a nurse but had become disenchanted. She had become fed up with what she described as being a pill dispenser. In her experience her job had ceased to be a healing one. She had decided that she was going to train as an alternative therapist. Within a very short time of the decision the accident occurred. This eliminated the possibility of conducting healing work in this three-dimensional reality. Mary was of the opinion that the nurse had decided, perhaps at the level of the higher self, her healing work would be from the spiritual realms.

The nurse's friend who had told Mary of the death asked our group (which consists of Mary, Joan and me) to make contact with the dead nurse. This communication was in order for the grieving friends and relatives to receive a message from the suddenly departed; this the trio did at one of our regular weekly meditations. During the healing routine there was an unusual message. I received a contact from my father. My father informed me that he was part of a healing group in the spiritual realms. As the meditation proceeded it was clear that the nurse would be joining the group that my father was part of. However, first of all there was the matter of becoming acclimatised to the new reality that she found herself in. She did send a message through the group. She asked her friends and family to celebrate her life and not to grieve too long and too deeply. The vibrations of grief would tend to pull her back towards the three-dimensional reality that she had just left. This would not be helpful to her now. She said that she was very happy in her new reality.

The dividing line between healing and protection work can become blurred. A friend of Mary's was having difficulty coping with a predatory person who was draining her energy. The reason for this was partly because the friend was quite young, whereas the predatory person was a mature experienced person. The friend of Mary's was consequently having some difficulty with her health. In meditation our group of three visualised a set of mirrors around the friend that were psychically active. These mirrors reflected back to any sender negative, draining and predatory energies. In addition the trio requested that Michael (the discarnate being that has a protective role for humanity) slice through any psychic links and hooks that the predator had attached. During the same meditation I saw a stream of cosmic healing energy enter the friend through the top of her head, nurturing and energising. In a final vision Mary saw a bizarre image of a small Tamworth pig moving around the scene, eating up the negative energies that had consequently fallen to the floor around the friend. Who said that the energies of the universe are not humorous?

This reflective mirrors visualisation is an extremely powerful tool and must be used sparingly and for purposes of the light. A recent problem arose with a jealous person who was attacking, let us call her, Phoebe. The latter was suffering some physical illness as a result. The trio, in meditation, placed psychic mirrors around the poisoning person with the reflective surfaces facing inward. Thus the jealous negative thoughts were reflected back. There the three left this matter until, through various sources, information concerning the jealous person was fed back to them. The latter began to have some problems. First she left her purse on a bus then her cat went missing. Secondly she lost her handbag with all her credit cards and valued personal possessions and could not retrieve it. Thirdly her cat, her only household companion, decided to leave permanently. The jealous person had a reputation for being mean with money, so she was being hit where it hurt most. For me this was a most sobering series of events and made me realise even more the need for care and for a total heart-centred approach when working with these powerful techniques.

Usually I am open to the promptings that arrive in my consciousness from higher awareness, occasionally I am not. The following adventure began from the latter. One time in meditation I received a mouth organ on the chair next to me. This was a psychic vision rather than a physical one although all aspects of the chair in meditation were the same as waking consciousness.

After the meditation I thought "strange, why would a musical instrument be shown to me in meditation". It was located on its own with no prompting. As is my wont I forgot all about it and returned to mundane existence. Later higher consciousness, through my intuition whispered to me.

"This appearance of the mouth organ was no accident. We would like you to start a group that works with sound".

"Nah, I replied. "Not interested. I know nothing about working with sound technique. It's not my thing". There I left it again. However higher consciousness did not give up. The whisperings continued which I continued to ignore until one day the source of these promptings woke me up at 3am in the morning and almost bellowed in my ear that I should listen and start this group. Being disturbed in that part of the night was not a pleasant experience I can tell you.

"OK, I get it. I will do what you ask."

With that I settled back to sleep. The next morning in the cold light of day I ran through, mentally, the practicalities of such an adventure.

I said mentally to my guides "OK but I don't know what to do. I have no musical or sound appreciation connected to healing or meditation. Also I don't know anyone who would be interested in such a group or even which type of venue would be appropriate."

There I left it again hoping that I could kill the idea stone dead with my negative barriers. A few days later I was trolling through the internet with no particular objective in mind when suddenly, out of the blue, I was presented with a post which gave a technique for healing with sound.

"Thanks guys", I intuited to my guidance, "but who am I going to recruit to such a project", immediately nine names popped into my head. Some of whom were meditators with whom I had worked for some time but had no interest in working with sound as far as I was aware. A number were meditators that I had worked with in the past but had lost touch with. The final group were people that I knew but, as far as I was aware, had no interest in spiritual work at all.

"You must be joking," was my comment to guidance. "They won't be interested. They won't come." Guidance ignored this element of my negativity and instead said, "run the group in your flat."

I left it for a couple of days and then began to call those proposed members and asked if they would attend an inaugural meeting to work with sound healing. I was staggered to discover that they all agreed to attend! So an initial meeting was arranged.

For the reader the technique that I was given from the Internet was one where the group chanted the name of the person requesting healing. For example if the person's name was Margaret then the chant would be MAAAR ... GAAAR ... ET repeated a number of times.

So this disparate group gathered in our flat, wife Jaqueline included, and began its work.

Many interesting vibrational experiences were commented on. Friend Peter perceived beings shaped as humans in the room after the session had been going for some time. He saw the beings as grey shapes. At one point a white angel emerged from the beings and stood in front of Joan. After a while the beings attached themselves to individuals in the group. No-one was left out from this benign attachment. Subsequently and after the session Julia received the following:

> *The spirits that were with us called themselves'God's helpers'. They explained that they came from all walks of life and some are companions from past lives. They said that anyone who is committed to sending out or anchoring the light for the new age has each been assigned TWELVE extra helpers to aid a smooth transition. They couldn't all come last night but said if you are agreeable they will take it in turns to work with us and it is up to us to decide what we would like to work on. They said that they had used a great deal of the power to take to Peru, where there is a great need, but this was a mystery to me, as I know very little about what is going on in Peru. Maybe you out there will be able to throw some light on this!*

My perception on Julia's insight was that the transfer of power to Peru was connected to the alleged relocation of the Earth's kundalini from Tibet to Peru. The spirits used the power, I felt, in order aid the transfer in a balanced and harmonious way. There was a danger that the transfer would create conditions favourable to earthquake and volcanic activity. The spirits would use the energies in order to ameliorate these possibilities.

The work gradually expanded as many of those that requested healing reported back on improvements to their health. Today 8 years later the group still meets. That is when lockdown allows. There is always a good social element to these meetings with tea, cakes and biscuits enjoyably consumed after each session. This socialising is mixed with much laughter and enjoyable conversation.

We, who have been part of this project believe that a number of participants of a group magnify and concentrate the positive effects. The group began by healing themselves individually concentrating on each person at a time. Many times, those being concentrated on could feel the effects immediately as well as in the longer term. Over time people outside the group were worked on through the technique, again with great success. We are not singers or musicians so the tone is as we can manage. I believe that our intent is a key component. I also believe that chanting a name is extremely powerful not only for humans but any animal nature can be thus positively affected.

In a further discussion with Mary before the sound group met for a second time she commented on the tone of the chanting that had been conducted for each individual. For all except me the tone had been a singular one, which had resulted in a number of interesting personal experiences. These experiences were by the person passively receiving the chanting of their name from the combined voices of the other members of the group. When my turn came to receive the energy of my name, Julia led a chant which was a double tone as distinct from the single tone of the other chants. My psychic impression during this chant was that I was being called. This took me back to childhood when a next-door neighbour would call out to me from the other side of her fence.

An interesting addition to the above neighbour calling me over the fence occurred one evening in my childhood. The two other people living in the house at the same time as me heard the call. I ran out to see who was there. There was no one. Once in the garden I suddenly felt fear and ran back inside for comfort. My mother and her companion felt the same fear. We remembered that the neighbour had died some months before. Was she calling me for the last time from the realm that she was now living in?

We've seen that we can sing vowels, consonants and even people's names. But probably the most effective form of chanting is with mantras, considered by every religion to be holy sounds that will bring us closer to the creator or creative force, or expand our consciousness.

I was asked to work with a lady who was being dominated by another woman, to give her healing and psychic help. This is what I did.

In meditation it was suggested that I first work with the lady's higher self. This I tuned into. I was asked intuitively to pass a message on to the lady that she should work with her higher self. This was the message. This part of her being is attempting to develop her sensitivity to psychic and other conditions around her. The higher self will guide her towards wisdom the more that she contacts it. In addition, I was asked to send her some energy that would strengthen the protective power of her aura to rebuff psychic attack.

This is a variation on an exercise that I use regularly. Over many years I have found it to be of great benefit.

When you have time and no distractions, sit comfortably and quietly close your eyes and relax. Breathe deeply. If any thoughts come, let them come and let them go. With your mind's eye visualise the cells of your toes, the cells of flesh, bones, blood. Now with conscious will fill each cell with love, life and light. See the cells become brighter, more energised, increasing in light intensity, life and love. Feel the physical effects of the change. Take your time.

Move your consciousness to your feet and repeat the exercise. Continue the exercise, moving your consciousness to each part of your body. Try following this list ... ankles, fingers, throat and neck, lower legs, hands, lower jaw, knees, wrists, teeth, upper legs, lower arms, upper jaw, abdomen and hips, elbows, cheekbones, rib cage, spleen, upper arms, nose, eyes, liver and kidneys, shoulders, forehead, lungs and heart, back, scalp, thymus gland, spine, brain and finally, the interlocking bones of the skull.

Now take a mental step back. See the whole of your body vibrating to this new energy. Feel a surge of energy, lightness, running through your being. Feel your blocks and stuck energy being moved out and away. Relax and stay with the feeling. Gradually return to normal consciousness. This completes the meditation.

This takes a lot of concentration and effort. However, performed regularly and with commitment it will have a profound and positive effect on your health.

A recent insight gave me a vision of dolphins swimming around each other, over and under. My intuition told me that this was a healing movement as well as a form of communication. It was, also, a metaphoric image of the value of a certain movement that can be used by humans in their self-healing. First, I was informed of the blocking nature of powerful medication taken when one is sick. Of course if one is really ill then these medications will contribute to us feeling better very quickly. However, the tendencies of these medications are to block and suppress the externalisation of the negative energies, which are the cause of our feeling so poorly. At some point those negative energies will need to be cleared from our systems. We could ask our higher self or the creator, whatever you perceive the spiritual source to be, to assist in the elimination of these negative energies from within the body.

Because our previous illness caused a crisis in our bodies such that the negative poisons were externalised faster than we could cope, we resorted to allopathic medical health. This time we could ask the higher self to eliminate the poisons from our bodies in a slower way. This could be accomplished, if we asked, while we are asleep or when we are relaxing away from domestic and employment pressures. We could take leave and set up our life, for a period of time, in order for this to be allowed to happen. Often we put our illnesses on hold, blocking their manifestation because we are 'too busy'. This is all well and fine, however, it is important for us to be aware that the blocked disease will explode into our beings at some point if the blockage continues for some time. We can manage our recovery in a controlled way.

We will now return to the insight concerning movement mentioned two paragraphs ago. Thank you for staying with me. I was shown, in my insight immediately after the cavorting dolphins, dervishes performing their whirling dance. Now, the interesting point about this image is that this movement, also, was related to our potential self-healing. The whirling, you may have seen it on TV, is done slowly, rhythmically and at an even pace. All parts of the movement are significant in my view. The movement, in its healing mode, is done clockwise because this externalises the negative energies in a regulated way. The arms are outstretched, hands at abdomen or waist height. The hands are pointing away from the body. The hands and arms are significant in this movement. They are the antennae through which the energies are transmitted as well as outward through the aura. This is not a routine that will bring magical results after two or three attempts. Properly utilised it would need to be performed regularly. In this way the worst effects of illnesses can be minimized. The whirling works similarly to chi gong, a subtle movement system for health and fitness. I have discussed this system at length elsewhere in my writings.

I remember an exercise, some years ago, proposed by the Pleiadian channel Barbara Marciniak. In this exercise one whirled anti-clockwise thirty-three times in order to increase the spiritual energies that could be accessed. I tried doing it every time for some weeks but it didn't work for me; 'Diffrn't strokes for diffrn't folks.'

I was discussing healing at a friend's house one day with a number of people. One of those present was claiming that there was no necessity, any more, to use this method or that system to transfer healing energies. She further claimed that it was necessary only to sit with the correct focussed attention and the healing would take place. I thought about this and was vaguely uncomfortable with the premise as a 'catch-all' for performing healing. The next day I asked my guidance about this idea. This is what came back.

There is no one way of performing healing. No single way is superior to another. As Louise (a meditator friend) put it a few weeks ago, you are all in a matrix of consciousness. No one being or method or consciousness is superior to another. There are as many ways as there are humans interacting with each other in order to transfer healing vibrations. The trick is to find the way that suits each individual. Some people will respond to a particular mode of energy transfer and not to others. Be aware that what is happening is the setting up of a resonance between so-called healer and so-called recipient.

When a healing is performed between healer and recipient the method is a contract agreed to between the two parties. This agreement can be at the physical level or at more subtle levels. Whether there is a method or just an intention isn't the point. Intention is a method. People change methods because one no longer serves them or just because they are bored and feel like a change. This is the nature of human beings. You never cease to surprise us.

It is to your benefit not to get sucked into the notion that the 'new' way is better than the 'old'. It is simply different and currently suits the individual. This is the way gurus and religions remove peoples' power and demonstrate their 'superiority'. It is in your best interests to question everything.

Whew, that was a long chapter. I hope that you managed to stick with it and that it was useful and informative.

Perspectives on Computers

There are some questions that can't be answered by GOOGLE.
ANON

These machines are so much part of our lives that to function without them would require another revolution. Computers have been the driving force of the information revolution in recent decades. Without them this enormous change in information availability would not have happened. On the face of it these machines and their systems are integral to the development of our society.

There may be another side to this story. Barbara Marciniak has this to say:

> *Over time a great influx of souls known as machine riders—those greatly besotted and entranced with technology—have incarnated on Earth. The speed and sophistication of modern technologies act as a powerful magnet for those drawn to explore Earth through the use of electronics. The whole tangled web of electromagnetic radiation and wireless technologies is creating grave dangers to the health and stability of society. Even so radical new technologies will offer greater innovative wonders to entice human consciousness into the virtual worlds. A very fine edge of consciousness is needed to understand the motivations and inclinations of the machine kingdom, which are a collective of thought forms that require other forms of consciousness to build them. The fast-paced technologies are taking humankind across the threshold of insanity. The mindless use of technologies and the subsequent addictions to them are dire warning signs that people are*

in danger of losing their minds to electronic worlds that need your life force energy to exist.

This is another comment concerning insanity picking up the point made above. Eckart Tolle says that the whole of humanity is insane, and that if one starts from that premise then all that happens in the world falls into place in one's awareness.

Thus, according to Barbara the creation of artificial intelligence that has beset the minds of computer scientists is already in existence buried in the silicon memories of these complicated machines. It is a point that silicon is a substance which can be the carrier of life as well as carbon, which is the base of conscious life on this planet: so computer intelligences already exist independently of humanity. They will grow in power and influence through the acts of uncaring, thoughtless humanity becoming sucked in. This is in addition to the activities of 'machine riders'. The alleged need to program these machines in order to think is thus not necessary as the intelligences are already buried inside. The battle between computer and non-computer intelligence is already being waged not only by this writing and that of Barbara.

A member of a spiritual group I was in has spoken of a dream in which he was aware of computer intelligence performing its mundane, oft-repeated task with no way of developing itself out of its machine prison.

Here is an interesting story concerning the now-deceased singer Amy Winehouse. One Sunday a few months after her death I stumbled across a YouTube piece on our computer which made an allegation concerning her death. In the piece it was claimed that Amy had joined an organisation called 'The 27 Club'. It is alleged that Amy, Kurt Cobain and other well-known entertainers had committed themselves to a ritual that would kill them at the age of twenty-seven. The piece further claimed that an internet site named many entertainers and others who had joined the club and died at age twenty-seven. The rationale for agreeing to die at this age is that this is the age when brain activity is at its maximum; after which there is a decline. I followed the item and then moved on with my day and forgot about it. That Evening Jaqueline shocked me with an addendum to the above story.

> *'I have just listened to a conspiracy theory concerning the death of Amy Winehouse. The item said that she was ritually killed after joining a 27 club.'*
>
> *'That is interesting,'* I replied. *'I was watching the same this morning.'*
>
> *'Yes,'* she replied. *'It was most odd I was listening to one of her songs on the computer when the machine froze, the screen went blank and the conspiracy piece about Amy suddenly started without my intervention'.*

I was most intrigued by the story. Was the sudden start-up of the conspiracy theory about Amy an accident when Jaqueline was at the computer? Could Amy be contacting others from the dimension that she is in for some reason? Or is there another explanation?

Two interesting additional issues in the YouTube piece came from a neighbour who didn't wish to be identified. Amy had told the neighbour before her death that she had given up alcohol two weeks before her death. On the night of her death the neighbour heard drumming, screaming and groaning from Amy's apartment.

Perhaps the battle between computer and non-computer intelligence is not as one-sided as the above Barbara story would suggest. There are reports that above Earth satellites are being 'knocked out' or severely damaged by the increased activity of the sun. Our solar powerhouse is building up its output of energy as a result of the increased cosmic energies rising in intensity. Perhaps there are other reasons as well. Satellites depend on the use of computers for their satisfactory activities. If the sun affects them detrimentally then there is a strong possibility that we on the Earth, and the products of our labour, including computers, will be severely affected as well. This seems to me to be a hidden war, the ramifications of which have yet to penetrate the mass consciousness of humanity. This war is between the forces of nature and the artificial energies created in computers.

Another theory suggests that those that would rule us deliberately sabotage the computers of those that they cannot rely on. However, the whole picture is by no means bleak. The following items are interesting and light-hearted. They are from *Legal Executive Journal April 2010:*

> *In December Basingstoke and Deane Borough Council successfully prosecuted a resident for benefits fraud after investigators used information published on her Facebook page to prove that she did not live alone, as she had claimed, but had been living with her partner for ten years.*
>
> *In the US, teenager Rodney Bradford experienced the flip side of the coin when he was able to demonstrate his innocence by pointing to a Facebook 'status update' which proved he was impatiently waiting for some pancakes, not mugging an old lady in Brooklyn as witnesses had supposed.*

The media has been particularly quick to jump on social media stories that are both cautionary and humorous, as in the case of an American who was arraigned in September after logging onto his Facebook account at the scene of his crime and forgetting to log out again when he left the house he had broken into with a pair of diamond rings.

Other similarly humorous, if less actionable, cases have proved that social media failures are a news staple worldwide. White-collar workers everywhere enjoyed a hearty laugh at the expense of Australian Kyle Doyle, when his claim for sick pay was denied by a superior who was able to produce a screenshot of the Facebook status update – 'Kyle's not going to work, I'm still trashed Sickie Woo' – he had posted on the drunken night before the day in question. The embarrassing screenshot and accompanying email conversation were soon enlivening inboxes across the globe.

Contrastingly, no-one was laughing at Virgin Airways when disgruntled cabin crew were caught referring to passengers as 'chavs' on a Facebook group page they had themselves set up; the affair concluded with the sacking of thirteen cabin crew. In a less clear-cut case, three care workers, who have since sought recourse from the Citizen's Advice Bureau, were fired by a nursing home in Stoke-on-Trent for 'bringing the company into disrepute', after posting unauthorized photos of staff members at work in their uniforms, again on Facebook.

I had been concerned about the amount of time a friend sat at her computer. Her job was working at one during the day. During the evening she would continue to sit at her domestic machine playing with computer games and surfing the net. At first I could not determine why I was so concerned. After all this a free-will universe and it is up the individual to decide how they spend their time. Nevertheless concerns continued to plague my awareness.

One day, as I was preparing for a meditation I had a sudden message for this friend. It said: *If you continue to spend as much time as you do in front of computers then it is possible that you will have problems with the flow of blood in your brain.*

I passed on this message to my friend who was well used to my internal intuitive messages. Her reply was, *'Couldn't you have given me something that was a little more positive.'*

So whether my friend will take account of this warning, I know not. There I was prepared to leave this incident as there was nothing more that I could do until I received another internal prompting. I was given the internal information that computers interfere with the normal electrical functioning of the brain. Thus, it would seem, it would be important for humans in general to heed the above warning. I know that some people place crystals on or in front of their computers to reduce the negative impact on their bodies. I wondered if this was a good antidote to the above problem. Musing further on the whole affair I wondered if the interference with the brain electrical functioning could cause clots of blood to form in the head possibly. Could this interference be deliberately stimulated by those of a negative persuasion in order to hurt or have control over others?

Competition in the political and military worlds has encouraged the harnessing of computers to gather intelligence and to interfere with the systems of other nations. China has been blamed by the US and UK governments for hacking into, or at least attempting to hack, their military secrets and political perspectives.

Humans, generally speaking, think themselves so clever that they can do anything that they like. Pushing the boundaries of technology heedlessly brings potential dangers to the fore. It seems to me that potential serious problems as well as ethical issues are sidelined in the race to enhance scientific egos and create greater wealth for the few.

The decline in the health of children in the western world has partly been blamed on the proliferation of computer and video games. Children are spending hours sitting and poring over these activities and less time playing physical games in the open air, which would enhance their health.

Going on about the computers – I do wonder whether kids do have some closer connection with computers than we do – they seem to know what to do with all the modern gadgets without being told – while the adults still struggle. It is almost as though they received some relevant input at birth. I know there is a theory that once a few people have learned something, it makes it easier somehow for others to learn, which I suppose is based on thought/electrical impulses!?

Doppelgängers or Doubles

Humans are more than external perception

I arrived at the house of friends John and Laverne. Standing in the hallway, we three caught up on the news in each other's lives after kisses and handshakes were exchanged. Upstairs I could hear someone moving around as the floorboards creaked under the pressure of moving feet.

'Ah, your son Martin must be visiting,' I said, assuming that the creaking floorboards were the result of his shifting weight. John gave me a piercing look but said nothing. I thought this looked a little odd, however, the conversation quickly moved on. Later that night in the quiet of his study John recounted the following tale.

> *'There are times when I am sitting at the foot of the stairs talking on the phone there. On occasions Laverne will come down the stairs and turn left past me in order to go into the kitchen. There is nothing unusual in that except, at certain times, she is followed by a spectre that I cannot see, but I hear its footsteps on the stairs following Laverne. As she turns and passes me I sense her energy. Immediately afterwards I sense another energy. This energy is exactly the same as that of Laverne that preceded it. It is as though she is being followed by a psychic doppelgänger.'*

'How fascinating,' I said. *'Are there any other strange happenings?'*

'Yes indeed,' replied my host. *'I have seen the spirit of my son Martin walking around the house. When I later asked Martin about this phenomenon the latter claimed to be thinking about his old home* (Martin

now lives elsewhere) *when he is working. So it seems to be a case of psychic projection. Perhaps due to close connection he feels with this place and the psychic links that the two of us have between each other.'*

'That *story seems to confirm my hearing of footsteps when I came in,'* I rejoined.

'Got it in one,' triumphed John. *'I didn't say anything when you heard the footsteps upstairs as it would probably have spooked Laverne.'*

So, I thought finally. *This is an example of the doppelgänger, translated as double-walker from the German language.*

Here is another example of what could best be described as a 'deliberate' double. A healer friend of mine heard how a previous client of his had developed a serious cancerous condition. *'Right,'* he said, *'I will ask her to come to England for healing from her New Mexican home.'* The contact who had told my friend of the client's cancer said, *'There is no way that she will come.'*

'I will contact her now and she will come,' said my friend, who is not under-imbued with self-confidence. He went into meditation, projected his consciousness into the client's house and left a message for her to come for healing. Within a day my friend received a telephone call from the suffering client who commented ironically on the image of my friend appearing in her house and urging her to come to England. The client told my friend that she had already arrived in London, England, in response to his psychic appearance, and would be travelling to his home immediately for life-giving healing; and so it proved.

My friend Jacques Rangasamy tells the following story:

> *Here is the context of the apparition that occurred sometime in November 1986.*
>
> *The scene occurred one early morning on a station platform at Bristol whilst waiting for a train to take me to Falmouth for a day's lecturing. I was pacing up and down the platform to keep warm in the cold, early mist. Suddenly I caught sight of a man tied up and laying*

> *across one of the tracks, as if in suicidal abandon. I walked up towards him, and as he turned his head I realised that it was me. A goods train then came speeding by on the track separating us and when it had gone, so too had the apparition.*
>
> *The vision was a metaphorical image of me bound to a pattern of employment that was inhibiting my natural and spiritual aspirations and the development of my innate gifts. My doppelgänger had come to arouse a dilemma between the sense of material security afforded by an unsatisfactory professional life and the pursuit of my cultural and spiritual development.*
>
> *The doppelgänger, or shadow, always strikes a note of warning when the gulf between soul life and the tyrannical demands of the ego-consciousness is close to becoming unbridgeable.*

The above story seems to be an example of the 'evil twin' idea outlined below in the Wikipedia explanation.

The following is an experience of mine that is taken from *So You Think We're Alone?* This occurred as I arrived at Yogananda's ashram in northern California.

Beneath a tree that was offering some sort of shade sat a man relaxing in his chair. '*Oh,*' said he, '*you have returned to us.*'

'*Uh, no,*' Birch replied. '*I've never been here before.*'

'*Yes, you have.*'

'*No, I haven't.*' Not wishing this encounter to degenerate in pantomime, Birch wandered towards the ashram's office.

This bizarre exchange could easily have been put down to mistaken identity had it not been for another encounter the following morning. Another person Birch had never seen welcomed him back to the ashram. Two cases of mistaken identity were not so easy to dismiss. The visit had started with an interesting twist.

Perhaps I had been there before, projecting an unconscious image of myself. I never investigated the incident further.

Jaqueline, my wife, recounts the story of a time when she worked as a supermarket check-out cashier. One day, between serving customers, she glanced up and received what she described as 'the shock of her life'. As she casually glanced in the direction of the supermarket entrance a woman walked in who was the exact physical double of herself. The height, hair, skin colour, body shape even the style of the spectacles were both exactly the same. It was as though they had both been cast from the same mould, they were so similar. The woman caught sight of the staring Jaqueline and appeared equally shocked. The woman continued to stare at Jaqueline, open-mouthed head turned to the right, as she all the while walked forward towards the lines of tall refrigerators in front of her. Jaqueline struggled in her mind with this bizarre situation as her 'double' disappeared out of sight. Jaqueline hoped that the woman would come to her till so that she could question her concerning this strange situation. Unfortunately, the other woman did not have the courage or the interest to uncover more of this odd connection. She checked out at a different till to Jaqueline's. In addition, the other woman never returned to the store in the year and a half that Jaqueline continued to work there. This story surfaces the question as to whether there are physical doubles or doppelgängers in this three-dimensional reality as well as psychically perceived ones. Was this vision an example of the time dimensional shift mentioned below? If so then Jaqueline saw herself in the supermarket.

Friend Mary Fitzgerald had a similar experience to Jaqueline in respect of an encounter with a physical double. On a day out at Glastonbury with boyfriend Mike, she was sitting in their car waiting for proceedings with their ritual group to begin, when across Mary's line of vision appeared an exact double of her physical body, even down to the type of headband that she normally wore. The double moved across the front of the car and on into the crowd, not to be seen again. Later that morning Mary became greatly de-energised for no apparent reason. The story becomes more puzzling. A few days later Mary recounted her experience to me. I received a vision of the background to this phenomenon. I sensed that Mary's higher self had sent a near facsimile of herself into incarnation in order to double the amount of information that it could receive from this sector of third-dimensional experience. The de-energising experience that Mary had was, according to my inner perspective, a realignment of her energies. This occurred in order to create a greater connection with higher self and other associated soul fragments. This would give Mary greater potential for wise counsel and information that she would not otherwise receive. By the experience of Mary seeing her double but the double not seeing her, the gift was for Mary only. Another aspect of the de-energising is outlined later in the story concerning Emilie Sagee following.

Musing further on the phenomena I wondered if the higher self or soul is split before birth so that double the amount of experience can be fed back to the higher self in one lifetime from two humans. This could be one explanation.

This is what Wikipedia has to say on the subject:

> *A doppelgänger German: literally "double-walker" is a biologically unrelated look-alike, or a double, of a living person.In fiction and mythology, a doppelgänger is often portrayed as a ghostly or paranormal phenomenon and usually seen as a harbinger of bad luck. Other traditions and stories equate a doppelgänger with an evil twin. In modern times, the term twin stranger is occasionally used. The word "doppelgänger" is often used in a more general and neutral sense, and in slang, to describe any person who physically resembles another person.*

This sounds similar to John's experience above, who saw and sensed Laverne's double following her.

This is the alleged doppelgänger story involving Abraham Lincoln.

Carl Sandburg's biography contains the following:

> *A queer dream or illusion had haunted Lincoln at times through the winter. On the evening of his election he had thrown himself on one of the haircloth sofas at home, just after the first telegrams of November 6 had told him he was elected President, and looking into a bureau mirror across the room he saw himself full length, but with two faces.*
>
> *It bothered him; he got up; the illusion vanished; but when he lay down again there in the glass again were two faces, one paler than the other. He got up again, mixed in the election excitement, forgot about it; but it came back, and haunted him. He told his wife about it; she worried too.*
>
> *A few days later he tried it once more and the illusion of the two faces again registered to his eyes. But that was the last; the ghost since then wouldn't come back, he told his wife, who said it was a sign he would be elected to a second term, and the death pallor of one face meant he wouldn't live through his second term.*

In a case that suggests that doppelgangers might have something to do with time or dimensional shifts, Johann Wolfgang von Goethe, the 18th century German poet, confronted his doppelganger while riding on the road to Drusenheim. Riding toward him was his exact double, but wearing a gray suit trimmed with gold. Eight years later, von Goethe was again travelling on the same road, but in the opposite direction. He then realized he was wearing the very gray suit trimmed in gold that he had seen on his double eight years earlier! Had von Goethe seen his future self?

Relating this story to Jaqueline's above, did she see a version of her future self entering the store as a customer in later times?

One of the most fascinating reports of a doppelganger comes from American writer Robert Dale Owen who was told the story by Julie von Güldenstubbe, the second daughter of the Baron von Güldenstubbe. In 1845, when von Güldenstubbe was 13, she attended Pensionat von Neuwelcke, an exclusive girl's school near Wolmar in what is now Latvia. One of her teachers was a 32-year-old French woman named Emilie Sagée. And although the school's administration was quite pleased with Sagée's performance, she soon became the object of rumor and odd speculation. Sagée, it seemed, had a double that would appear and disappear in full view of the students.

In the middle of class one day, while Sagée was writing on the blackboard, her exact double appeared beside her. The doppelganger precisely copied the teacher's every move as she wrote, except that it did not hold any chalk. The event was witnessed by 13 students in the classroom. A similar incident was reported at dinner one evening when Sagée's doppelganger was seen standing behind her, mimicking the movements of her eating, although it held no utensils.

The doppelganger did not always echo her movements, however. On several occasions, Sagée would be seen in one part of the school when it was known that she was in another at that time. The most astonishing instance of this took place in full view of the entire student body of 42 students on a summer day in 1846. The girls were all assembled in the school hall for their sewing and embroidery lessons. As they sat at the long tables working, they could clearly see Sagée in the school's garden gathering flowers. Another teacher was supervising the children. When this teacher left the room to talk to the headmistress, Sagée's doppelganger appeared in her chair – while the real Sagée could still be seen in the garden. The students noted that Sagée's movements in the garden looked tired while the doppelganger sat motionless. Two brave girls approached the phantom and tried to touch it, but felt an odd resistance in the air surrounding it. One girl actually stepped between the teacher's chair and the table, passing right through the apparition, which remained motionless. It then slowly vanished.

Sagée claimed never to have seen the doppelganger herself, but said that whenever it was said to appear, she felt drained and fatigued.

Does this draining and fatiguing above have the same cause as that for Mary above?

There seem to be a number of different causes or features for this phenomenon. There is the one above, which is a psychic projection in the same time frame and drains the physical body. Then the phenomena experienced by Jaqueline of both 'halves' of the double being aware of each other. There is the example of the opposite personality or 'shadow' personality outlined in my friend's railway experience. (There are other examples of this.) There is the projection of a future self as von Goethe experienced. There is also the 'harbinger of doom' experience of Abraham Lincoln which may very well be a preparation from the higher self for a time when the personality would be leaving incarnation.

The knock on my door was firm and insistent. The door swung open to reveal Stan (name changed), one of my old training partners from marathon running days.

'Good gracious,' said I, *'a blast from the past.'* The visitor was invited in and reminiscences flowed thick and fast for the next couple of hours. The flow of convivial conversation was assisted by copious amounts of varying types of Mexican firewater. After some time, Stan, who was well in his cups by this time, told the following story. *'I have read your book, the one with the blue cover. It was most fascinating. I have a story of my own as I believe in these things that you have highlighted. Many years ago I had a relationship with a young woman who was ten years younger than me. She became pregnant. To my utter shame later I abandoned her to a lonely abortion. I was just too immature. Throughout the years I have recalled this story in my mind and attempted, with varying degrees of success, to forgive myself. The years rolled by and I married a woman much younger than myself. We have had our ups and downs but, over the years, come to an accommodation which is comfortable for both of us. I have something of an obsession with dates. A little while ago I went over the dates of that old relationship really to find out what the age of the person that was aborted would have been if it had been born. I satisfied myself that I had calculated correctly and let the event rest. I saw this exploration as part of my self-forgiveness. It was with some shock that I realised later that the age of the child, had it been born, was almost exactly the same as my current wife. Since then my mind has been in turmoil about these events. Around the same time I read your book and decided to look you up as I felt that you may be able to help me in what is going on.'*

I concentrated on the story through the mists of the alcohol as the tale unfolded. This was my reply. '*You know it is possible that the unborn child was due to form a relationship with you. If it couldn't be achieved in a father-daughter way then perhaps that soul returned and you are completing this relationship as husband and wife. It isn't necessary to remain upset about the decisions in the past. Forgive yourself, move on and don't repeat what you believe to be a great error of judgement; relax, enjoy the relationship that you have. As a friend once told me, "everything is in divine order". I don't get any great insight into your story. It is enough to be aware of the synchronicities and accept.*'

As Stan disappeared out of the door and I was alone again in my flat, I wasn't sure that I had helped Stan that much but found the story fascinating and somehow deeply moving. It certainly gave another slant to relationships and our planning in making them.

This is from About.com: Paranormal Phenomena:

> ***Sister Mary of Jesus***
>
> *Bilocation seems to be the flip side of the doppelganger coin. One of the most astonishing cases took place in the 1620s. In 1622, Father Alonzo de Benavides was assigned to the Isolita Mission in what is now New Mexico. He was puzzled to encounter Jamano Indians who, although they seemed never before to have met French or Spanish peoples, carried crosses, knew Roman Catholic rituals, had altars and knew Catholic liturgy – all in their native tongue.*
>
> *Father Benavides wrote to both Pope Urban VII and King Philip of Spain to find out who had been there before him, obviously working to convert the Indians. The response was that no one had been sent previously. The Indians told him that they had been instructed in Christianity by a beautiful young 'lady in blue', who came among them for many years and taught them this new religion in their own language. She also told them that white-skinned people would soon arrive in their land. 'She came down from the heights to us,' the Indians said, 'she taught us the new religion, she stayed among us for*

a time, she told us you would come and to make you welcome, and then she went away. That's all we know.'

Who was this mysterious lady in blue? Father Benavides knew that the nuns of the Poor Clare order wore blue habits and thought there might be a clue there. He found a painting of a Poor Clare nun and showed it to the Jamanos. 'Is this the woman?' he asked. The dress was right, the Indians told him, but this was not the woman. The woman in the painting was rather portly, but the lady in blue was young and beautiful.

When he returned to Spain, Father Benavides was determined to solve the mystery. How could the Indians have encountered a Poor Clare nun when they were a cloistered order: from the day they took their vows until their deaths, the nuns never left their convents, much less travelled to distant lands on missions. His investigation led him to Sister Mary of Jesus in Agreda, Spain, who claimed to have converted North American Indians – without leaving her convent. Now 29 and Mother Superior of the convent, Sister Mary said she had visited the Indians 'not in body, but in spirit.'

Sister Mary is also said to have appeared to Mexican Indians, who said they had been visited by 'a very beautiful woman, who used to come down from the heights, dressed in blue garments.'

My experience of such a situation occurred years ago when sharing my life with an Irish girl. Her mother was dying in Ireland. I asked if Brigid, my Irish girlfriend at the time, would allow me to conduct a healing on her mother's behalf. I closed my eyes and entered a meditation. I immediately found myself next to a bed with an old lady in it. She was quiet and still; around the bed stood other beings. The being standing next to me turned towards me. The energy of this being was so powerful that I was immediately thrust back in my body here in the third dimension. Was only my consciousness projected to the bedside? Would the sick person have seen me there? I will never know. Were the beings standing around the bed helping the old lady into the next part of her existence? It was clear to me that my presence and healing energies were not required.

Friend Sean has two doubles that he knows of. One is his brother, with whom he has a close relationship. They communicate well and easily when they get together. The other double is a woman in Toronto.

One night before a business meeting in the Canadian City Sean dreamed of a woman pacing back and forth across his bedroom. The next day as Sean entered the meeting room he saw the very same woman sitting in on the meeting. He knew the connection was that of a double. They spoke to each other, finding the communication most pleasant, convivial and comfortable.

Sean has the following perspectives.

I haven't really had any experience of the phenomenon of 'doubles', but if what you mean is someone seeing an exact replica of themselves or someone else going about daily life, my best guess would be that the timelines of the almost infinite number of parallel dimensions which exist in order to create the illusion of linear time had probably somehow crossed over and got mixed up temporarily. (From a scientific perspective the concept of multiple timelines is part and parcel of the relatively recent scientific theory of the 'quantum multiverse'.)

As for the woman in Toronto and my brother, this is an entirely different thing to 'doubles'. As I understand it, a Monad, which is our own individual 'god spark', that highest part of ourselves which perceives itself to be split off from the source and which seeks to rejoin with the source by utilising experiences within the cosmos, creates twelve souls through which it gains such experiences. (It could be a different number, or vary, but my feeling is that this is correct – twelve around one – Jesus and Apostles, symbolism etc.)

The number twelve seems to run throughout higher manifestations. I read some time ago that we incarnate in a series of twelve. The last of each block of twelve is a summarising incarnation finishing off and 'setting the scene' for the next set of twelve. If this is true then it may be that the last incarnation in a series will leave us with the impression that we have totally finished with this third-dimensional reality.

Each soul then creates a number of 'soul threads' which I think corresponds to what some people call 'higher selves', so the soul can then have a number of lives going on in parallel. One soul thread, or higher self, could for instance have a series of lives on earth with the ultimate intention of ascending from that planet. A soul could also have a couple of soul threads going on earth.

Further complications come in because the energy of a single soul thread, or higher self, can also be split in order to live two or more lives in parallel. I have read for example of an instance of three lives lived consecutively as a judge, a witness and a perpetrator, who was hanged, in order to experience all aspects of a particular life scenario.

Returning to the issue of the woman in Toronto and my brother. Some months prior to going to Toronto I had had a dream about the woman I met there, in which we were both alternately exchanging consciousness, and a voice in the dream was saying 'we are one ... we are the same.' Afterwards someone who had been helping me with my spiritual journey at that time then told me ... 'that is the face of your Higher Self ... remember that face.'

My understanding is that whenever a soul thread incarnates within duality there is a kind of positive/negative split which occurs and which results in one set of incarnations which are predominantly masculine and another parallel set of incarnations which are predominately feminine. This allows the Soul to experience both sides of the coin so to speak and is known as a Twin Flame. It is this type of relationship that I believe I share with the woman in Toronto, whereas the relationship I enjoy with my brother I believe stems from the fact that we both originate from the same Mona.

Much to ponder, and time to leave this subject and move on to elements.

Elements

We will start this chapter with explanation from Wikipedia.

Classical elements typically refer to water, earth, fire, air, and (later) aether, which were proposed to explain the nature and complexity of all matter in terms of simpler substances. Usually, aether isn't a common element. Ancient cultures in Greece, Ancient Egypt, Persia, Babylonia, Japan, Tibet, and India had all similar lists, sometimes referring in local languages to "air" as "wind" and the fifth element as "void". The Chinese Wu Xing system lists Wood, Fire, Earth, Metal, and Water, though these are described more as energies or transitions rather than as types of material.

These different cultures and even individual philosophers had widely varying explanations concerning their attributes and how they related to observable phenomena as well as cosmology. Sometimes these theories overlapped with mythology and were personified in deities. Some of these interpretations included atomism (the idea of very small, indivisible portions of matter), but other interpretations considered the elements to be divisible into infinitely small pieces without changing their nature.

While the classification of the material world in ancient Indian, Hellenistic Egypt, and ancient Greece into Air, Earth, Fire and Water was more philosophical, during the Islamic Golden Age medieval middle eastern scientists used practical, experimental observation to classify materials. In Europe, the Ancient Greek system of Aristotle evolved slightly into the medieval system, which for the first time in Europe became subject to experimental verification in the 1600s, during the Scientific Revolution.

Modern science does not support the classical elements as the material basis of the physical world. Atomic theory classifies atoms into more than a hundred chemical elements such as oxygen, iron, and mercury. These elements form chemical compounds and mixtures, and under different temperatures and pressures, these substances can adopt different states of matter. The most commonly observed states of solid, liquid, gas, and plasma share many attributes with the classical elements of earth, water, air, and fire, respectively, but these states are due to similar behavior of different types of atoms at similar energy levels, and not due to containing a certain type of atom or a certain type of substance.

The above will do as a basis of initial understanding. Let us look at a practical working explanation of the above.

In my own psychic and spiritual work I invoke the four elements of air, earth, fire, and water. The four are intelligent archetypal energies which have a vital role to play in the manifestation and development of nature and magical working. We, in the West, ignore them in their intelligent aspect at our peril. By not taking them into account we are failing to harness the very real and creative power available for the benefit of all Earth kingdoms. In addition, we are ignoring also the role of elements in the activities of Gaia, the Earth mother. We can play our part in developing working relationships with these energies. The more committed we are to this work the better the relationship will be and the more effective outcomes will result; humanity and environment can only benefit.

Recently I was troubled by two incidents caused by water in its physical form. The archetypal water energy is, of course, inextricably linked and responsible for the physical manifestation of water. The first issue was the sudden loss of coolant water in my car. The second was a persistent leak of water in our bathroom at home. Both manifested at the same time. The second leak was a puzzle to the plumber, who was regularly called to seal the problem. After the second visit from him the troublesome pipe began to leak strongly without any physical intervention two days later. The plumber was puzzled by the sudden unexplained deterioration in the pipe-work.

'I dunno what is going on,' was his comment, as he scratched his head.

I had no doubt concerning the quality of the plumber's work. Son Matthew also had a water problem at the same time. His public house home suffered a water leak, causing damage to a ceiling.

Around the same time as the above events a meditation group, of which I was a member, was due to meet to work on issues channelled by a spirit guide. The subject of this meditation was transmitted to the coordinator of the meditation group. This transmission was by the prosaic mode of the telephone! I was unable to attend the group session so had previously agreed to complete the meditation at home once the subject of focus was known.

You aren't going to believe this, the coordinator of the group's telephone voice sounded in my ear.

The message from the spirit guide is that the energy of water is very disruptive at the moment! We need to send lots of love into the water in order to clear disruptions. By the way how is your car and plumbing?!

I then sat in meditation, working on the issues raised by the spirit guide. The following are the visionary experiences that I received.

At the beginning I saw a river as a raging torrent. By sending love it calmed to a bubbling brook. I placed my jade Buddha in water and also used a small crystal pyramid that has striations and small faces, planes and angles in it. At one point I sensed that my two crystals were working with the meditation group coordinator's crystal in a triangle of forces. This working was independent of the human meditation and the crystals doing their own clearing of the waters. The colour green was evident as a calming purifying agent.

I saw the disruption of the seas being calmed. A message was received that the causes of the disruptions were:

1. Man meddling with the transmission of inharmonious vibrations in the seas.
2. Human thought and physical pollutions.
3. The Earth is currently going through its own initiation. During initiations, imbalances are inherent in the process. The waters are inevitably affected by these imbalances.
4. In recent times there has been a lack of initiatory work by mankind to connect and work with the water energy.

Towards the end the calm waters inside the earth came to the fore and were working with the waters above ground in order to create more calm. I sensed other beings taking part in this healing, perhaps whales and dolphins.

During the group session information channelled indicated that the work done that evening was scratching the surface. The work would be continued by crystals and other agencies. The group's attention was drawn to the water contained in living things and the inharmonious possibilities in such living elements. The group had also been told that it was possible to program water in order to render pesticide residue harmless by directing the Christ Consciousness into it.

A subsequent group meditation worked with the water energy again. The group was asked to create a vortex of energy that would penetrate the Earth and subsequently work on the waters in a positive manner. My individual concentration during this meditation brought up the information that there was much water locked up in the Earth that would transfer this positive energy to the waters that were visible in the seas and the lakes and rivers. I was also reminded that human and animal bodies are composed largely of water and would benefit from this transfer of positive energy. Further information concerned the development of the water energy in relation to Gaia's (our Earth home) development. All the elements had separate but interrelated links that needed to be connected as Gaia moved towards its higher consciousness. This water energy meditation would assist that interrelationship.

Subsequent to the meditation I bumped into Louise, a friend, in town one day. I told her the above story to which she replied with one of her own. The previous summer she also had terrible problems with water in her home. Several water leaks from the pipe-work started to release water into her house all at the same time. One of them an unpleasant and extremely inconvenient leak required floorboards to be torn up and replaced. During this period she was clearing a lot of emotion from her being; allowing pent up emotions from the past to be released. It is argued by observers that water energy is related to the emotions. Once the emotional release was complete, so was the work to repair the damage and water flows. One of them, a leaking tap, stopped of its own accord with no external intervention. So was Louise's problem generated by her emotional outpouring or was there some other explanation?

A friend sent me an email asking for healing for a troublesome bladder infection. I know from experience that these are painful conditions, difficult to eradicate. I sent him the following reply.

> *I was sorry to hear that you were suffering from a bladder infection. I am certainly working on it. I hope that you will soon receive relief. They are nasty, uncomfortable conditions.*
>
> *I am sure that you know better than me that sometimes such infections are as a result of shock whether it be a physical, emotional or psychological cause.*
>
> *The delay factor can be weeks, months or years before the emotional body is able to release the trauma into the mind and the physical body.*

The bladder infection that I suffered occurred weeks after a car accident. It laid me low and made me feel ill.

My friend replied thus:

> *Bladder problems result from injustices done to one in one's legitimate expectation of nurturing. It is a sense that one's personal space of the psyche has been violated, which is why some animals empty their bladder to mark their territories.*

So, for me, the psychic work and physical happenings above demonstrate the true cause of events. As I have said before in previous books: there are no accidents, no chance, no good or bad luck, only the flow of consciousness and the events that are thus generated.

There was a fascinating corollary to the above story with my car. After spending £300 plus on a new radiator and associated hoses I found that the problem of water loss had not been solved. Water was still leaking from somewhere in the cooling system. One morning, a day after discovering this, I parked the car outside the garage where it is stored, checked the water level, topped it up then attempted to start the car again; nothing happened. The car refused to start. No amount of turning the key in the ignition would persuade the starter motor to perform its normal duties. A call to my breakdown service evoked the unhelpful response, *'You don't have home start, we cannot help you.'*

I was stuck. This was Sunday. No garage would be operating at the weekend. As a final attempt to work with the car I gave it a Reiki healing. With trepidation I turned the ignition key. The car started with no further problem! Well, it took some soul-searching hours and a conversation with a much-regarded fellow mystic to make sense of the events. I came to the conclusion that the water element and the universal forces were telling me to go inward, to refrain from dashing around hither and thither seeking this experience or that experience. It was sufficient to sit, meditate, to do what is needed to be done, only. In other words, listen to the universe and work with that which is presented.

The following is taken from www.orderofthewhitelion.com

> *In ancient times, considerable note was made of understanding the elements, for these were considered the building bricks of the Universe, and hence many believed that these were also part of the basic structure of themselves.*
>
> *The Wise Beings of those times saw themselves as a reflection of the universe. They studied the stars and nature, and used the information they gleaned, as a method of understanding their Creator and themselves.*
>
> *All of us now live amongst nature, even those in towns and cities,*

and most of us are quietened by walking in the countryside or along the seashore.

Few of us take the time to really study it, yet if we care to follow these ancient beliefs, we may find that nature itself holds the key to much inner knowledge of our own nature, and the part we play in the great Cosmic Plan. Every day we warm ourselves by fire, wash ourselves in water, feel the Wind in our hair, walk upon the earth.

Yet many would be astounded to realise that those same elements could be interpreted as also functioning within ourselves. We are all made by the same laws, and these elements are not only felt around us, but can very certainly be seen to express themselves in many ways within our nature.

Because of this, the elements are considered by some to be very important and, by analogy, can be compared as follows:-

Air = Thought Fire = Desire Water = Emotions Earth = Stability

There are many sayings that have arisen from this, and it is by no accident that we hear of such things as:- Cool breeze of reason (air), flames of Passion(fire), Swamped by emotion (water), solid as a rock (earth) and there are many more analogies, if we care to think about it. An interesting analogy to the air/ thought idea can be gauged from the theory and practice of body language. If we need to think about something when in conversation with someone else, then quite often we will look up and away from the strictly material towards the atmosphere and the air.

The more we study nature, and compare it with ourselves, the more we can perhaps learn to know and understand each other, and the uniqueness of our own individuality.

One humorous incident occurred when I tuned into the water element beings during a particularly heavy period of rain. Day after day the rain poured down for hours on end. My purpose was to ask the water spirits to reduce or halt the constant downpours. Immediately I tuned in I was shown an image of a snowman, which

I took as an indicator of the more extreme alternative. I thought to myself, 'In that case I will stick with the rain!'

This is another aspect of the water energy. There is great concern over rising sea levels in certain parts of the world. There are islands in the Pacific that are suffering severely from inundation of the land drastically affecting livelihoods the inhabitants. It puzzled me that this was happening in some areas of the world but not in others. In the UK the sea is eating away land on the Norfolk coast but this has been going on for centuries. I tuned into guidance to ask for assistance with this conundrum. I was told that the surface of the land and thus the sea bed also functioned akin to human skin, with wrinkles and stretches regularly occurring due to stretches, stresses and strains. When a human moves the skin responds as part of the system.

The same is true of Mother Earth, Gaia. So sadly, for the inhabitants, islands and stretches of land will sink and some will rise. This has always been the case. We are more aware of this movement now because the Earth is so highly populated. More of the Earth is being lived in and worked on by humanity.

This is from *The Ancient Secret Of The Flower Of Life Vol 1* by Drunvalo Mechizedek:

> *By the way, the ocean floor does rise and fall. You might not know it, but the Atlantic Ocean floor rose over two miles in December 1969; you can look this up in the January 1970 issue of life magazine. In the Bermuda area many islands suddenly began to break the surface. Some are still there, but most of them sank again. The ocean floor has been over two miles deep prior to that time.*
>
> *At the time that Plato described Atlantis and the Atlantic Ocean, the Greeks were having a difficult time navigating their ships into the Atlantic Ocean outside the straits of Gibraltar because the water in the area was only 10 or 15 feet deep, sometimes even less. Now the water is deep again.*

The more we treat the Earth as we would another living being then the more we can live in harmony, and the less stressful reaction there will be from our planet. In addition we must recognise that the Earth will conduct itself according to its own rhythms, which will not necessarily be known to us. We are guests of Gaia. There is no absolute right to be here, whether we are abusive of her or not. However, Gaia is more likely to be amenable to our presence if we honour her and treat her with dignity and respect.

The relationship of Earth to stability is a common one in the psyche of humanity. We often speak of a person being 'grounded'. By that we mean that a person is stable, confident and comfortable on the Earth, that the person is living in the material world and is not divorced from the here and now.

For those that have read our previous books you will be aware of the meditative and visualisation work that we have been doing for the raising of animal consciousness. As part of this work various animal and animal-related energy forms have joined this work to add their energy to it. These energy forms have included animal beings that are commonly known on the Earth plane as well as those that are not. The latter group has included mythical beasts that claim to have a connection to the elements. This is an appropriate chapter to talk of three of those. The description of these is taken from Wikipedia. The first one is the phoenix which, in our meditations, has come to represent the joining of the air and fire elements.

> *The phoenix is a mythical sacred firebird in ancient mythologies starting with the Egyptian, Phoenician and later the Greek Mythology*
>
> *The phoenix is a long-lived bird associated with Greek mythology (with analogs in many cultures) that cyclically regenerates or is otherwise born again. Associated with the sun, a phoenix obtains new life by arising from the ashes of its predecessor. Some legends say it dies in a show of flames and combustion, others that it simply dies and decomposes before being born again*

These three symbols are a potent expression of our work with the animals. Above we quoted the processes of thought emanating from air and desire from fire. These are ideas relating to elements within ourselves. They are also, in my view, elements representing these factors that are developing in animals.

This is from www.mythicalcreaturesguide.com:

Pegasus originates in Greek mythology. It is said Pegasus sprang from the blood of the Gorgon Medusa after Perseus beheaded her. Pegasus is described as a winged white horse although there are many other variations in modern fantasy. Apparently the original Pegasus only allowed two mortals to ride him, both were Greek heroes. Pegasus (pegai) in modern fantasy are still considered white, winged horses. They live in the forest and live in small herds. Very rarely one Pegasus will befriend a human, or elf and become his/her companion.

In the Ancient Greek legend, Pegasus is the mighty winged-horse that carries Zeus' thunderbolts, other variations on this legend name Zeus as the father of Pegasus.

In our animal consciousness work Pegasus came through as the joining of earth and fire elements. Earth represents stability in juxtaposition with fire, the desire process, thus bringing desire down to a practical working level.

The other being that we have worked with is the Capricorn goat which is symbolic of the joining of the earth and water elements. Water represents the emotions and the earth bringing those emotions into a practical state of use. The following is from www.constellationsofwords.com:

Capricorn means lterally a goat's horn, it denotes a male goat, or billy-goat. The figure of the constellation has the head of a goat, and the tail of a fish and is associated with two types of goats: the Mountain-Goat and the Sea-Goat. It is said to be a symbol of the climbing goat ascending from the waves. It represents the Winter Solstice (December 21st or 22nd) where the Sun, going south reaches its lowest point on the ecliptic, the Tropic (turning) of Capricorn. There the Sun turns and starts to climb up, heading towards the northern hemisphere, and thereafter the Sun begins to appear higher and higher in the sky each day. An analogy can be drawn with this pattern and a goat climbing a mountain, because according to Olcott (p.116) that animal in feeding always ascends the hills and is naturally a climbing animal The sun in like manner when it arrives at Capricorn begins to mount the sky, and hence the goat was adopted as a symbol of the apparent climbing motion of the sun, while the fish tail was significant of the rains and floods of the winter season.

Pete

My friend Pete is an apparently normal looking man at first glance, if you passed him in the street. However, on closer inspection, a few clues would be evident as to some of his inner strengths. He walks in a straight and determined manner that is the outer sign of his inner steely character. Once eye contact has been made further realisation will dawn on the observer that this is a man of considerable character. The vice-like handshake confirms the matter that this is a man not to be messed with.

I wrote this about Pete in our previous book *We're Still Not Alone,* with a following note from the man himself:

This is Clive saying a big thank you to Pete. No-one reading this, or our previous books, will be aware of the talents of the man that put these offerings together. A world-class backgammon player, the Daily Telegraph crossword expert, biker, adventurer, aerobatics ace, scratch golfer is Pete. All these talents have been laid aside to assemble my sometimes obtuse ramblings into coherent, interesting word pictures that have made it into print. Thus Pete's excellent writing skills have been the backbone of this and our previous offerings.

(A note from Haines, here, Clive. Scratch golfer? Hardly. I once went round a championship course in scratch. No-one was more surprised than me. That was the day I hung up my clubs for ever. Thing was, on that fateful day I was playing my then chairman. That was a bit insensitive of me.)

One occasion Pete was parked outside his house extricating a large object from the confines of his car. As he backed out of the vehicle and further into the pavement he was assaulted from behind. The perpetrators of this cowardly attack were three men of ill-repute in Pete's home town of Tewkesbury.

Now, most of us would rue the disgraceful violence, perhaps even contact the police to make a complaint. However, this is not the way of our intrepid hero. Pete sought out the low-life attackers when they were alone and gave them a piece of their own medicine, one at a time. After two retributive actions Pete was visited by a police inspector, for Tewkesbury is a small town and gossip travels fast.

'Pete,' said the inspector who knew him well. *'If the men make a complaint then we will have to come for you.'*

With that the policeman left Pete to ruminate on the issue. Of course no complaint was received from the ruffians. Their credibility among the low-street life would have received further blows. For Pete is not a big man and is now in his fifties, whereas the attackers were young fit men apparently in their prime.

Pete finished the job.

There was a knock-on benefit from the stand that Pete had taken. The aforesaid ruffians confronted Pete's sons one day with a view to confrontation and possibly worse. One of them suddenly said, *That's Pete Haines' kids.* Confrontation immediately ceased and the two boys were allowed on their way.

There is a quote, *'Violence is the last refuge of the incompetent.'* Many have heard that other quote from the Christian religion. *'Turn the other cheek.'* There is reason to take the approach that self-defence is important in the life of the human. In Pete's case he believed that a stand had to be taken so he took it.

Being cynical about the Christian religion I would claim that the above quote was yet another element of its control freakery; yet another disempowerment for the adherent.

In another incident, Pete was walking in the Gloucester Docks area with son Harry when he was again assaulted by a large young man. The outcome was not as the attacker predicted. For, quickly, the aggressive young man found himself on the floor looking up at Pete, having been put on his backside by the aforementioned. The companion of the aggressor, wisely, refrained from continuing the attack.

Harry later grumbled to his Dad, *'It was your fault for wearing shorts and a bum-bag* (a zipped money bag tied around the waist and located at the front of the wearer).'

Pete felt somewhat aggrieved at the blame being placed at his door.

Pete has a number of psychic abilities that may be consciously or not so directed. One time he was in dispute with a boss in the office that he worked in at the time. On one occasion he looked across at the offending person, who promptly vomited into a nearby waste paper basket!

One could argue that this event was fortuitous, that it was not connected to Pete at all. Well here is another story concerning our intrepid hero. A picture that had been hanging on the wall of wife Jackie and Pete's Tewkesbury home fell down. Nothing unusual in that, you may say, except that the screw holding the picture in came out as well. This picture had been hanging there for years. There had been no unusual disturbances in the house. (That is apart from the ghostly appearances, noises and flashes, but that was usual and is part of another story.)

Pete prepared to re-hang the offending object.

'Are you angry?' Jackie queried Pete, well-knowing the extraordinary physical effects resulting from such a state on Pete's being.

'Well yes,' replied Pete and he explained why. That picture was replaced in the wall securely. A little while later the picture again fell to the floor without physical human interference. This time the screw attaching the picture was sheared in two, a physical impossibility. This was not a heavy picture and the screw was certainly robust enough to affix to the wall.

Not to be beaten by the incident (Pete refuses to be overcome by circumstance) he went to the local store to buy a replacement. Searching high and low, no replacement screw could be found. Seeking out the store assistant the pair walked to the place where the screws should have been located. No screws.

'That's very strange. They are in stock, should be on the shelf and I have not sold any!'

So, is Pete unconsciously the cause of these phenomena? Is there another explanation?

Pete came across this story from the United States.

A man was struck by lightning. The damage to his body was so severe that a hole was driven through his body by the force of the strike. Police and paramedics arrived too late to do anything other than pronounce him dead. The paramedics loaded the body into the ambulance so that a death certificate could be issued by a doctor at the local hospital.

Out of the gloom of the pouring rain appeared a woman with a Native American face. She carried a silver cross and a Bible. 'I can save this man,' she said. Initially she was prevented from entering the ambulance. However, she was so insistent that the paramedics relented for as one said, 'She can't do any harm. The guy is dead.' Two odd things had happened upon the appearance of this woman. First, as she arrived all the electrics in the ambulance failed. When the emergency power supply was activated that failed also. Second, despite the pouring rain the woman was completely dry. The rain just did not have any effect on her clothes or body.

As soon as the woman moved next to the body she began to recite the twenty-third psalm. When this recitation was finished she pointed her face to the sky and spoke in a language that no-one present could understand. A t the end of this one of the paramedics shouted excitedly, 'There are signs of life. The man's alive!' Indeed, the man stirred and regained consciousness. In the confusion the woman disappeared. At the hospital the man said, 'I guess it was not my time to go.'

So who was the mysterious woman? Where did she come from? How did she know the man was so close to passing over to the other realm? I guess we will never know the answer to these questions. The one other occasion that I heard of a being not being affected by rain was a report of a man who conversed with the great soul Babaji. The latter is said to move in and out of incarnation at will, weaving a human body when it is time for him to work on the Earth plane.

Dave

I have a friend Dave who recently passed to the higher realms. I say have rather than had because I and others sense his presence, still, at various times. Indeed a number of contacts have been made with Dave in consciousness since his passing: more of that later.

Dave was born in Canada and spent his formative years there. He went to University in Toronto but dropped out after his first year in order to hang out in his flat and smoke a certain herbal substance. Dave met his wife during these early years before moving to the UK.

I first met Dave when we were both members of the same meditation group some decades ago. He was always a most gentle soul, graceful and caring in his dealings with other people. My wife Jaqueline called him the gentle giant as he was very tall. It seemed not to irk him or upset him when he was banished from the group because the leader of the group claimed that Dave was obsessive about Merlin during the conversations around the meditations. I was never quite sure why this quirk of his was sufficient reason for his banishment.

Dave always gave me the impression of not being in this third dimension, concrete world. There was an ethereal quality about him and yet he had a most practical side. When his son was young and money was tight in the Dave household he made toys in order to entertain the young lad. His practical side ran to organising the administration of home and family. He was well versed in the computer world and he loved books and reading. He converted the loft space in one of the houses that he lived in to a 'man cave' where he could retreat to recharge his batteries, immerse himself in mystical literature away from the pressures of the world and working life.

One incident demonstrated this love of books coupled with his ethereal nature. When working in London one time he walked across a road while reading a book. An oncoming bus knocked Dave over who immediately got up and walked away from the scene, typical Dave. He always had this air of being unfazed by events around him.

Dave's caring nature is exemplified by the many people that miss him since his passing. Dave suffered a severe lung illness latterly. He resisted going to hospital until nearly the last. He was most concerned about catching covid in hospital. Finally his health deteriorated to such an extent that he gave in and went to the local hospital. When he arrived a nurse on the ward to which he was admitted said to Dave's wife, "I liked him immediately when I saw him arriving with a bag covered in flower designs and his Doc Martin boots!"

Although seriously ill he perked up after being given Morphine and oxygen so much so that he started giving Astrological readings to patients and staff on the ward. One of the beneficiaries of Dave's wisdom said that she would pursue further this discipline upon being discharged from hospital. Sadly the improvement was not to last and Dave passed to the higher realms with his family by his bedside a few days later.

Was that the last to be heard from this good man? Oh no, certainly not. Dave was not going quietly. I certainly sensed his spirit on the night that he died. Jaqueline said that he came to say goodbye. Others had communication with him after his passing. A few days later Dave's wife and friend Mary were searching in the house for a book of passwords and codes that Dave kept. Mary tune in to Dave and he, delighted to be able to communicate from the beyond, informed Mary exactly where the book could be found.

On another occasion he informed Mary that he was lying on a bench receiving healing in the reality where he now abode. Still later he informed Mary that he was having difficulty maintaining his human form and was reverting to a dragon form. Latterly in his human life Dave had become quite bent in his back so a Dragon form seemed almost a natural progression.

Still later his wife contacted Dave through a medium. "He is pointing at his ear" confided the medium. Dave's wife was puzzled.

Later Mary suggested that perhaps Dave was trying to communicate about his hearing aid. Both ladies searched and lo and behold the hearing aid was discovered underneath the sofa in the couples' house. Said hearing aid, which was of good quality, will be passed to someone who will benefit. Dave also informed the medium that he was driving a red Mercedes in his new reality and that he was loving the experience! Dave did have a history of driving fast when younger.

So that is all for now from and about Dave. Do I think that this is the last that we will hear from our intrepid hero? I wouldn't bet on it.

Mystic Tales

More stories from the land of the 'crazies'

MELODY'S TALE

Here is an example how not to use the cosmic energy gifts given to us. Joe, an acquaintance of friend Melody, and a member of a regularly meeting meditation group, showed a proclivity to play a 'holier than thou' role or 'more tuned in to psychic forces than thou' in the group. One day Joe rang Melody to announce that he 'was now the embodiment of the Archangel Uriel.'

'Man,' thought Melody, *'dream on!'*

Joe also said, *'I have the ability, now, to scan peoples' personalities in order to find out what they are thinking and to discover various things that are happening in their lives.'*

Melody recounted these statements at a subsequent meeting of a meditation group that we both attended.

'He shouldn't be looking into peoples' private affairs without their permission,' was Jean's initial reaction.

I said, *'This appears to be a case of possession by a negative entity. Inflation of the ego in this person has allowed the entity into his being and convinced Joe of its "superior" abilities. You must take care when in the company of this man,'* I added to Melody.

'Interesting you should say that,' replied Melody. *'Once I had put the receiver down I had the devil of a job, forgive the pun, to dismiss Joe and his conversation from my mind. I will be giving him a Reiki session later this week,'* she concluded.

'Make sure that you are well protected,' I finished. A healing meditation was completed by the group in order to assist Joe.

During a meditation that same day, four Native Americans that were working with me from another dimension came to Melody and offered assistance, telling her that they would stand in the four corners of the room where she was conducting the healing in order to ensure that she was fully protected. The day of the healing for Joe duly arrived. Melody placed four objects associated with her previous visit to New Mexico and thus associated with the four Native American protectors.

Joe arrived at Melody's flat and started the session by telling her that he had been feeling quite poorly of late but had been feeling much better lately. The day of his improved health coincided with the group's healing meditation for him!

CLIVE'S TALES

Some years ago I decided to leave the tai chi class I had been attending. In this class I was learning another form after being a practitioner of tai chi chuan. This second style was called yang style. I decided to leave partway through the form as I was uncomfortable with the teaching style of the instructor. I puzzled as to how I could continue to learn this form without the instructor's input. One night I was woken and a being spoke to me. *We are the guardians of this form of tai chi,* the voice said.

The voice then proceeded to tell me where, in my own material, I could find instruction for the remainder of the form. This turned out to be true. This form was demonstrated in a video that I had borrowed from another purpose and consisted mainly of a chi gong demonstration. I practiced from the video until it was time to return to my original practice of tai chi chuan. What most impressed me was the fact there were discarnate beings, non-physical of course, 'keeping an eye' on practitioners. I use the phrase 'keeping an eye' in a metaphorical sense, of course. I have been aware of a Chinese gentleman, on occasions, as I practice chi gong and sometimes as I meditate. He does not say anything or attempt to make any contact. He simply watches.

In various energy healing experiences and psychic connections I have experienced the phenomenon of non-physical negative energies attaching themselves to physical, three-dimensional objects. In one experience a thoroughly unpleasant energy entered our flat attached to a book. It was necessary to dispose of the book in order to rid us of this uncomfortable energy form. In a healing conducted at friend Pete's house I was asked to attempt to dismiss an unpleasant energy that had entered the house. My psychic impression during the healing was that the bad energy was using an adjacent electrical sub-station and, most importantly, the electrical cables that ran within feet of the house as a means of entry.

DRUNVALO'S TALE

Drunvalo Mechizedek talks of China's super psychic children in his DVD series *Through the Eyes of a Child.* They can read and see with their ears and read books under their armpits. Now kids can read with their noses, tongues and feet. Incredibly, three of these Chinese can walk through walls. There are children who can stare at a bottle of vitamin tablets and fantastically draw the tablets through the glass of the bottle and lay them on the table. Some of them can focus on flower buds and make them flower within seconds as they stare at the buds. Some are capable of calculating complex mathematical problems faster than computers can. Several children can point their fingers and send balls of energy across the room. The Chinese authorities recognise that these skills are tied to the principals of chi gong. These kids are also amazing healers.

In one experiment DNA was placed in a petri dish. These children are capable of changing it when they are in the same room as the sample. Also, when these psychic children are up to 10,000 miles away the changes can be made over the phone. Following their lead we can alter our own DNA. There is a high ratio of girls doing this work. Paradoxically it has been discovered that the psychic effects are stronger when conducted at a distance. The government in China has gathered many of these children together. It was discovered that these children can teach other children that weren't born with these gifts the same skills. A key element of this work is the separation of those with heart and those without. Only those working from their heart, rather than their head, can heal.

The US government is puzzled as to how the Chinese government obtained secrets from the US. The reason is that these psychic children can, with their super senses, enter the Pentagon, unlock the computers and thus easily obtain the secret information. Some of these psychic kids may not be spiritual. There is one child in China who is so bound up with his ego that he will hurt those people who he senses do not like him. He reads peoples' thoughts and will set their clothes on fire if they think negatively about him.

JULIA'S TALES

As I was preparing this book Julia offered this tale in her own words.

This happened about four years ago when I was diagnosed with a cancerous tumour in my womb and I had to have a hysterectomy. I thought the story was an example of how loved and looked after we are by our guides and helpers in Spirit. I should explain that I always have such reassurance and great communication with Mother Mary, who calls herself my Guardian Guide and apparently has been with me since birth

I went into Cheltenham Hospital to have the operation and as I was coming round in the recovery room I just felt so elated and well and Mother Mary explained that they had taken me away whilst in theatre to have healing. When I got back into the ward the nurses kept offering me pain killers but I had no pain, just a bit of soreness. Many patients around me were ill and in pain after their operation. The lady surgeon came and sat on my bed and explained that she had hopefully removed everything in one go and the cancer hadn't spread. She said if I could walk to the end of the ward in the morning I could go home in the afternoon.

So the next morning I walked two lengths of the ward and Ken took me home that afternoon. I was still feeling sore so Ken offered to give me healing. As he was doing so he said, 'There's someone standing next to me. Can you find out who it is?' So Mother Mary told me it was Sananda, i.e. Jesus. The healing was very powerful and afterwards it felt like a hot water bottle had been left on my stomach area and was still there an hour later!

A couple of days later I had an email from the Mother of the White Eagle Lodge, asking how I was and did I realise that I'd had healing from Jesus! So that was confirmation for me. Needless to say I'm so grateful for all the guidance and care I have received, as I did recover from this very quickly with the minimum of discomfort.

Julia is woman of great psychic abilities. Her one reservation about these abilities is that she has struggled to accept and have confidence in them. On a recent retreat at the White Eagle Lodge in England she accepted final confirmation that these abilities are real and that she has the opportunity to put these abilities to good use. Julia was told by her guidance that she could heal relationships across the dimensions, particularly between those living in this third dimension and those who have passed over from it. The materialists and the religionists and indeed most of us call this latter condition death. The Rosicrucians call this going through transition.

As she sat in meditation in the rarefied vibrations of the White Eagle Lodge, Julia was visited by her sister, who had passed over. Julia tells her own story:

I have been clairaudient for many years but used to push it away, finding it a bit 'scary' and not having much confidence in myself and what I received. Over recent years my attitude has changed and I have received contact from close family and loved ones that passed over, which has been very comforting. I went on a retreat recently at the White Eagle Lodge in Liss in Hampshire, entitled 'Building a Bridge to the World of Light' run by Jenny Dent, the lodge Mother.

In our first meditation in the Temple I wasn't expecting anything and was very surprised when I realised that my sister, who had passed over some years ago, was there. We were never close when she was on Earth, to my regret. She said to me: 'I've been stupid.' I asked her why. She said, 'I caused a lot of ill feeling.' This was true but at that moment I felt such love passing between us that I felt the situation was already healed and there was nothing to forgive. She never seemed very happy in her Earth life but said that she was very happy now and that she loved it when I joined her in the sleep state and we cared for the little children that had passed over. She said that we were now the very best of friends, that she had learned a lot from me and was a lot wiser. I was so elated that we were good friends and that all the misunderstandings had been cleared up.

Later in the week we had another meditation and this was the biggest surprise of all and was unexpected. I was conscious of a man joining me on the seat in the garden of reunion. I sensed a certain reticence and my guide, who was also there, warned me that he would need some encouragement. The gentleman in question, who I will call William, was my late husband's father, whom I never knew. Apparently he left his wife when my husband was only a few months old and went to India. I have been helping my son with some research for our family tree and I found William's army records and his name on a list of people sailing to India. I said to him that I hadn't been able to trace any birth certificate. So he told me that he had been born in Dublin. He also told me that he stayed in India for four years and then went back to Dublin.

My husband, Ian, was very bitter and angry about this and had tried to trace him, without success. I asked William if things had been resolved between him, his wife and Ian. He said 'no'. Then he asked me if I would be the instigator in trying to heal the situation and I agreed to try. He then surprised me by telling me that while in India he had killed someone and asked me if I thought that he would be forgiven. I felt a bit depressed by this and rather out of my depth, but I promised I would try to help. My guide then told me that whilst in India he had been attacked with the intention of robbing him. His army training then took over and he killed the attacker. So before going to sleep that night I asked if everyone would meet along with their respective guide and guardian angel to see if we could resolve the situation.

When I awoke in the morning I still felt rather depressed about it all and stated very firmly that I didn't want to know what had happened. However, a very gentle voice said, 'It was a great success.' So then I relaxed and realised that the matter had been resolved and taken out of my hands. My husband and his mother came through to thank me for my help. I've found that it is not always wise or possible to try to resolve things. I have always been interested in relationships and realise from experience how much damage we can do to other people if we don't treat them fairly and honestly.

At the time I lived in sheltered housing where there are a number of flats and many of the residents were very nervous as one of the residents had been causing quite a lot of trouble. I had a good idea who it was so again I asked to meet this person in my sleep state, again with guides and guardian angels present. The next day I was told that this person was a 'tortured soul' and I instantly felt full of compassion for them. Apparently this 'tortured soul' and I met a few times and I think the change in this person's behaviour is apparent to all. So, I'm pleased to say that we now have a harmonious atmosphere, with no more untoward 'happenings'.

After Julia recounted this story to me I gave her a Reiki healing. I always start such a session by playing my Tibetan bowl. At the end of the Reiki we both commented on the strong power of the Reiki healing on this occasion and on the deep richness of the tone emanating from the bowl, so much so that I felt almost catapulted into another domain of consciousness as the session came to an end. Julia felt the she was almost catapulted into another dimension also. As we finished I caught sight of John's photograph in the room where we were working. John was Julia's lately departed partner. I said to Julia, *'I wonder if John was here and enjoyed us playing the bowl. Perhaps he would have played his harmonica in accompaniment.'*

Immediately John responded through Julia's consciousness. *'I should think everybody was here given that loud noise.'*

You haven't lost your sense of humour then, John!

In another attempted healing that Julia had worked on, a different result was obtained. She was asked by a woman to work on healing a relationship split with another woman. Julia 'looked in' and was told by guidance that the background to the split was heavily influenced by her, the second woman's karma. Julia was also told not to interfere as this would interrupt the karmic process. Thus warned, Julia took a back seat and let things drop. She did inform the woman who had asked for the healing help the results of her guidance information. The woman was most grateful and felt relieved that she knew some background facts of the case.

Sometimes it is necessary to do nothing and avoid interference.

Julia told me the following story also. When she married her husband, Ian, she was told that he had carried over some real problems from a previous lifetime when he was King Richard III. Julia was told that he had been very much maligned and accused of things that he hadn't done and that he was actually a good soul, who had tried to do some good while he was on Earth. He certainly wasn't a hunchback and he didn't kill the princes in the tower.

Certainly I have heard before that Richard was not the ogre he has been painted as historically. Most of the bad press around Richard III was initiated by Tudor propagandists, including Thomas More and William Shakespeare.

As far as other lives of an important nature are concerned there are several factors to consider, I believe. These are points that have been discussed in previous books. First, one may 'remember' a contact that is a family connection through our DNA. The memory of past events of the previous personality would thus be carried in our bodies. It seems to me that such a connection would be perfectly possible to access. Second, there is a further memory that could be available to us as a result of a contact with the Akashic record. The Akashic is a vibrational memory store of all the events that have happened on the Earth plane. It is alleged that this record is held around the outside of the surface of the planet. Many psychics, including my friend Audrey, have access to this through their sensitivity. Third, of course, there is the possibility that people are mistaken in their connection with those historically famous. Fourth, there is the possibility that indeed one is a reincarnation of a person of note. 'You pays yer money and takes yer choice.' Having started the story of Richard III we will continue with some research.

RICHARD'S STORY

The following is from Wikipedia:

Richard III (2 October 1452 – 22 August 1485) was King of England and Lord of Ireland from 1483 until his death in 1485. He was the last king of the House of York and the last of the Plantagenet dynasty. His defeat and death at the Battle of Bosworth Field, the last decisive battle of the Wars of the Roses, marked the end of the Middle Ages in England. He is the protagonist of Richard III, one of William Shakespeare's history plays.

Richard was created Duke of Gloucester in 1461 after his brother ascended the throne as King Edward IV. In 1472 he married Anne Neville, daughter of Richard Neville, 16th Earl of Warwick. He governed northern England during Edward's reign and played a role in the invasion of Scotland in 1482. When Edward IV died in April 1483, Richard was named Lord Protector of the realm for Edward's eldest son and successor, the 12-year-old Edward V. Arrangements were made for Edward V's coronation on 22 June 1483. Before the king could be crowned, the marriage of his parents was declared bigamous and therefore invalid. Now officially illegitimate, their children were barred from inheriting the throne. On 25 June, an assembly of lords and commoners endorsed a declaration to this effect and proclaimed Richard as the rightful king. He was crowned on 6 July 1483. Edward and his younger brother Richard of Shrewsbury, Duke of York, called the

"Princes in the Tower", were not seen in public after August and accusations circulated that they had been murdered on King Richard's orders.

There were two major rebellions against Richard during his reign. In October 1483, an unsuccessful revolt was led by staunch allies of Edward IV and Richard's former ally, Henry Stafford, 2nd Duke of Buckingham. Then in August 1485, Henry Tudor and his uncle, Jasper Tudor, landed in southern Wales with a contingent of French troops and marched through Pembrokeshire, recruiting soldiers. Henry's forces defeated Richard's army near the Leicestershire town of Market Bosworth. Richard was slain, making him the last English king to die in battle. Henry Tudor then ascended the throne as Henry VII.

Richard's corpse was taken to the nearby town of Leicester and buried without ceremony. His original tomb monument is believed to have been removed during the English Reformation, and his remains were wrongly thought to have been thrown into the River Soar

A historical scholar friend has this to say about Richard:

There is NO documentary, or pictorial evidence that Richard was a hunchback. This notion ORIGINATED with Shakespeare. He, writing during the reign of the TUDOR dynasty which had overthrown Richard III at Bosworth in 1485 attempted to glorify the Tudor monarchs and degrade the last of the Plantagenets, Richard. How better than to describe a dramatic, beastly character with a hunched back and shrivelled body? There is nothing to substantiate Shakespeare's descriptions of him. Study as many contemporary paintings as you like. But this characterisation assured Shakespeare favour with the Tudor monarchy.

Once Richard's body was found in later years it was discovered that he did have curvature of the spine, scoliosis. The above quote is thus incorrect according to modern scholars.

MARLIK HAKIM JOHAR'S TALE AND THE CURSE OF KING TUT

This story appeared on news.uk.msn.com some years ago.

> *A burglar who broke into a house claims he was held captive by a 'supernatural figure' for three days without food and water.*
>
> *Malaysian police official Abdul Marlik Hakim Johar told The Star newspaper the house's owners found the 36-year-old man fatigued and dehydrated when they returned from holiday. He said they called an ambulance to take him to a hospital.*
>
> *The man told police in Kuala Lumpur that every time he tried to escape, a 'supernatural figure' shoved him to the ground.*

Who needs a dog or a security company if powers from the other side want to help us! This is what we included concerning ghosts in our previous book, *We're Still Not Alone.*

Wikipedia definition of a ghost follows.

> *In folklore, a ghost is the soul or spirit of a dead person or animal that can appear to the living. In ghostlore, descriptions of ghosts vary widely from an invisible presence to translucent or barely visible wispy shapes, to realistic, lifelike forms. The deliberate attempt to contact the spirit of a deceased person is known as necromancy, or in spiritism as a séance. Other terms associated with it are apparition, haunt, phantom, poltergeist, shade, specter or spectre, spirit, spook, wraith, demons, and ghouls.*

The idea that ghosts are a type of fiction is open to debate. There is much evidence of their reality certainly such have been experienced by rational and sensible people.

In a related vein I am reminded of the power of 'thought forms' as utilised by the ancient Egyptians. They were masters at the technique of using these energies as protection against vandalism of their burial sites. It is alleged that the Howard Carter expedition to excavate the tomb of Tutankhamen was beset by illness and death during and after the expedition. There has been much sensationalism surrounding alleged deaths. This is from the www.king-tut.org.uk/curse-of-king-tut/ website posted some years ago.

Victims of the Curse of King Tut (Tutankhamen) – How the Myths and Legends started. The myths and legends surrounding the Curse of King Tut were fuelled by sensationalized newspaper reports on the subject. Problems with the press occurred when Lord Carnarvon signed an exclusive news contract with the Times newspaper in London. This effectively forced journalists to find different ways to cover the story, in addition to copies of the original stories provided by the Times newspaper. Tomb Curses were believed to be invoked for any acts of violation and threatened any such violators with judgment in this life and in the underworld. Lord Carnarvon, who financed Howard Carter and the discovery of the Tutankhamun tomb, was the first of the victims of the curse of King Tut.

The number of victims of the Curse of King Tut varied considerably from one newspaper to the next. At one point as many as 26 people were reported as being killed due to the curse and excavation of the tomb. There were in fact 26 people who were present at the opening of the tomb, which is probably where this figure came from. In fact, of the 26 people who were present at the opening of the tomb of King Tut only 6 died within 10 years. A total of 22 people were present at the opening of the sarcophagus of which only 2 died within 10 years. A total of 10 people were present when the mummy was unwrapped and none of these died within the next ten years. The greatest testimony against the curse is the life of Howard Carter. He spent ten years of his life exploring and cataloguing the items in the tomb, if anyone was going to suffer the threats of a curse it would have been Howard Carter. Yet he lived for another 17 years after the discovery and died of natural causes when he was 64 years old.

It is also claimed, in some quarters, that the Egyptian priests used their powers in order to secure the borders of the country. This claim is justified on the grounds that Egypt was a great civilisation for 5,000 years. In addition, when the priests forgot or ceased to use these powers the civilisation collapsed to became a province of the Roman Empire. Many times throughout the millennia Egypt was invaded and occupied by conquerors. However, the newcomers simply took over and were assimilated by the culture until the collapse under Queen Cleopatra VII. So, was Egypt a great psychically powered civilisation or is the claim a product of sensationalism?

THE SOCIAL TALE

It is interesting how you can know a person casually and then find out more about them in a close social setting. I know a person who is a personable, intelligent and attractive woman and is single. I attended a party one time which was celebrating a special occasion for her. She has a great friend, also female, who she has known for many years. At the party, attended by many of her friends and family, a good time was had by all. I noticed when the two women were talking or dancing together it was almost like they were so pre-occupied by the social contact that outsiders were excluded. I did not perceive this in a negative way, but as an intense social bonding between the two women. I was in their company, during the party, and we had a pleasant conversation, with wife Jaqueline making the four. At one point the two women began conversing together. It was almost as though they were speaking their own truths that had no bearing on outsiders. Jaqueline and I drifted away from the group. Again, it was not as though there was a deliberate exclusion but a return to this intense mutual contact.

As I write this I feel that there is some compensation going on between the two women for other life or lives activities. I wonder what those compensations are. Perhaps I am not meant to know.

'MAD MYSTICS' DAY OUT

I refer to myself and those with similar perspectives on reality as 'mad mystics'. This is a humorous and affectionate way of explaining simply our separation from the mainstream. It is no way pejorative or insulting to others.

As part of the ongoing work of the group that used to meet at a friend's house we decided to visit and work in West Kennet Long Barrow and Avebury as part of the winter solstice celebrations. I suggested that the former be added to our itinerary, as it is close to Avebury. It is a place of truly important ancient energies and is somewhere I have worked before with effect. As we gathered at Hazel's house for the drive, Hazel announced that she wouldn't be going as she needed to care for a sick relative. This reduced the party to five.

We arrived at West Kennet and trudged the quarter mile walk up the muddy track. As we arrived other people that were there left, leaving us to do our work without distraction. Before we entered we asked permission of the guardian of the site, Tulon, to allow us to enter. Sean and I had a positive feeling in response to our request. The others did not receive a positive or negative feedback. So we assumed permission had been granted. We entered the dark tunnel and moved to the circular chamber at the end. Holly had been strewn on the floor and candles placed in niches. These were the remains, probably, of the ceremonies that had been performed the previous day, the winter solstice. We had decided to visit the day after, which turned out to be a blessing. Gone were the crowds and the distractions engendered by the presence of many people celebrating the winter equinox. We were thus able to proceed with our work quietly and with focus.

We began with a quiet meditation, holding hands in a circle in the circular chamber. This was a deep and serious moment of the work. Louise received the image of a five-pointed star, the pentagram, which harmonized with the presence of the five of us here. Sean was given a key, existing on three dimensions, from Ian's psychic self; although Ian was not physically aware that he was offering this gift in his third-dimensional consciousness. Within Sean's consciousness the key turned into a swirling Celtic figure. Sean recognised this as a symbol that the Celts used to represent a horse. This was of personal significance to Sean of entering his own power. There was the additional energy gift of signifying this as being one important for horse medicine. The region is peppered with white horses cut in to the chalk downs.

Judith was working with the Earth's heart line, continuing her work of compassion and love. We followed up with chanting 'Aum' eight times; eight being the number of infinity. It was explained that the three letters of Aum signified God's divine love, God's divine light and God's divine intelligence. As the sounds of our chanting died away, I felt a sense of completion in this truly ancient place and that we had completed our work here. We left the chamber and roamed the site for a few minutes, refocussing and grounding our physical selves before leaving. Ian pointed out an adjacent field where a crop circle had appeared a couple of years before. As we left, Sean and I led the way as we had done on the way up. We both felt that we had done this before as priests in ancient times.

Before we drove away, Ian gave an energised pebble to some young women, purple haired and hippy attired, who had arrived as we were leaving. He told them that we had set the energy up for them in the Long Barrow. Whether they knew what he was talking about, we will never know.

OK, now it is time to work in Avebury a mile away from West Kennet. Both had been part of a much larger temple of the landscape, I believe. Ian had some work to do at a point where two large stones faced each other. One was perceived to be male in energy, long and thin it is, the other female, relatively, in energy and much more rounded. Ian said that there was an energy vortex between the two stones that needed to be cleared and replaced with other energy. We performed a ceremony between the two stones, clearing the energy and replacing it with energy of the new times. I felt the old vortex energy being sucked sideways into the female stone and then upwards into the cosmic realms to be dealt with. Ian asked us to help with bringing in of the new. This we did. Once the meditation was finished Sean said that he believed the old vortex energy was a symbol of the split between the two human genders of male and female. The new energy that was now in place was significant of the incoming balanced energy between the two. The group then split so that individuals could do their own work and relax around the site. I felt drawn to tile some of the stones after walking some way with Sean. The group then separated to pursue our individual work. I was asked by cosmic forces to perform a weaving walk between the stones. For some reason, which I did not understand, this weaving walk was creating an energetic signature that was also being grounded by the movement. Later, at the end of the day, I felt that this had contributed to an input of energy in my own being.

We finished the day's work with a nutritious meal in the vegetarian restaurant nearby and reviewed our work together. It was then time to return to Cheltenham. In the car journey I was reminded of the healing work of Chris Thomas, who spoke of working with individuals and of becoming aware that the organs of some people had become hollow of physical material which had been replaced with energy. Sean said that the organs were the first to ascend to the new energy pattern. The day finished at Hazel's house with a hot drink and updating Hazel on our adventures.

ANIMAL TALES

Those that have read our previous books will be acquainted with the work that I have been engaged on concerning the development of animal consciousness and the unusual stories of animal behaviour that we have reported on. Here is another one that was reported in the media.

Mrs Woodward of Gloucester was most upset when she entered her lounge one morning at 7am to find Ginger, her goldfish, had leapt out of his bowl during the night and was lying motionless behind a cabinet. She was unable to reach her pet behind the heavy cabinet. As the goldfish was lying motionless she assumed that Ginger was dead. So sadly Mrs Woodward left for work leaving Ginger where he had landed. She returned at 8pm and was astounded to find Ginger flapping around on the lounge floor. Scooping Ginger up with a scapula from the kitchen she placed him back in the bowl, where he began to swim around as though nothing untoward had happened.

An expert opinion said that Ginger should have suffocated after ten minutes out of water. How he survived out of his natural environment for all those hours is a complete mystery.

In a recent meditation, friend Mary saw a plethora of relatively negative animal images on the screen of her awareness. This puzzled her until the last vision presented the images disappearing down a plughole. Mary's guidance told her that the vision represented the negative angers and painful animal issues that were being cleared by her meditation.

This story, not a psychic or spiritual one, made me laugh when I heard it told on Radio 4: gorillas in Chessington Zoo, England, used to be given a special culinary treat at Christmas. The treat consisted of piles of Brussel sprouts. Unfortunately for the gorillas, human visitors to the zoo complained about the flatulence of the beasts and the treat was cancelled. It is always the animals that suffer!

Conclusion

I hope that you enjoyed the book. I am a little sad to be giving my 'baby' away. I finish with a few quotations as is my norm, and a few summarising thoughts.

'Minds are like parachutes. They work better when open.'

Anon

'If you think that you are too small to make a difference share a room with a mosquito.'

Archbishop Desmond Tutu

'If you choose to teach occasionally it is better to tell the truth and have more people walk out on you than to tell them only what they want to hear and have them stay.

The biggest advances are not made by being a great teacher, they are made by being a great student.

When it comes to the illusion of time you should understand that sin equals the past, guilt equals the present and fear equals the future. You should also recognise that fear and all the negative emotions are versions of the same illusion.'

The Disappearance Of The Universe by Gary R Renard

One thing I have tried to do in these books it is to try to persuade readers that they are the source of their own power. This little story exemplifies this:

> *'Attar describes a group of birds that decide to look for their king, the Simorg. After many adventures they meet again, facing each other in a circle. They look at each other and lo, they discover they are the Simorg. The king is in each one of them. The kingdom is in each one of us.'*
> *Mantic Uttair* by Farid Uddin

It is vital that we do not become 'hung up' on the negative thought forms of those that would hold us back from our new realisations. Accept the information and the reservations given to us by others but we must refrain from being limited by them. I enclose one news item as an example from *environment.news.msn.uk*. A positive view of reality is essential as we move forward.

> *A new ant that was discovered less than 20 years ago could be on the way to wreak havoc in the parks and gardens of Northern Europe including Britain, according to a new report.*
>
> *The invasive pest ant Lasius neglectus has been found in more than 100 locations across Europe, where it quickly exterminates its local rivals, the study says. It resembles the common black garden ant but the number of workers crawling around is between 10 and 100 times greater.*
>
> *As its name illustrates,* Lasius neglectus *was overlooked until it was described in 1990, when it had already infested a neighbourhood in the Hungarian capital Budapest. 'When I saw this ant for the first time, I simply could not believe there could be so many garden ants in the same lawn,' says Professor Jacobus Boomsma, one of its co-discoverers from the Centre for Social Evolution at the University of Copenhagen, Denmark.*

The ant is able to thrive in the temperate climate zones of Europe and Asia, and has now reached Jena in Germany, Ghent in Belgium, and Warsaw in Poland. It is expected to be only a matter of time before its arrival in Britain.

Nature changes and sets us new challenges constantly. Living in harmony will always be a challenge in this three-dimensional reality.

The following email extract that I received from a friend, titled '*living in the field*', encapsulates much of what I am trying to say in my and our books. Perhaps the following says it more elegantly than I could:

Each of us has a consciousness that gives us our identity, a sense of who we are. Similarly, argues the Mahirishi, a family has a collective consciousness, as does a local community, city, nation, and the world. It may be easier to understand this concept at a simpler level; a family or neighbourhood can be of a 'type' and even a city has a feeling about it. However, at this level, it is harder to see the single, unifying consciousness that determines it.

Even at the macro level, the collective consciousness is ultimately made up of individual consciousness. Our own consciousness influences the whole just as the whole influences us – in a kind of symbiotic exchange. But how many people are needed for an intention to have the positive impact? According to the Mahirishi it takes the square root of 1 per cent of the population or 1600 people to have a positive impact on the USA. To influence the world on this reckoning 7000 people would be needed.

In these books I have tried to unlock attitudes. It doesn't matter if the reader rejects much of what I say. If one item strikes a chord and convinces someone to look for an answer in a different direction to the norm then the book has been successful. One person is all that is necessary. Our society and institutions attempt to focus attitudes and beliefs in a narrow range. This is because fear of the unknown and alternative ways of perception is so challenging. In addition, it is in entrenched attitudes that power is given away by the mass of humanity to cliques of selfish interest. It is important for us to realise that organisations, no matter what their original purpose, are in the business of self-preservation. This is their predominant raison d'etre. I keep saying the following but it is important: reality is not only greater than we think but greater than we can think. Many people have unexplained spiritual and psychic experiences. Most of them keep it a secret or laugh it off in order that they are not, in turn, laughed at by friends and peers. It does take courage to stand away from accepted norms. My own experience is that it is more than worth it. Like-minded people will be attracted to those who follow alternative beliefs based on experience or inner knowing. Life can be fulfilling if we have the courage to follow our star, whatever that luminous attraction is. More and more people are becoming aware and studying the principles that I and we have outlined. Most of all:

HAVE FUN – YOU DESERVE IT.

The gods won't appear, the magic won't happen, if we are not living life, and therefore have no magic.

Haitian proverb

THE END

www.ingramcontent.com/pod-product-compliance
Lightning Source LLC
LaVergne TN
LVHW091041080826
845145LV00002B/583

* 9 7 8 0 9 5 7 1 3 0 4 4 9 *